Activity Anorexia
Theory, Research, and Treatment

Activity Anorexia
Theory, Research, and Treatment

Edited by

W. Frank Epling
W. David Pierce

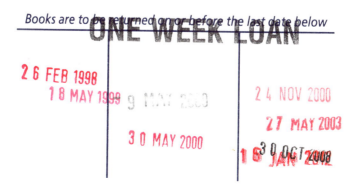

Lawrence Erlbaum Associates, Inc., Publishers
10 Industrial Avenue
Mahwah, NJ 07430

Cover design by Gail Silverman

Library of Congress Cataloging-in-Publication Data

Activity Anorexia : theory, research, and treatment / W. Frank Epling
& W. David Pierce (eds.).
        p. cm.
    Includes bibliographical references and index
    ISBN 0-8058-1929-0 (cloth : alk. paper)
    1. Exercise addiction. 2. Anorexia nervosa. I. Epling, W.
    Frank. II. Pierce, W. David.
RC569.5E94A28   1996
616.85'262—dc20   96-5984
                                                   CIP

Books published by Lawrence Erlbaum Associates are printed on
acid-free paper, and their bindings are chosen for strength and dura-
bility.

Printed in the United States of America
10 9 8 7 6 5 4 3 2 1

Contents

Contributors

Paul F. Aravich   Eastern Virginia Medical School, Department of Anatomy and Neurobiology, 700 Olney Road, P.O. Box 1980, Norfolk, VA 23501, USA

Terry Belke   Department of Psychology, Mount Allison University, Sackville, New Brunswick, E0A 3C0, Canada

William M. Beneke   Department of Social and Behavioral Sciences, Lincoln University, 310 Founders Hall, Jefferson City, MO 65102-0029, USA

Clare C. Beumont   McKenzie Carrick Pty Ltd., Level 2, 44 Miller, Street, North Sydney, NSW, 2060, Australia

Pierre J. V. Beumont   Department of Psychiatry, University of Sydney, Sydney, NSW, 2006, Australia

David Cumming   Department of Obstetrics and Gynecology, Division of Endocrinology, The University of Alberta, Edmonton, Alberta, T6G 2R7 Canada

Caroline Davis   343 Bethune College, York University, 4700 Keel Street, North York, Ontario, M3J 1P3, Canada

Lee E. Doerries   Christopher Newport University, Newport News, VA 23606-2998, USA

W. Frank Epling   Department of Psychology, The University of Alberta, Edmonton Alberta, T6G 2E9, Canada

Elizabeth Geer   Women's Health Center, St. Luke's-Roosevelt Hospital Center, 1000 Tenth Avenue, New York, NY 10019, USA

Jack L. Katz   Department of Psychiatry, North Shore University Hospital, 400 Community Drive, Manhasset, NY 11030-3815, USA

W. David Pierce   Department of Sociology, The University of Alberta, Edmonton, Alberta, T6G 2E9, Canada

K. M. Pirke   Department of Psychoendocrinology, Center for Psychobiological Research, University of Trier, Postfach 2920, 5419 Trier, Germany

Thomas S. Rieg   Department of Psychology, Christopher Newport University, 50 Shoe Lane, Newport News, VA, 23606, USA

James C. Russell   Department of Experimental Surgery, The University of Alberta, Edmonton, Alberta, T6G 2E9, Canada

Diane Symbaluk   Department of Sociology, The University of Alberta Edmonton, Alberta, T6G 2E9, Canada

Stephen W. Touyz   Westmead Hospital, Westmead, NSW, 2145, Australia

Jerry G. Vander Tuig   Human Nutrition Research Program, Lincoln University, Jefferson City, MO 65102-0029, USA

Michelle P. Warren   Reproductive Endocrinology, Women's Health Center, St. Luke's-Roosevelt Hospital Center, 1000 Tenth Avenue, New York, NY 10019, USA

Garry Wheeler   Physical Education and Recreation, University of Alberta, Rick Hansen Center, W1-67 Van Vliet, Edmonton, Alberta, T6G 2H9, Canada

Alayne Yates   Division of Child and Adolescent Psychiatry, University of Hawaii, 1319 Punahou Street, Honolulu, HI 96826, USA

Preface

This volume represents an attempt to provide researchers and clinicians with an insight into recent developments in activity anorexia. Much of the basic research on the topic has come from the animal literature. This is not surprising; the theory of activity anorexia is built on an animal model of self-starvation. Rats that are placed on a single daily feeding run more and more over days, stop eating, and die of starvation. Additionally, experiments that for ethical or practical reasons could not be done with humans may be conducted with other animals. The animal research is extending our understanding of biologically based reward mechanisms that regulate eating and exercise, environment–behavior interactions that affect anorexia, and the biochemical changes that accompany physical activity and starvation.

Increasingly, however, the impact of physical activity on human anorexia is being directly investigated. As a matter of interest, 8 out of 14 research chapters in this volume are based on human research. Some researchers are interested in the impact of hyperactivity and caloric restriction on human reproductive function (changes in menstrual cycle and sex hormone levels accompany anorexia). Other authors are investigating physically active subgroups of people considered to be at risk for anorexia. Finally, several clinician-researchers suggest how physical activity and extreme dieting interact for anorexia nervosa patients.

Chapter authors were asked to present their views independent of our argument that, when it is present, physical activity is central to anorexia. Many of the chapter authors disagree with us about the details of activity anorexia. A few contributors to the book suggest that excessive physical activity is either incidental to, or an epiphenomenon of, anorexia. Most authors are, however, in accord with the view that physical activity reduces food consumption which further drives up activity that results in even less caloric intake and so on. No matter what their perspective, all contributors agree that hyperactivity frequently accompanies self-starvation in humans and other animals. We hope that the end result is a book that is lively and that provides a source of ideas for both researchers and practitioners.

ACKNOWLEDGMENTS

We would like to thank Alberta Mental Health Research Council who funded our research on activity anorexia. Dr. Judy Cameron gave us the idea for organizing the present volume, and we thank her for that and for her encouragement and advice.
—*W. Frank Epling*
—*W. David Pierce*

I

Principles and Processes of Activity Anorexia

1

An Overview of Activity Anorexia

W. Frank Epling
W. David Pierce
University of Alberta

Activity anorexia is a biologically based self-starvation syndrome that is triggered by diet and exercise routines. The syndrome occurs in several species of animals including rats and humans. For humans who live in affluent parts of the world, type of diet and exercise patterns are largely determined by sociocultural factors. For other animals, diet is a function of food availability, and exercise is mostly due to response feedback or stimulation from the environment.[1] Whatever factors produce it, severe food restriction in combination with excessive physical exercise can lead to what we call *activity anorexia*. Activity anorexia occurs when food intake declines, and this reduction in caloric intake results in an increase in physical activity. Increased physical activity causes an additional decline in food intake, which further increases activity, and so on. This simple negative feedback loop organizes several diverse research literatures with regard to human anorexia.

Many animals exposed to a significant reduction in caloric intake respond by increasing their physical activity. At first glance this does not seem to make sense. Why would an organism that is challenged by food reduction increase its caloric expenditure? Some animals do, in fact, reduce their energy output when food is scarce. For example, some species (e.g., ground squirrels) that are routinely exposed to food depletion survive by reducing their metabolic rate and by hibernating

---

[1]The environment, in our use, includes internal–physiological events such as neural conduction, hormonal changes, and so forth.

through periodic famines (see Mrosovsky & Sherry, 1980, for other examples). Consider, however, an organism that is dependent on a stable year-round food supply. If an environmental catastrophe threatens starvation, the animal that becomes mobile may travel to a new and plentiful food patch.

Chaotic dieting, excessive activity, and physiological abnormalities are associated with human anorexia. Willful self-starvation by humans is usually diagnosed as anorexia nervosa (AN), and patients are treated as mentally disordered. Our contention is that most cases of AN are in fact instances of activity anorexia (see Epling & Pierce, 1991, for detailed evidence). Activity anorexia is functionally defined and occurs when a decline in food consumption increases physical activity. Central to this description is that as physical activity becomes excessive, food intake is reduced, and the reduction in caloric intake leads to more activity, and so on. Eventually this feedback cycle may lead to starvation and death.

The chapters in this book represent a wide diversity of opinion and findings about the role of physical activity for anorexia. Topics range from reproductive function and eating disorders in humans to neurotransmitters and activity in semistarved rats. Several authors argue that the excessive activity observed in anorectic patients is mediated by cognitive factors; others focus on neuroendocrinology, biology, or behavioral processes. Some researchers are trying to discover the fundamental nature of the locomotor activity that food-restricted rats and patients with AN exhibit. Others suggest that the activity seen in activity anorexia is a side effect of more central processes and that the syndrome is thus incorrectly labeled. Despite these differences of opinion, all would agree that excessive physical activity is a prominent feature of self-starvation for anorectic animals and for AN patients.

ACTIVITY ANOREXIA

We have developed an animal model of the process of activity anorexia and a biobehavioral theory (chapter 3) that incorporates the animal results as well as convergent evidence at the human level. In this chapter we describe activity anorexia in rats and outline the convergent evidence from several literatures for a human variant of activity anorexia.

A Laboratory Model of Activity Anorexia

Under certain environmental conditions rats self-starve, and this phenomenon appears to be functionally similar to so-called willful starvation by humans (AN). In our laboratory, adolescent rats, approximately 60 days old, are placed in a cage that is attached to a running wheel. The wheel and side cage can be separated by closing a sliding door (Fig. 1.1). During the first 5 days of an experiment, the door that separates the side cage from the wheel is closed. Food is freely available in the cage and each animal can eat as much as it wants. The amount eaten is measured

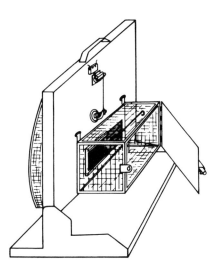

FIG. 1.1.   A standard 1.1-m Wahmann running wheel with an attached side cage. A sliding door prevents or permits access between cage and wheel. Reprinted from W. F. Epling and W. D. Pierce (1991). *Solving the Anorexia Puzzle: A Scientific Approach.* Toronto: Hogrefe & Huber. Reprinted with the permission of Hogrefe & Huber Publishers, Seattle Toronto Bern Göttingen.

daily and the rats are also weighed each day (see Pierce & Epling, 1991, for a more complete description).

The food and weight measures provide baseline points for the experimental interventions, which combine food restriction and opportunity to run on a wheel. In a typical experiment, the animals are restricted to a single 60- or 90-minute daily meal. Following the meal, the doors to the wheels are opened and experimental animals are allowed to run. Control animals receive the same treatment, but the wheels will not turn.

Several procedural points are noteworthy. Experimental animals are given continuous access to the wheels except during the feeding period. In this way, running does not compete with eating. When wheels are available, there are no programmed contingencies for running. The animals can stay in their cages, sit in the running wheels, walk rather than run on the wheels, or respond in any other way.

The initial effect of placing animals on 1 meal a day is a large drop in food consumption (see Fig. 1.2). This is not surprising because the animals have not experienced a rapid change in food supply and are not adapted to the new feeding schedule. When food restriction and the opportunity for wheel-running occur together a number of interesting effects are observed. As shown in Fig. 1.2, experimental animals begin to run on the wheels. They increase running behavior over time even though there is no requirement to do so. This is an unusual response, because energy expenditure increases at a time when food intake is limited. Within a week, increases from several hundred to thousands of revolutions a day. Impor-

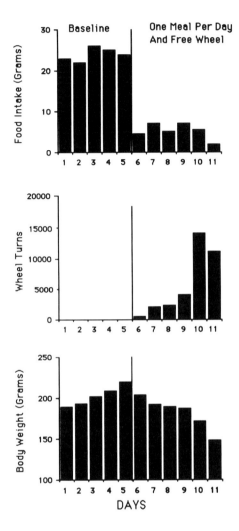

FIG. 1.2. Effects of food restriction (one 60-minute meal a day) and access to a running wheel for a typical rat. The figure shows food intake in grams (top), number of revolutions of a 1.1-meter wheel (middle), and body weight in grams (bottom). The thin solid line represents baseline from experimental phases.

tantly, control animals, who cannot run, adapt to the feeding schedule within several days and remain healthy.

A more startling effect is that food intake at the meal declines as running becomes more and more excessive. At the end of 1 week, the animal may not eat at all. The physical activity does not appear to be stressful (Spigelman, McLeod, & Rockman, 1991), and failure to eat is not due to the development of activity-stress ulcers (Doerries, Stanley, & Aravich, 1991). Recent findings by Belke and Heyman (1993; chapter 4, this volume) indicate that running generated by food restriction has reinforcing properties (opportunity to run will support lever-pressing by rats on variable-interval schedules). The animals in the activity anorexia experiment give up eating based on a reinforcement process that involves increasing energy expenditure through wheel-running. A typical rat may run up to 15 kilometers per day at the peak.

If the process of activity anorexia is allowed to continue, animals become weaker and weaker, food intake declines, activity subsides, and they die of starvation. The seemingly willful starvation and excessive exercising of these animals appears similar to many cases of AN.

Animal and Human Anorexia

Observations like these suggest clinical applications. This is because the laboratory phenomena appear to be functionally similar to what has been labeled AN in humans (see chapters 15 and 16). We suggest that activity anorexia, not AN, is the issue. That is, many cases of activity anorexia have been incorrectly called AN. One way to establish functional similarity between an animal model and human pathology is to gather convergent evidence, which involves documenting diverse findings from various sources that together support or refute the relationships observed in the laboratory. The strongest form of convergent evidence occurs when a researcher is unable to predict the outcome of this search. In order to extend the activity anorexia model to the human level, we suggest six levels of functional similarity by convergent evidence (Pierce & Epling, 1991).

Excessive Physical Activity is Associated With Anorexia in Humans.   Based on our early animal research (Epling, Pierce, & Stefan, 1981), we wondered if anorectic patients were in fact hyperactive. Epling, Pierce, and Stefan (1983) and Epling and Pierce (1988) reported on the mounting evidence for a relationship between physical activity and AN. We found numerous reports of hyperactivity in anorectic patients (Blitzer, Rollins, & Blackwell, 1961; Crisp, 1965; Halmi, 1974; Katz, 1986; King, 1963; Kron, Katz, Gorzynski, & Weiner, 1978; Slade, 1973). Kron et al. (1978) conducted a retrospective study of hospitalized anorectics and concluded that hyperactivity is a central feature of AN.

To illustrate, Katz (1986) reported that a physician became anorectic, going from 175 to 115 pounds, after starting a running program that increased to 50 miles per week. Hip pain made running difficult and the man compensated by extensive walking and cycling. Beumont, Beumont, and Touyz (chapter 15) point out that there is commonality of presentation between obligatory runners and anorectic patients and that overactivity is an important clinical feature for many anorectic patients. Davis, Kennedy, Ralevski, and Dionne (1994), using an in-depth interview technique, obtained a lifetime sport and exercise profile for anorectic patents. They concluded that sport and exercise can be central, causative, or both for anorexia (see also chapter 16).

Katz (chapter 17) noted that there are problems with most reports of excessive exercise in anorectic patients (e.g., most studies do not have a control group, but see Davis, Kennedy, Relevski, & Dionne, 1994, for an exception). Nonetheless,

Katz said that the available data suggest that 65% to 75% of anorectic patients exercise excessively. In a respected series of papers, Yates and her coworkers (chapter 14, this volume; Yates, 1991, 1992; Yates, Leehey, & Shisslak, 1983; Yates, Shisslak, Allender, & Crago, 1992) noted that obligatory runners and anorectics engage in similar behavior. Further, Yates (chapter 14) suggests that the overtrained athlete (who is close to collapse but will not stop exercising), the exercising anorectic patient, and the anorectic rat running on an activity wheel seem similar to one another. They all appear to be locked into a compulsion to exercise.

Physical Activity Reduces Food Intake.   Research on nutrition and behavior confirmed our speculation that humans reduce food intake when physical activity becomes excessive (Edholm, Fletcher, Widdowson, & McCance, 1955; Epstein, Masek, & Marshall, 1978; Johnson, Mastropaolo, & Wharton, 1972; Mayer, Roy, & Mitra, 1956; Watt, Wiley, & Fletcher, 1976). For example, Edholm et al. (1955) reported that military cadets ingest less food on drilling days than they do on days of lower activity. Epstein et al. (1978) found that obese school children would voluntarily reduce food intake following a prelunch exercise period.

Generally, increasing physical activity reduces food consumption. This effect occurs when physical activity is increasing against an individual's base rate and subsides when activity stabilizes (Epling & Pierce, 1984, 1989). Once activity stabilizes, food intake recovers and may increase in order to compensate for the additional caloric expenditure (Tokuyama, Saito, & Okuda, 1982). Of course, when starvation becomes extreme, activity decreases. This lethargy is also observed in our laboratory rats near the end of the activity anorexia cycle.

Lower Food Consumption Increases Physical Activity.   There is other evidence that lower food consumption increases physical activity in humans (Blanton, 1919; Howard, 1839; Russell-Davis, 1951) and in rats (Boer, Epling, Pierce, & Russell, 1990; Russell, Epling, Pierce, Amy, & Boer, 1987). A controlled experiment on human starvation was conducted by Keys, Brozek, Henschel, Mickelson, and Taylor (1950). In this study, 36 conscientious objectors to World War II were required to undergo 6 months of semistarvation. Although Keys et al. emphasized the inactivity of the men, their procedures may have masked the expected increase in physical activity when food is restricted. The men were required to participate in a regular physical activity program, hike 22 miles a week, and walk 2 to 3 miles a day back and forth to the mess hall. Each man was also required to do a weekly 30-minute test on a motor-driven treadmill at 3.5 miles per hour on a 10% gradient.

In spite of this, there is evidence that food deprivation induced excessive physical activity. The researchers stated, "Some men exercised deliberately at times. Some of them attempted to lose weight by driving themselves through periods of excessive expenditure of energy" (p. 828). Keys et al. interpreted this exercising as a deliberate attempt by the men to lose weight in order to have their food ration increased. A more likely explanation is that these men were experiencing the activity anorexia cycle. Overall, the study by Keys et al. and other evidence indicate that humans increase physical activity when food intake declines and become inactive when starvation is severe (see Epling & Pierce, 1988, 1991; Epling, Pierce, & Stefan, 1983, for reviews).

The Onset of Anorexia in Humans and Animals Develops in a Similar Manner.
Another line of convergent evidence shows that the onset of anorexia in humans is
consistent with the pattern observed in animals. In the laboratory, food restriction
generates excessive physical activity that interferes with eating. A similar pattern
is reported for anorectic patients (chapter 15, this volume; Beumont, 1991; Beumont, Booth, Abraham, Griffiths, & Turner, 1983; Katz, 1986). Beumont et al.
(1983) asked 25 anorectic patients to identify their symptoms and the order of
occurrence. Of the 28 reported symptoms, only "manipulating food servings" and
"increased sport activity" were present in all patients. Generally, the ordering of the
symptoms indicated that behaviors involving dieting and food restriction occurred
early in the sequence. These changes in food allocation were followed by increased
sport activity and "exercising alone." Thus the pattern of onset in humans parallels
the development of activity anorexia in laboratory rats.

*Reproductive Function is Disrupted for Physically Active Rats, Athletes, and
Anorexia Patients.* The estrus cycle is disrupted for female rats that are food
deprived and that run excessively on an activity wheel (Watanabe, Hara, & Ogawa,
1992). Anorectic humans are hyperactive and have problems with menstruation
(chapter 10, this volume; Kaye, Picker, Naber, & Ebert, 1982). Physical activity
can also produce menstrual difficulties for female athletes (chapter 11, this volume;
Mansfield & Emans, 1989). Olympic and college track and field athletes often
experience delayed onset of menstruation (Cumming & Rebar, 1983, 1985; Frisch
et al., 1981). Ballet dancers who are very active also have a high incidence of
menstrual problems and other symptoms of anorexia nervosa (Frisch, Wyshank, &
Vincent, 1980; Garner & Garfinkel, 1980). Lower serum testosterone and higher
serum cortisol levels have been observed for male athletes who engage in strenuous
physical activity and food restriction, suggesting a disruption of reproductive
function similar to that of female athletes (chapters 12 and 13, this volume; Wheeler,
McFadyen, Symbaluk, Pierce, & Cumming, 1992; Wheeler, Singh, Pierce, Epling,
& Cumming, 1991; Wheeler, Wall, Belcastro, & Cumming, 1984).

*Social Reinforcement Based on Cultural Practices Encourages People to Com-
bine Dieting and Exercise in a Way That Leads to Activity Anorexia.* An apparent problem for the laboratory model is that food restriction is imposed on the
animals, whereas humans impose food restriction or diet on themselves
(Mrosovsky, 1984). However, food restriction is imposed on both animals and
humans: The experimenter imposes food restriction on the animals, whereas social
pressures of Western culture toward thinness and fitness ensure that many people
go on extreme diets and exercise to excess (see review in Epling & Pierce, 1991).
To illustrate, young women who are thin and fit are verbally reinforced by their
peers for meeting the slim and trim beauty standard. In contrast, obese people are
criticized, occasionally laughed at, and sometimes shunned. In other instances, job
or sports requirements require food restriction and intense exercise (e.g., ballet
dancers, college wrestlers). In short, cultural contingencies of reinforcement ensure
that numbers of individuals restrict their caloric intake, and many people who do
this combine dieting with intense exercise. For an elaboration of the evidence
supporting this contention see chapter 3.

SUMMARY

Overall, the convergent evidence for activity anorexia in humans is strong. We argue that the anorexia observed in laboratory animals is functionally similar to a large number of cases that are labeled as AN in humans. In other words, many cases of anorexia nervosa are in fact instances of activity anorexia. Based on several years of research by Epling, Pierce, and colleagues, a theory and animal model of human anorexia has been proposed (Epling & Pierce, 1988, 1989, 1991; Epling, Pierce, & Stefan, 1983, 1981). This theory of activity anorexia is updated and presented in chapter 3. Theoretical considerations involve evolutionary biology, behavior, and physiology.

ACKNOWLEDGMENT

Preparation of this chapter was supported by research grant #51-25009 from the Alberta Mental Health Research Council.

REFERENCES

Belke, T. W., & Heyman, G. M. (1993). *An application of Herrnstein's hyperbolic equation to the study of the reinforcing efficacy of wheel-running in rats.* Unpublished manuscript.

Beumont, P. J. V., Booth, S. F., Abraham, D. A., Griffiths, D. A,. & Turner, T. R. (1983). Temporal sequence of symptoms in patients with anorexia nervosa: A preliminary report. In P. L. Darby, P. E. Garfinkel, D. M. Garner, & D. V. Coscina (Eds.), *Anorexia nervosa: Recent developments in research* (pp.129–136). New York: Alan R. Liss.

Beumont, P. J. V. (1991). Forward to solving the anorexia puzzle: A scientific approach. In W. F. Epling & W. D. Pierce (Eds.), *Solving the anorexia puzzle: A scientific approach* (pp. ix–xv). Toronto, ON: Hogrefe & Huber.

Blanton, S. (1919). Mental and nervous changes in children of the Volkschulen of Trier, Germany, caused by malnutrition. *Mental Hygiene, 3*, 343–386.

Blitzer, J. P., Rollins, N., & Blackwell, A. (1961). Children who starve themselves. *Psychosomatic Medicine, 23*, 69–38.

Boer, D. P., Epling, W. F., Pierce, W. D., & Russell, J. C. (1990). Suppression of food deprivation-induced high-rate wheel running in rats. *Physiology and Behavior, 48*, 339–342.

Crisp, A. H. (1965). Clinical and therapeutic aspects of anorexia nervosa: A study of thirty cases. *Journal of Psychosomatic Research, 9*, 67–68.

Cumming, D. C., & Rebar, R. W. (1983). Exercise and reproductive function in women. *American Journal of Industrial Medicine, 4*, 113–125.

Cumming, D. C., & Rebar, R. W. (1985). Hormonal changes with acute exercise and with training in women. *Seminars in Reproductive Endocrinology, 3*, 55–64.

Davis, C., Kennedy, S. H., Relevski, E., & Dionne, M. (1994). The role of physical activity in the development and maintenance of eating disorders. *Psychological Medicine, 24*, 957–967.

Doerries, L. E., Stanley, E. Z., & Aravich, P. F. (1991). Activity-based anorexia: Relationship to gender and activity-stress ulcers. *Physiology and Behavior, 50*, 945–949.

Edholm, O. G., Fletcher, J. G., Widdowson, E. M., & McCance, R. A. (1955). The energy expenditure and food intake of individual men. *British Journal of Nutrition, 9*, 286–300.

Epling, W. F., & Pierce, W. D. (1984). Activity-based anorexia in rats as a function of opportunity to run on an activity wheel. *Nutrition and Behavior, 2*, 37–49.

Epling, W. F., & Pierce, W. D. (1988). Activity-based anorexia: A biobehavioral perspective. *International Journal of Eating Disorders, 7*, 475–485.

Epling, W. F., & Pierce, W. D. (1989). Excessive activity and anorexia in rats. In K. M. Pirke, W. Wuttke, & U. Schweiger (Eds.), *The menstrual cycle and its disorders: Influences of nutrition, exercise and neurotransmitters* (pp. 79–87). New York: Springer-Verlag.

Epling, W. F., & Pierce, W. D. (1991). *Solving the anorexia puzzle: A scientific approach.* Toronto: Hogrefe & Huber.

Epling, W. F., Pierce, W. D., & Stefan, L. (1981). Schedule-induced self-starvation. In C. M. Bradshaw, E. Szabadi, & C. F. Lowe (Eds.), *Quantification of steady-state operant behaviour* (pp. 393–396). Amsterdam: Elsevier/North Holland Biomedical Press.

Epling, W. F., Pierce, W. D., & Stefan, L. (1983). A theory of activity-based anorexia. *International Journal of Eating Disorders, 3*, 27–46.

Epstein, L. H., Masek, B. J., & Marshall, W. R. A. (1978). A nutritionally based school program for control of eating in obese children. *Behavior Therapy, 9*, 766–778.

Frisch, R. E., Gotz-Welbergen, A. V., McArthur, J. W., Albright, T., Witschi, J., Bullen, B., Birnholtz, J., Reed, R. B., & Herman, H. (1981). Delayed menarche and amenorrhea of college athletes in relation to the onset of training. *Journal of the American Medical Association, 246*, 1559–1563.

Frisch, R. E., Wyshank, G., & Vincent, L. (1980). Delayed menarche and amenorrhea in ballet dancers. *New England Journal of Medicine, 303*, 17–19.

Garner, D. M., & Garfinkel, P. E. (1980). Socio-cultural factors in the development of anorexia nervosa. *Psychological Medicine, 10*, 647–656.

Halmi, K. A. (1974). Anorexia nervosa: Demographic and clinical features. *Psychosomatic Medicine, 36*, 18–26.

Howard, R. B. (1839). *An inquiry into the morbid effect of deficiency of food chiefly with reference to their occurrence amongst the destitute poor.* London: Simpkin, Marshall.

Johnson, R. E., Mastropaolo, J. A., & Wharton, M. A. (1972). Exercise, dietary intake, and body composition. *Journal of the American Dietetic Association, 61*, 399–403.

Katz, J. L. (1986). Long distance running, anorexia nervosa, and bulimia: A report of two cases. *Comprehensive Psychiatry, 27*, 74–78.

Kaye, W. H., Picker, D. M., Naber, D. & Ebert, M. H. (1982). Cerebrospinal fluid opioid activity in anorexia nervosa. *American Journal of Psychiatry, 139*, 643–645.

Keys, A., Brozek, J., Henschel, A., Mickelson, O., & Taylor, H. L. (1950). *The biology of human starvation.* Minneapolis: University of Minnesota Press.

King, A. (1963). Primary and secondary anorexia nervosa syndromes. *British Journal of Psychiatry, 109*, 470–479.

Kron, L., Katz, J. L., Gorzynski, G., & Weiner, H. (1978). Hyperactivity in anorexia nervosa: A fundamental clinical feature. *Comprehensive Psychiatry, 19*, 433–440.

Mansfield, M. J., & Emans, S. J. (1989). Anorexia nervosa, athletics, and amenorrhea. *Pediatric Clinics of North America, 36*, 533–549.

Mayer, J., Roy, P. & Mitra, K. P. (1956). Relation between caloric intake, body weight, and physical work: Studies in an industrial male population in West Bengal. *American Journal of Clinical Nutrition, 4*, 169 175.

Mrosovsky, N. (1984). Animal models: Anorexia yes, nervosa, no. In K. M. Pirke & D. Ploog (Eds.), *Psychobiology of anorexia nervosa* (pp. 24–34). New York: Springer-Verlag.

Mrosovsky, N., & Sherry, D. F. (1980). Animal anorexias. *Science, 207*, 837–842.

Pierce, W. D., & Epling, W. F. (1991). Activity anorexia: An animal model and theory of human self-starvation. In A. Boulton, G. Baker, & M. Martin-Iverson (Eds.), *Neuromethods, Vol. 18: Animal models in psychiatry 1* (pp. 267–311). Clifton, NJ: Humana Press.

Russell, J. C., Epling, W. F., Pierce, W. D., Amy, R., & Boer, D. (1987). Induction of voluntary prolonged running by rats. *Journal of Applied Physiology, 63*, 2549–2553.

Russell-Davis, D. (1951). Studies in malnutrition. *M.R.C. special report series no. 275.* London: H.M. Stationery office.

Slade, P. D. (1973). A short anorectic behavior scale. *British Journal of Psychiatry, 122*, 83–85.

Spigelman, M. N., McLeod, W. S., & Rockman, G. E. (1991). Caloric vs. pharmacologic effects of ethanol consumption on activity anorexia in rats. *Pharmacology Biochemistry and Behavior, 39*, 85–90.

Tokuyama, K., Saito, M., & Okuda, H. (1982). Effects of wheel running on food intake and weight gain of female rats. *Physiology and Behavior, 23*, 899–903.

Watanabe, K., Hara, C., & Ogawa, N. (1992). Feeding conditions and estrous cycle of female rats under the activity–stress procedure from aspects of anorexia nervosa. *Physiology and Behavior, 51*, 827–823.

Watt, E. W., Wiley, J., & Fletcher, G. F. (1976). Effect of dietary control and exercise training on daily food intake and serum lipids in post-myocardial infarction patients. *American Journal of Clinical Nutrition, 29*, 900–904.

Wheeler, G. D., McFadyen, S. G., Symbaluk, D., Pierce, W. D., & Cumming, D. C. (1992). Effects of training on serum testosterone and cortisol levels in wrestlers. *Clinical Journal of Sport Medicine, 2*, 257–259.

Wheeler, G. D., Singh, M., Pierce, W. D., Epling, W. F., & Cumming, D. C. (1991) Endurance training decreases serum testosterone levels in men without change in lutinizing hormone pulsatile release. *Journal of Clinical Endocrinology and Metabolism, 72*, 422–425.

Wheeler, G. D., Wall, S. R., Belcastro, A. N., & Cumming, D. C. (1984). Reduced serum testosterone and prolactin levels in male distance runners. *Journal of the American Medical Association, 252*, 514–516.

Yates, A. (1991). *Obligatory running and the eating disorders: Toward an integrated theory of activity.* New York: Bruner/Mazel.

Yates, A. (1992). Biologic considerations in the etiology of the eating disorders. *Pediatric Annals, 21*, 739–745.

Yates, A., Leehey, K., & Shisslak, C. M. (1983). Running— An analogue of anorexia? *New England Journal of Medicine, 308*, 251–255.

Yates, A., Shisslak, C., Allender, J., & Crago, M. (1992). Comparing obligatory and nonobligatory runners. *Psychosomatics, 33*, 180–189.

2

Validity Criteria for Animal Models of Anorexia Nervosa Involving Activity Anorexia

Thomas S. Rieg
Winona State University

Animal models of eating disorders are desirable for numerous reasons. Such models allow for the simulation of eating problems under controlled conditions with unlimited numbers of subjects. Through the use of animals, it is possible to study the effects of various manipulations, including pharmacological and physiological variables that would not otherwise be possible. Finally, whereas human pathology is usually only studied after the disorder presents itself, animals can be used to develop cause-and-effect statements between antecedent events and subsequent behavior.

This chapter defends several models of anorexia from the common criticism of lack of validity from both colleagues and the general public. In order to achieve this goal, the criteria for an animal model are presented, then criteria of validity and their applications to various models of anorexia nervosa (AN). Finally, various animal models of AN, are presented with a focus on the activity component of the disorder. Each is evaluated in terms of its validity.

MODELS OF PSYCHOPATHOLOGY

The use of animals to model human psychopathology has a long history in psychology (Bond, 1984). Underwood (1957) defined *models* as representations or likenesses of certain aspects of a complex event structure or system; these representations are made by using symbols or objects that in some way correspond to what is being modeled. The advantage of using animal models is that these representations produce, under controlled conditions, phenomena analogous to naturally occurring mental disorders. It is important to note that models are not theories. Theories require a formalized set of logically intertwined propositions that are more robust than models (Marx & Goodson, 1976). Direct empirical testing of multifaceted theories of anorexia is often difficult, if not impossible. Therefore, models have been constructed based on components of the theory.

To a large extent it is this misunderstanding of the distinction between a model and a theoretical explanation that has caused people to be suspicious of the use of animal models to study anorexia nervosa. Many hold expectations that models explain all features of AN including psychological, physiological, and psychosocial symptoms. Experimenters have argued that models do not provide enough psychological complexity to explain truly the associated human psychopathology. It is this schism that has deprived animal researchers of acceptance of their work and in many cases has been the cause of rejected grant applications.

A model is a conceptual framework that will provide the researcher with a guide as to how a problem might be pursued. Often this framework will be a guide whereby findings in one area might be applied to another domain. In psychology, theories dictate how and what to model in the animal. In the psychopathology of AN, clinical findings dictate how and what will be modeled in nonhuman animals.

Human anorexia is characterized by significant weight loss, intense fear of becoming obese, distortion of body shape, and amenorrhea (American Psychiatric Association, 1994). Anorexia occurs with alarming frequency among women and men with a 50% relapse rate within the first year (Yates, 1989). Its mortality rate remains at 6% (Yates, 1989). Four common behaviors engaged in by individuals with anorexia that result in weight loss are dieting, laxative abuse, purging, and excessive activity or exercise.

The question for researchers becomes which and how many of these features can be modeled in the nonhuman animal. Animals do engage in natural anorexias involving voluntary fasting. For animals, this time of voluntary fasting is associated with a reduction in metabolism (Mrosovsky & Sherry, 1980). The male emperor penguin loses up to 40% of its body weight while incubating its egg (Le Mayo, 1977). Other obvious examples of animal anorexias involve defense of territory and harem, migration, and molting (see Mrosovsky & Sherry, 1980, for a review). However, although these anorexias may be similar to human AN, they differ in a number of important features (Mrosovsky, 1983). Animal anorexias provide the organism with a reproductive advantage, are associated with a reduction in metabolism, and stop short of total energy exhaustion.

None of these anorexias accurately characterizes AN in humans. Animals do not consume foods that normally make them sick or cause weight loss in one form or another. Bolles (1970) contended that each species has a set of built in, species-specific defense reactions that leads to its survival. Rats will sample small amounts of a novel food, and if the food produces no ill effects it will become part of the rats' diet. No animal is known to regurgitate with the intent of losing weight. Such behaviors, most characteristic of birds, are designed to nurture their offspring. Some species of animals even lack the ability to regurgitate. In contrast, activity is one behavior that is observed in humans and in animals that in excess will lead to death.

Increased Activity in Anorexia

It is argued that increased activity is a primary feature of AN (Beumont, Arthur, Russell & Touyz, 1994; Kron, Katz, Gorzynski, & Weiner, 1978). Kron et al. (1978) reported that 64% of patients diagnosed with AN were highly active prior to the onset of the disorder. Individuals with AN expend more energy in the form of physical activity than do control subjects (Casper, Schoeller, Kushner, Hnilicka & Trainer Gold, 1991). Furthermore, even during early treatment AN patients continue to show increased activity levels (Falk, Halmi, & Tryon, 1985). This compulsive need to exercise has even been used in an operant conditioning paradigm in which access to physical activity can be made contingent on weight gain (Blinder, Freeman, & Stunkard, 1970). Subpopulations in whom exercise is encouraged are at risk for developing AN (Katz, 1986; Smith, 1980; Yates, Leehey, & Shisslak, 1983).

Validity and Animal Models

When evaluating an animal model, an issue that is frequently overlooked is the extent to which different types of validity affect acceptance of the model. In terms of acceptance, content validity is usually the first step in establishing an animal model of psychopathology. Content validity involves face validity and refers to the extent to which a model appears to measure what it is supposed to measure. Because human AN patients present such features as weight loss, distorted body image, food or weight phobia, and increased activity levels, an animal model must have as its primary dependent variable changes in at least one of these. The ideal model would, of course, incorporate more than one of these features. Increasing face validity has the advantage that both researchers and the lay public will have more confidence in the model.

A model has construct validity when the independent and dependent variables in an experiment accurately reflect what they are intended to measure. Construct validity involves the possibility that an experimental manipulation that is meant to represent one particular construct may be interpreted in terms of another or even more than one construct. What might be viewed by one researcher as an aspect of a particular psychopathology might be viewed by another as an aspect of a different disorder. For example, although excessive exercise by the individual with AN might be considered an essential feature of the disorder specifically designed to reduce calories, it might also be construed as an example of the frequently reported obsessive or compulsive component of AN (Kasvikis, Tsakiris, Marks, Basoglu, & Noshirvani, 1986).

The third type of validity is criterion-related validity (or concurrent or predictive validity) that deals with predicting a certain observation in some setting outside of the model or at some time in the future. The issue in animal models becomes one of determining whether the findings in one model are correlated with those of another model. For example, are the metabolic changes reported in one experimental manipulation similar to those reported when animals undergo another procedure? If each model predicts similar changes or abnormalities in some measure, then those models can be considered to have concurrent or predictive validity.

EXERCISE MODELS FOR AN

Several animal models that focus on an essential feature of AN, exercise or activity, have been proposed to investigate anorexia. In this section, each model is presented, discussed, and evaluated in terms of its merit as a model and with respect to the various types of validity as outlined above. Although it might be possible to review a variety of models of AN, the discussion is limited to those models that involve activity as an essential component.

Contingent Exercise

Early research showed that when reinforcement was made contingent on wheel running, postreinforcement pauses resembled those observed in rats during lever-pressing for food (Skinner & Morse, 1958), indicating no differences between these two operants. There also seems to be an inverse relationship between wheel-running and eating. When an activity wheel was made available, rats reduced their daily food intake, whereas food intake was increased with removal of the wheel (Premack & Premack, 1963). Furthermore, when wheel-running was made contingent on lever-pressing, rats showed an inverted U function to their level of food deprivation as measured by percent body weight (Pierce, Epling, & Boer, 1986). Rats pressed the lever more at 75% of their body weight than at their free feeding weight (100%). Finally, in the paradigm of open economies, where animals can choose among different behaviors, rats spend most of the time engaging in wheel-running (Collier & Rovee-Collier, 1981). These studies indicate the interplay between wheel-running, eating, and food deprivation. One interpretation is that wheel-running in the laboratory is analogous to seeking food in everyday settings. Increased activity may allow animals to find food when the food supply is reduced by famine or other circumstances.

The model of contingent wheel-running may have its greatest usefulness when applied to situations where humans associate physical health, derived from exercise and weight reduction, with psychological health. Hayes and Ross (1986) indicate that exercise and good physical health improve psychological well-being. This trend toward increased athleticism may be because only 55% of the population was satisfied with its health and that dieting has become the norm in our society. Seventy-eight percent of adolescent girls wish to weigh less (Eisele, Hertsgaard, & Light, 1986), and 70% had engaged in some weight-reducing activity within the previous year (Wadden, Foster, Stunkard, & Linowitz, 1989). The findings derived from contingent wheel-running follow those reporting a link between exercise and well-being (Hayes & Ross, 1986). In this case, exercise is seen as an adaptive behavior, unlike AN, for which exercise exacerbates and perpetuates the disorder. The model therefore lacks face validity in that it merely establishes a correlation between activity and food intake. It has both construct and criterion validity to the extent that exercise is considered voluntary or even reinforcing and the findings generalize to other models. Table 2.1 contains a summary of the model and its associated criterion for validity.

Forced Exercise

The use of an acute forced treadmill exercise is one experimental manipulation that models activity in the rat. In this paradigm, rats are trained over numerous sessions to run on a flat-belt treadmill. The intensity of the exercise can be modified by increasing the angle or the speed of the treadmill. In order to ensure that the animal continues to run on the belt, an electrified grid (generally 50 V DC, 60 mA) is positioned at the rear of each compartment (Nikoletseas, 1980). Rats quickly learn to avoid receiving shocks by running and are exercised for approximately 1 hour each day. Animals that fail to learn to run are discarded from the protocol.

Forced exercise has its similarities in human athletes who are encouraged to exercise as a part of the training regimen. Depending on the type of sport, data indicate that high school athletes reduce their body fat to 5% (Smith, 1980). This model seems to be similar to the human condition in terms of weight reduction and therefore has face validity. However, the exercise is not voluntary and seems to be specific to one type of activity (i.e., treadmill), unlike what is observed in humans with anorexia (Richert & Hummers, 1986). Finally, the metabolic and physiological changes associated with forced exercise are consistent with those of other models of anorexia (Nickoletseas, 1980). Based on these observations, the forced exercise model lacks construct validity but achieves criterion validity (see Table 2.1).

Forced Swimming

Forced swimming (Richter, 1957) exposes rats to prolonged or repeated chronic exercise. The animal model was originally designed as a model of depression

TABLE 2.1

Types of Activity-Based Animal Models of AN
and their Associated Types of Validity

Type of Model	Face	Construct	Criterion
Contingent Wheel Running	no	yes	yes
Forced Exercise	yes	no	yes
Forced Swimming	no	no	yes
Activity-Based Anorexia	yes	yes	yes

(Porsolt, LePichon, & Jalfre, 1977). In this model, rats swim in a Plexiglas cylinder and are tested until they meet a criterion of immobility. Rats generally continue to exercise for 10 to 20 minutes before they give up. In some protocols, weights have even been tied to the animals' tails in order to prolong swimming (Asano, Suzuki, & Minamitoni, 1986; Guilland, Moreau, Genet, & Klepping, 1988). Some researchers might argue that this is an adequate model for anorexia; however, various problems are associated with its implementation. The fact that animals learn to adapt to their predicament by becoming immobile, especially with respect to repeated exposure (O'Neil & Valentino, 1982), defeats its purpose as a model of anorexia, as an essential feature of AN is increased activity. A second problem with this model is that the subjects die in one session without experimenter intervention or if the water temperature is increased or reduced from what appears to be the ideal water temperature (Richter, 1957; Bruner & Vargas, 1994).

Like the treadmill exercise paradigm, this model involves acute exercise and can be considered chronic only to the extent that animals are exposed to daily swimming sessions. This model, then, seems to lack both face and construct validity for AN as discussed above (see Table 2.1). More recently, Kramer, Dijkstra, and Bast (1993) have modified the swimming task to resemble a treadmill paradigm where rats swim against a current of water. The uses of this apparatus remain to be determined. This model has some similarities to depression where the animal is said to be depressed when it ceases to swim. It is interesting to note that serotonin abnormalities observed in forced swimming are similar to those reported in models of anorexia, and therefore it retains criterion validity.

Voluntary Exercise

An animal model of AN has been described with two important features of the human disorder: dieting and exercise. Almost 40 years ago Reid and Finger (1957) reported that animals starve themselves to death when given restricted access to food and access to a running wheel. This phenomenon has been given various names, including *self-starvation* (Routtenberg & Kuznesof, 1967), *activity–stress ulcer* (Pare & Houser, 1973), *activity-based anorexia* (ABA); (Epling & Pierce, 1988; Epling, Pierce, & Stefan, 1983), and *semistarvation-induced hyperactivity* (Broocks, Liu, & Pirke, 1990). Experimentally, the effect is simple to produce. Rats are deprived of food and fed once per day for 60 to 90 minutes. During food deprivation they are given free access to a running wheel. Under these conditions animals increase their activity levels and reduce their daily food intake. Experimental animals die if experimenters do not intervene (Routtenberg, 1968). Control animals on the same feeding schedule but not given wheel access increase their food intake and stabilize their body weight (Epling & Pierce, 1984).

Ideally, the experimental manipulation is set up as a 2×2 factorial design involving wheel access and food access (Aravich, Rieg, Ahmed, & Lauterio, 1993; Aravich, Rieg, Lauterio, & Doerries, 1993). Experimental animals (ABA) are deprived of food and fed for 90 minutes per day and given wheel access for 22.5 hours per day. Controls consist of body weight matched (BWM) rats that are deprived of food so that their percentage weight loss equals that of the ABA animals. The exercise control rats (EXC) are not deprived of food but are allowed access to the running wheel, whereas the last group of rats (ADL) is given ad libitum food and no running wheel. Animals are exposed to this paradigm until the ABA rats reach a criterion of 25% or 30% body weight loss (Doerries, Stanley, & Aravich, 1991). Depending on a number of subject variables, including sex, weight, and age of the animal prior to introduction to the protocol, ABA rats will meet the criterion within approximately 10 days, although exceptions have been noted (Rieg, Maestrello, & Aravich, 1994).

The model involves voluntary and chronic running by the animals and, compared with other paradigms both of exercise and other animal models of anorexia, meets all the validity criteria for a model of AN (see Table 2.1). Its particular strength may be related to the fact that activity becomes a sensitive measure to determine the effectiveness of the independent variable. Not only does the model generalize the effects of food deprivation, but it is also applicable to restricted water access (Rieg, Doerries, O'Shea, & Aravich, 1993). Finally, it is sensitive to other manipulations affecting feeding, activity, and weight loss (Rieg & Aravich, 1994).

CONCLUSIONS

In terms of models for the activity component of AN, activity-based anorexia seems to have the best chances for gaining widespread acceptance. It meets the criteria of a model, has the three forms of validity as previously discussed, and produces the associated physiological correlates (discussed elsewhere in this volume) of anorexia nervosa in humans. Much remains to be determined about the predisposing, precipitating, and perpetuating factors involved in AN, and ABA at this point holds the most promise for elucidating these elements.

REFERENCES

American Psychiatric Association. (1994). *Diagnostic and statistical manual of mental disorders* (4th ed.). Washington, DC: Author.

Aravich, P. F., Rieg, T. S., Ahmed, I., & Lauterio, T. J. (1993). Fluoxetine induced vasopressin and oxytocin abnormalities in food-restricted rats given voluntary exercise: Relationship to anorexia nervosa. *Brain Research, 612*, 180–189.

Aravich, P. F., Rieg, T. S., Lauterio, T. J., & Doerries, L. E. (1993). Beta-endorphin and dynorphin abnormalities in rats subjected to exercise and restricted feeding: Relationship to anorexia nervosa? *Brain Research, 622*, 1–8.

Asano, S., Suzuki, K., & Minamitoni, K. (1986). The effects of endurance swimming on the serum lipoproteins and post heparin serum lipolytic activity in rats. *Journal of Sports Medicine, 26*, 194–202.

Beumont, P. J. V., Arthur, B., Russell, J. D., & Touyz, S. W. (1994). Excessive physical activity in dieting disorder patients: Proposals for a supervised exercise program. *International Journal of Eating Disorders, 15*, 21–36.

Blinder, B. J., Freeman, D. M. A., & Stunkard, A. J. (1970). Behavior therapy of anorexia nervosa: Effectiveness of activity as a reinforcer of weight gain. *American Journal of Psychiatry, 126*, 1093–1098.

Bolles, R. C. (1970). Species-specific defense reactions and avoidance learning. *Psychological Review, 77*, 32–48.

Bond, N. W. (1984). *Animal models of psychopathology.* Orlando, FL: Academic Press.

Broocks, A, Liu, J., & Pirke, K. M. (1990). Semistarvation-induced hyperactivity compensates for decreased norepinephrine and dopamine turnover in the mediobasal hypothalamus of the rat. *Journal of Neural Transmission, 79*, 113–124.

Bruner, C. A., & Vargas, I. (1994). The activity of rats in a swimming situation as a function of water temperature. *Physiology & Behavior, 55*, 21–28.

Casper, R. C., Schoeller, D. A., Kushner, R., Hnilicka, J., & Trainer Gold, S. (1991). Total daily energy expenditure and activity levels in anorexia nervosa. *American Journal of Clinical Nutrition, 53*, 1143–1150.

Collier, G., & Rovee-Collier, C. K. (1981). A comparative analysis of optimal foraging behavior: Laboratory simulations. In A. C. Kamil & T. D. Sargent (Eds.), *Foraging behavior: Ethological, ecological and psychological approaches* (pp. 39–76). New York: Garland STM Press.

Doerries, L. E., Stanley, E. Z., & Aravich, P. F. (1991). Activity-based anorexia: Relationship to gender and activity-stress ulcers. *Physiology & Behavior, 50*, 945–949.

Eisele, J., Hertsgaard, D., & Light, H. K. (1986). Factors related to eating disorders in young adolescent girls. *Adolescence, 21*, 283–290.

Epling, W. F., & Pierce, W. D. (1984). Activity-based anorexia in rats as a function of opportunity to run on an activity wheel. *Nutrition and Behavior, 2*, 37–49.

Epling, W. F., & Pierce, W. D. (1988). Activity-based anorexia: A biobehavioral perspective. *International Journal of Eating Disorders, 7*, 475–485.

Epling, W. F., Pierce, W. D., & Stefan, L. (1983). A theory of activity-based anorexia. *International Journal of Eating Disorders, 3*, 27–46.

Falk, J. R., Halmi, K. A., & Tryon, W. W. (1985). Activity measures in anorexia nervosa. *Archives of General Psychiatry, 42*, 811–814.

Guilland, J. C., Moreau, D., Genet, J. M., & Klepping, J. (1988). Role of catecholamines in regulation by feeding of energy balance following chronic exercise in rats. *Physiology & Behavior, 42*, 365–369.

Hayes, D., & Ross, C. E. (1986). Body and mind: The effect of exercise, overweight, and physical health on psychological well-being. *Journal of Health and Social Behavior, 27*, 387–400.

Kasvikis, Y. G., Tsakiris, F., Marks, I. M., Basoglu, M., & Noshirvani, H. F. (1986). Past history of anorexia nervosa in women with obsessive–compulsive disorder. *International Journal of Eating Disorders, 5*, 1069–1075.

Katz, J. L. (1986). Long-distance running, anorexia nervosa, and bulimia: A report of two cases. *Comprehensive Psychiatry, 27*, 74–78.

Kramer, K., Dijkstra, H., & Bast, A. (1993). Control of physical exercise of rats in a swimming basin. *Physiology & Behavior, 53*, 271–276.

Kron, L., Katz, J. L., Gorzynski, G., & Weiner, H. (1978). Hyperactivity in anorexia nervosa. *Comprehensive Psychiatry, 19*, 433–440.

Le Mayo, Y. (1977). The emperor penguin: A strategy to live and breed in the cold. *American Scientist, 65*, 680–693.

Marx, M. H., & Goodson, F. E. (1976). *Theories in contemporary psychology* (2nd ed.). New York: Macmillan.

Mrosovsky, N. (1983). Animal anorexias, starvation and anorexia nervosa: Are animal models of anorexia nervosa possible? In P. L. Darby, P. E. Garfinkel, D. M. Garner, & D.V. Coscina (Eds.), *Anorexia nervosa: Recent developments in research* (pp. 199–205). New York: Liss.

Mrosovsky, N., & Sherry, D. F. (1980). Animal anorexias. *Science, 207*, 837–842.

Nikoletseas, M. M. (1980). Food intake in the exercising rat: A brief review. *Neuroscience & Biobehavioral Reviews, 4*, 265–267.

O'Neil, K. A., & Valentino, D. (1982). Escapability and generalization: Effect on "behavioral despair." *European Journal of Pharmacology, 78*, 379–380.

Pare, W. P., & Houser, V. P. (1973). Activity and food-restriction effects on gastric glandular lesions in the rat: The activity-stress ulcer. *Bulletin of the Psychonomic Society, 2*, 213–224.

Pierce, W. D., Epling, W. F., & Boer, D. P. (1986). Deprivation and satiation: The interrelations between food and wheel running. *Journal of the Experimental Analysis of Behavior, 46*, 199–210.

Porsolt, R. D., LePichon, M., & Jalfre, M. (1977). Depression: A new animal model sensitive to antidepressant treatments. *Nature, 266*, 730–732.

Premack, D., & Premack, A. J. (1963). Increased eating in rats deprived of running. *Journal of the Experimental Analysis of Behavior, 6*, 209–212.

Reid, L. S., & Finger, F. W. (1957). The effect of activity restriction upon adjustment to cyclic food deprivation. *Journal of Comparative and Physiological Psychology, 50*, 491–494.

Richert, A. J., & Hummers, J. A. (1986). Patterns of physical activity in college students at possible risk for eating disorder. *International Journal of Eating Disorders, 5*, 757–763.

Richter, C. P. (1957). On the phenomenon of sudden death in animals and man. *Psychosomatic Medicine, 9*, 191–198.

Rieg, T. S., & Aravich, P. F. (1994). Systemic clonidine increases feeding and wheel running but does not affect rate of weight loss in rats subjected to activity-based anorexia. *Pharmacology Biochemistry & Behavior, 47*, 215–218.

Rieg, T. S., Doerries, L. E., O'Shea, J. G., & Aravich, P. F. (1993). Water deprivation produces an exercise-induced weight loss phenomenon in the rat. *Physiology & Behavior, 53*, 607–610.

Rieg, T. S., Maestrello, A. M., & Aravich, P. F. (1994). Weight cycling alters the effects of d-fenfluramine on susceptibility to activity-based anorexia. *American Journal of Clinical Nutrition, 60*, 494–500.

Routtenberg, A. (1968). "Self-starvation" of rats living in activity-wheels: Adaptation effects. *Journal of Comparative and Physiological Psychology, 66*, 234–238.

Routtenberg, A., & Kuznesof, A. W. (1967). Self-starvation of rats living in activity wheels on a restricted feeding schedule. *Journal of Comparative and Physiological Psychology, 64*, 414–421.

Skinner, B. F., & Morse, W. H. (1958). Fixed-interval reinforcement of running in a wheel. *Journal of the Experimental Analysis of Behavior, 1*, 371–379.

Smith, N. J. (1980). Excessive weight loss and food aversions in athletes simulating anorexia nervosa. *Pediatrics, 66*, 139–142.

Underwood, B. (1957). *Psychological research.* New York: Appleton.

Wadden, T. A., Foster, G. D., Stunkard, A. J., & Linowitz, J. R. (1989). Dissatisfaction with weight and figure in obese girls: Discontent but not depression. *International Journal of Eating Disorders, 13*, 89–97.

Yates, A. (1989). Current perspectives on the eating disorders: I. History, psychological and biological aspects. *Journal of the American Academy of Child and Adolescent Psychiatry, 28*, 813–828.

Yates, A., Leehey, K., & Shisslak, C. M. (1983). Running—An analogue of anorexia? *New England Journal of Medicine, 408*, 251–255.

3

Theoretical Developments in Activity Anorexia

W. David Pierce
W. Frank Epling
University of Alberta

In this chapter, a theory of activity anorexia is outlined that involves three levels of analysis: culture, behavior, and biology. In humans, cultural practices concerned with dieting and physical fitness place people at risk for activity anorexia. Risk increases when a person is encouraged to combine stringent dieting with intense exercise. At the behavioral level, food restriction enhances the reward value of exercise, and as physical activity increases the reward value of food declines. These behavioral relationships involve physiological processes that motivate and maintain anorectic behavior.

Figure 3.1 shows the interrelations among culture, behavior, and biology that account for activity anorexia. The theory explains how the physical and psychological symptoms attributed to anorexia nervosa are by-products of starvation and social learning. It is hypothesized that activity anorexia results from behavioral and biological processes that in Western societies are initiated by cultural practices based on the values of fitness and thinness.

CULTURE AND ACTIVITY ANOREXIA

Contingencies of reinforcement set by Western culture encourage people to diet and exercise, thereby increasing the chances that some individuals will combine

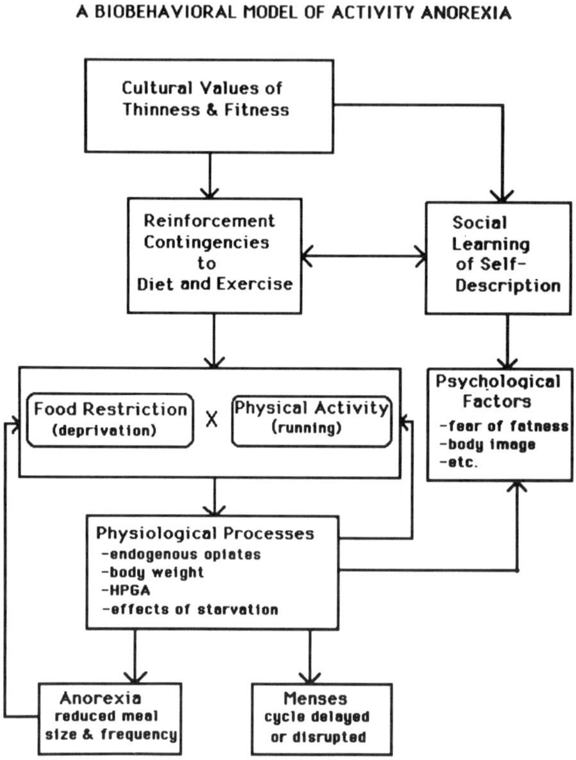

A BIOBEHAVIORAL MODEL OF ACTIVITY ANOREXIA

FIG. 3.1.   A biobehavioral model of activity anorexia. The model portrays the cultural impact on dieting and exercising. This behavior is suported by reinforcement contingencies set by family and friends. Under particular conditions, food restriction combines with physical activity to initiate the physiological processesof activity anorexia. Reprinted from *Solving The Anorexia Puzzle: A Scientific Approach* (p. 201), by W. F. Epling and W. D. Pierce, 1994, Toronto, ON: Hogrefe & Huber. Copyright 1994 by Hogrefe and Huber Publishers. Reprinted with permission of Hogrefe & Huber Publishers, Seattle Toronto Bern Göttingen.

food restriction and exercise in a way that initiates activity anorexia (Epling & Pierce, 1988, 1991; Epling, Pierce, & Stefan, 1983). Western culture currently values a thin, trim appearance in women (Lakoff & Scherr, 1984; Mazur, 1986) and physical fitness in both sexes (Beck, Ward-Hull, & McLear, 1976; Garner, Rockert, Olmstead, Johnson, & Cosina, 1985). Several researchers noted that in Western culture the mass media convey these values (Bruch, 1978; Kurman, 1978; Wooley, Wooley, & Dyrenforth, 1979), and people learn by observation (Bandura, 1986) to uphold and promote the beauty standards.

Acceptance of the thinness and fitness values means that people provide social approval, economic advantages, and privileges to individuals who attain the cultural beauty standards (Brigham, 1980; Green, Buchanan, & Heuer, 1984; Jones, Hannson, & Philips, 1978; Umberson & Hughes, 1984; Unger, Hilderbrand, & Madar, 1982). Because dieting and exercising are ways of achieving these standards, this behavior is reinforced (Garner et al., 1985). Importantly, social conditioning ensures that some people will inadvertently combine dieting with physical activity in a way that produces activity anorexia (Davies & Furnham, 1986; Dwyer, Feldman, & Mayer, 1970; Jakobovits, Halstead, Kelley, Roe, & Young, 1977; Miller, Coffman, & Linke, 1980). The more severe the increase in physical activity and the larger the drop in food consumption, the greater the chances of activity anorexia developing (Epling & Pierce, 1984, 1991).

Although the model (Fig. 3.1) emphasizes cultural factors as the major initiating conditions, it is important to recognize that the basic process may be triggered by other events. Famine, forced exercise, or any condition that combines food restriction and physical activity may increase the chances of activity anorexia. In addition, the psychological symptoms of anorexia are viewed as by-products of the activity–anorexia cycle. Katz (1986) reported that many of the psychological and physical symptoms of anorexia nervosa followed, rather than preceded, activity-induced starvation. Preoccupation with food, bingeing, vomiting, distortion of body image, loss of libido, and depression came after the onset of excessive exercise and food restriction (Beumont, 1991; Beumont, Booth, Abraham, Griffiths, & Turner, 1983; Keys, Brozek, Henschel, Mickelson, & Taylor, 1950).

Psychological factors as well as fear of fatness, body image distortion, and so on arise from starvation or from contingencies of reinforcement set by others (i.e., social learning). According to this analysis, family members, friends, and health professionals teach the anorectic to describe behavior, thoughts, and feelings. Also, reasonable responses to situational determinants of behavior are interpreted as personality symptoms. For example, a young woman who does not want to eat is said to resist treatment. Denial of illness, evidenced by resistance to treatment, is then taken as a symptom of anorexia nervosa (American Psychiatric Association, 1994). Psychological symptoms are also produced by the physiology of starvation. Keys et al. (1950) found that psychologically healthy men became neurotic, preoccupied with food, and bulimic when they were forced to starve.

EVOLUTION AND ACTIVITY ANOREXIA

The survival value of eating is obvious; the survival value of not eating is less obvious. However, anorexias do occur in many species that have resulted from natural selection (see Mrosovsky & Sherry, 1980, for a review and discussion). In these animals, anorexias often occur when the organism is engaged in other biologically relevant behavior (i.e., defending young, defending territory, molting, etc.). Organisms that are exposed to a periodic reduction in food supply (e.g., due to regular seasonal variation) may also become anorectic. For example, ground squirrels hibernate during the winter and will not eat when aroused. For these animals anorexia during hibernation contributes to energy efficiency. During hibernation, body temperature decreases and the kidneys do not function well. The kidneys remove waste products from the bloodstream and the animal must remain awake for efficient kidney function. Staying awake is energy-expensive because the animal must heat its body to normal temperature. Thus refusal to eat during hibernation relates to the energy cost of waking. In fact, the more squirrels eat the sooner they come out of hibernation (Mrosovsky & Barnes, 1974).

We contend that activity anorexia also had survival value and is an important variant of evolutionary-based anorexias. In this biobehavioral view, the interrelationships between physical activity and food intake are based on evolved structural features of organisms (i.e., physiological characteristics). Generally, natural selection favored those individuals (of some species) who became active during severe and unexpected food shortages. Animals that traveled to a new location found food, survived, and reproduced.

Anorexia induced by travel or migration to a new food patch probably had survival value. During a famine, food would be difficult to obtain and stopping to procure small amounts might be more energy costly than efficient. In other words, there may be a net negative energy balance between foraging for scarce (and difficult to obtain) food items and traveling to a more abundant food source.

BEHAVIORAL BASIS OF EATING AND PHYSICAL ACTIVITY

From a biobehavioral perspective, activity anorexia results from the interrelations of deprivation and food schedule on physical activity, and physical activity on food consumption. This multiplier effect between food restriction and physical activity is shown in Fig. 3.1. The multiplier effect results from two behavioral processes. Briefly stated, food deprivation increases the reinforcement value of exercise, and greater physical activity reduces the reward value of food. Thus a feedback loop based on reinforcement generates anorexia.

Reinforcement Value of Wheel-Running

Pierce, Epling, and Boer (1986) used 9 adolescent rats (4 males, 5 females) to test the reinforcement effectiveness of wheel-running as food deprivation changed. The animals were trained to press a lever to obtain 60 seconds of wheel-running. When the animal pressed the lever, a brake was removed and the running wheel was free to turn. After 60 seconds, the brake was again activated and the rat had to press the lever to obtain more time to run.

Once lever-pressing for wheel-running was consistent, each animal was tested when it was food deprived (75% of ad libitum weight) and when it was at free-feeding weight. In order to measure the reinforcement effectiveness of wheel-running, the animals were required to press the lever on an increasing fixed ratio for each opportunity to run. Specifically, the rats were required to press 5 times to obtain 60 seconds of wheel-running, then 10, 15, 20, 25, and so on. The point at which they gave up pressing for an opportunity to run was used as an index of the reinforcement effectiveness of exercise. Figure 3.2 shows the main results of this experiment and indicates that the reinforcement effectiveness of wheel-running increased with food deprivation for all animals.

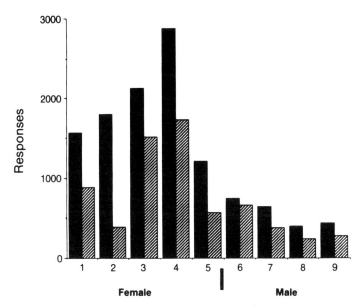

FIG. 3.2.   Maximum number of bar presses (responses) completed by 5 female and 4 male rats on a progressive ratio schedule. The animals pressed a lever to obtain 60 seconds of wheel running. Subjects were tested at 75% and 100% of free-feeding body weight. Female rats show greater response to food restriction than males. Reprinted from "Excessive Activity and Anorexia in Rats," by W. F. Epling & W. D. Pierce, in *The Menstrual Cycle and Its Disorders: Influences of Nutrition, Exercise and Neurotransmitters* (p. 84), edited by K. M. Pirke, W. Wuttke, and U. Schweiger, 1989, New York: Springer Verlag. Copyright 1994 by Springer Verlag. Reprinted with permission.

Female rats pressed more for the opportunity to run than males. Although it is tempting to suggest that this accords with a proportionally high number of women anorectics compared with males, there are other explanations. Female rats are considerably lighter than males, and the deprivation operation probably had a stronger impact on them. Also, female rats become highly active during estrus, and this may have affected the reinforcement value of wheel-running.

Overall, these results indicate that the reward value of wheel-running is sensitive to food allocation and deprivation (i.e., the behavior is related to food). When food is restricted, the reinforcement effectiveness of wheel-running increases; when the food supply is reinstated, the reinforcement value of wheel-running declines. The results support an evolutionary hypothesis that travel or migration is induced by reduction in food supply. Travel occurs because the reinforcement value of physical activity increases at times when food supply is diminished.

Food Supply and Wheel-Running

The sensitivity of wheel-running to fluctuations in the food supply has been investigated by Boer (1989) in our laboratory. Based on a procedure to induce voluntary prolonged running (Russell, Epling, Pierce, Amy, & Boer, 1987), five

6-week-old rats were given the opportunity to run on a wheel with an attached side cage. Over 10 days the animals were fed a fixed-restricted amount of food (15 grams per day) until wheel-running exceeded the criterion of 6,000 revolutions (6,600 meters). When an animal ran more than 6,000 revolutions in a day, the amount of food was increased to 18 grams. If the number of wheel turns fell below the criterion, food was reduced to 15 grams. This procedure established a steady-state level of wheel-running for each animal.

On day 10, some animals were fed 15 grams of food and others received 18 grams, depending on their level of wheel-running. Over the next 4 days, the rats were maintained on 15 or 18 grams of food (initial fixed amount of food). Following this period, the daily amount of food was titrated up and down relative to the initial fixed amount. Each titration was followed by a return to the initial fixed amount of food. For example, one rat received the food values of 15, 14, 15, 16, 15, 13, 15, 17, 15, 12, 15, 18, 15, 11, 15, 19, 15, 10, 15, and 20 grams, for consecutive four-day periods.

Results showed that the level of wheel-running tracked the changes in food supply. All animals ran less on days when food supply increased and ran more when the amount of food decreased. The number of wheel turns per day was sensitive to even a one-gram change in food supply. Also, larger fluctuations in the availability of food produced greater increases or reductions in the number of wheel turns per day. Interestingly, changes in wheel-running were not associated with changes in the animals' body weights. Body weights tended to increase over days, but wheel turns increased or decreased with changes in food supply.

Boer's (1989) results indicate that wheel-running is tightly regulated by changes in daily food supply. Moreover, the sensitivity of wheel-running to daily amount of food does not depend on changes in an animal's body weight (in contrast to Collier, 1969). It makes evolutionary sense that animals would begin to travel and search for food before their body weights reached a critical level. As the availability of food decreased, animals would increase their range of movement within a food patch or territory (see Devore & Hall, 1985; Loy, 1970, for evidence on primates). At a certain point, food supply would be so diminished that animals might trek long distances to find a stable source of food (Epling & Pierce, 1988, 1991; Pierce & Epling 1994).

This evolutionary analysis suggests it is possible that wheel-running in the laboratory is similar to travel within or between food patches in the natural habitat. Boer's (1989) work on moderate and prolonged running may model the daily movement of animals within a food area or location. If this is so, his results indicate that within-patch travel (i.e., search and procurement of food) is highly sensitive to small fluctuations in food supply.

On the other hand, Epling, Pierce, and Stefan (1983), among others (e.g., Routtenberg & Kuznesof, 1967), showed that severe food restriction may induce excessive and acute wheel-running. This behavior may be functionally similar to between-patch travel, where an animal moves rapidly over long distances from one food location to another (i.e., a trek for food). Interestingly, intensive running in the laboratory is also sensitive to aspects of food supply. For example, Kanarek and Collier (1983) reported that a single 60-minute daily meal generated excessive wheel-running, two 30-minute meals reduced the level of this behavior, and four 15-minute feedings prevented the occurrence of intensive running (and anorexia).

Thus excessive and acute wheel-running is regulated by the allocation and number of meals, when time of access to food is constant (60 minutes per day). A practical implication is that humans with anorexia who are hyperactive may benefit from an increase in the frequency of meals, holding daily intake constant. Hyperactivity is expected to subside and food intake increase with more frequent, small size, meals.

Reinforcement Value of Food

A second experiment, by Pierce et al. (1986), investigated the effects of exercise on the reinforcement effectiveness of food. Four male rats were trained to press a lever for food pellets. When lever-pressing reliably occurred, the effects of exercise on each animal's willingness to work for food was tested. In this case it was expected that a day of exercise would reduce the reinforcement effectiveness of food on the next day.

Reinforcement effectiveness of food was assessed by counting the number of lever-presses for food as food became more and more difficult to obtain. To illustrate, an animal had to press 5 times for the first food pellet, 10 for the next, then 15, 20, 25, and so on. As in the first experiment, the giving-up point was used to measure reinforcement effectiveness. Presumably, the more effective or valuable the reinforcer (i.e., food) the harder the animal would work for it.

As shown in Fig. 3.3, when test days were preceded by a day of exercise, the reinforcement effectiveness of food decreased sharply. Animals pressed the lever more than 200 times when they were not allowed to run, but no more than 38 times when running preceded test sessions. Food no longer supported lever-presses following a day of moderate wheel-running, even though a rest period in the home cage preceded the test. Although wheel-running was moderate, it represented a large change in physical activity because these animals were previously sedentary.

One rat (Subject 40) refused to run but was forced to do so on a motor driven wheel. As shown in Fig. 3.3, this animal sharply reduced lever-pressing for food after forced exercise. Because the reinforcement effectiveness of food decreased with forced exercise, it may be concluded that both forced and voluntary wheel-running produce a decline in the value of food reinforcement.

Taken together these findings support an evolutionary hypothesis that animals become anorectic during times of travel or migration. This conclusion is based on the assumption that wheel-running in the laboratory shares functional similarity to an animal's travel or migration in natural habitats. In this view, loss of appetite (anorexia) occurs because increases in physical activity reduce the reinforcement effectiveness of food. In terms of human behavior, people who increase their physical activity due to occupational requirements (e.g., ballet dancers) or for recreation may value food less and increase their chances of developing anorexia.

Opportunity for Activity and Anorexia

Because changes in physical activity alter the reinforcement value of food, Epling and Pierce (1984) reasoned that the incidence of anorexia would increase with the opportunity for physical activity. In fact, this is what happened as the amount of time that animals could run on their wheels was varied over a range of values.

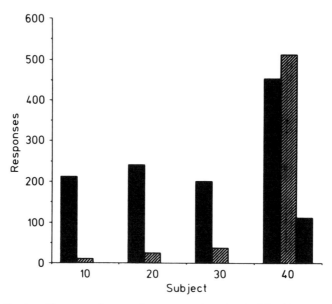

FIG. 3.3.   Number of bar presses (responses) on a progressive ratio schedule of food reintorcement for locked-wheel (dark) or open-wheel (striped) conditions. Subject 40 did not run when the wheel was open and was exposed to a forced-running procedure (third bar). Results show that wheel running reduces the reinforcement value of food. Reprinted from "Activity Anorexia: Interplay Between Basic and Applied Behavior Analysis," by W. D. Pierce and W. F. Epling, 1994, *The Behavior Analyst, 17,* p. 14. Copyright 1994 by the Association for Behavior Analysis. Reprinted with permission from *The Behavior Analyst* and the Association for Behavior Analysis.

In this study, adolescent male rats were randomly assigned to one of five activity conditions. The amount of time that animals could run on the wheels was 2, 6, 12, 18, or 22 hours a day. The only difference between the groups was the opportunity to run. As in other anorexia experiments, rats were freely fed and then changed to one 90-minute daily meal.

The opportunity to run influenced the amount of activity of the animals. Generally, the more the time the animals had to run the greater the change in daily activity was. Other results showed that food intake was affected by the amount of wheel-running. As the amount of running increased, food intake decreased. Animals were classified on a continuum of anorexia. Strongly anorectic animals showed clear suppression of food intake and sharply declining body weight. When animals were given 18 hours or more to run, 78% became strongly anorectic. Only 14% of animals who were given 12 hours or fewer of opportunity to run were strongly anorectic.

All cases of strong anorexia were accompanied by a specific type of activity curve, as shown in Fig. 3.4. This curve rapidly accelerates upward on a daily basis for anorectic animals. In other words, there is an exponential increase in daily activity. This change in daily rate of wheel-running is important for understanding the role of physical activity in anorexia. If activity slowly increases (i.e., linear) or remains the same from day to day, anorexia is less severe and less likely to occur. The opportunity to run influenced the likelihood of an accelerated activity curve; accelerated daily activity then determined the occurrence of strong anorexia (see also Epling & Pierce, 1989).

At the human level, people who combine dieting with rapidly increasing physical activity are expected to become anorectic. The athlete who substantially increases training, or the sedentary person who begins a physical fitness program, may be at risk if he or she is also restricting food intake (e.g., to alter appearance, to lose weight, or to incease performance). Research by Symbaluk (chapter 12, this volume) on subgroups of athletes provides some preliminary evidence for this training–food restriction hypothesis (see also chapter 13, this volume).

Behavior, Anorexia, and Evolution

These relationships among eating, activity, and environmental requirements (e.g., adjustments in reinforcement value, food supply or allocation, and opportunity for

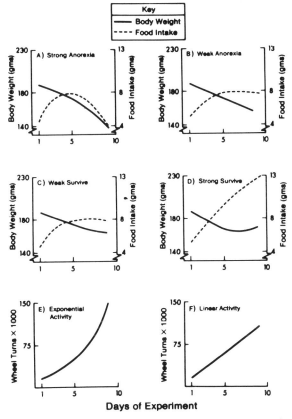

FIG. 3.4.   Idealized curves for body weight and food intake that allowed for the classification of two anorectic and two survival effects. Notice that the strong-anorectic effect (A) is characterized by rapidly declining food intake and body weight. This effect occurs when physical activity exponentially increases (E). Linear activity (F) may lead to weak anorexia (B) or weak survival (CA). Those animals that do not always run show the strong-survival effect (D). Reprinted from "Activity-based Anorexia in Rats as a Function of Opportunity to Run on an Activity Wheel," by W. F. Epling and W. D. Pierce, 1984, *Nutrition and Behavior, 2*, p. 45. Copyright © 1984 by John Wiley and Sons. Reprinted with permission from John Wiley & Sons.

physical activity) explain at a behavioral level why organisms do not eat on a famine-induced migration and why they eventually discontinue travel when a new food patch is found.

During a famine or drought, food is difficult to obtain and caloric intake is reduced. Because food is infrequently obtained, physical activity is highly reinforcing and the organism begins to move. As the animal increases physical activity, food becomes less effective as reinforcement, and the organism is unlikely to respond for food items that require extended effort. Only when food becomes abundant and more easily obtained is it eaten. As food from easily acquired sources is taken, the reinforcement value of traveling declines, and the organism stops moving. For these reasons, animals stop migrating once a new food patch is found. The behavioral relationships between eating and activity are a function of the organism's evolutionary history. Natural selection has resulted in physiological processes that are part of the contingencies regulating activity anorexia (see Fig. 3.1).

PHYSIOLOGY AND ACTIVITY ANOREXIA

Activity Anorexia and Endogenous Opiates

Epling and Pierce (1988, 1991) indicated that the excessive physical activity associated with anorexia could be maintained by the release of endogenous opiates. Recent evidence also implicates the opioid system in the regulation of food-seeking behavior. Finally, exercise and neural opiates have been implicated in control of fertility in anorectics and female athletes. These three roles of endogenous opiates are addressed next.

Physical Activity, Opiates, and Reinforcement. As we have noted, the release of endogenous opiates may function as reinforcement for physical activity. There is evidence of a dose response relation between intensity of exercise and plasma ß-endorphin; (Radosevich et al., 1989). This implies that ß-endorphin release in the central nervous system (CNS) is increased. As aerobic fitness increases, more and more exercise is required to attain maximal release of endogenous opiates (McMurray, Hardy, Roberts, & Forsythe, 1989). Thus physical activity is probably maintained on a schedule of reinforcement for endorphin release that requires greater and greater amounts of exercise.

In terms of wheel-running, opiate agonists (i.e., morphine) increase running following an initial period of hypoactivity (Babbini & Davis, 1972; Schnur & Barela, 1984; Schnur, Bravo, & Trujillo, 1983; Schnur, Bravo, Trujillo, & Rocha, 1983; Schnur, Hang, & Stinchcomb, 1987). For example, Schnur, Bravo, and Trujillo (1983) showed that low doses of morphine had a biphasic effect in golden Syrian hamsters, initially reducing physical activity and then increasing it. Analysis of wheel-running for each session indicated that the period of hypoactivity was less pronounced and diminished over 3 days. At the same time, hyperactivity increased and came to dominate most of the session.

The reinforcement hypothesis suggests that injection of an opiate antagonist will reduce the intense wheel-running of food-restricted animals. This is because the euphoric effects of opiates are diminished by antagonizing opioid receptors. In our laboratory, research by Boer (Boer, Epling, Pierce, & Russell, 1990) has explored the effects of the opiate antagonist naloxone on the food-restricted running of male rats. In this study, animals were made hyperactive by being fed a reduced amount of food and provided with a running wheel. Once wheel-running exceeded 5,000 revolutions per day (5 km) each animal was given I.P. naloxone (50 mg/kg in saline) or saline (.5 ml) on alternative days. Average daily wheel revolutions were approximately 5,800 for saline days and 4,800 on days when the animals were injected with naloxone, $p < .01$. These findings provided preliminary evidence for the hypothesis that food-restricted running is strengthened and maintained by the release of endogenous opiates (Arnsten & Segal, 1979; DeRossett & Holtzman, 1982; Potter, Borer, & Katz, 1983; Rodgers & Deacon, 1979).

However, studies of the effects of opiate antagonists on wheel-running using lower doses have typically not found effects. Carey, Ross, and Enns (1981) reported that 1 mg/kg and 10 mg/kg of naloxone suppressed food and water intake of rats, but had no effect on wheel-running. Schnur and Barela (1984) found no effect on wheel-running of naltraxone between doses of .3 to 10 mg/kg in golden hamsters.

Recent studies in our laboratory have refined and extended the work on opiate antagonists. We now have the ability to monitor in detail activity by rats in a steady-state wheel-running protocol (Boer et al., 1990) throughout the diurnal cycle. Preliminary experiments in our laboratory indicate that the response to a high dose of naloxone (50 mg/kg) is complex. The running decreases strongly in the time immediately following naloxone injection, with this effect intensifying daily over a 4-day series of naloxone treatment. There is a concurrent development of significant running later in the light portion of the diurnal cycle. At the same time naltraxone (1 mg/kg or 20 mg/kg) has no significant inhibitory effect on daily running, a finding in accord with Schnur and Barela (1984).

Taken as a whole, the research on opiate antagonists suggests a dose response relationship between the naloxone and food-restricted wheel-running, with lower doses having no effect and higher doses suppressing physical activity. This effect is not observed with the opiate blocker naltraxone. The effectiveness of higher doses of naloxone is consistent with an involvement of the kappa receptor in the modulation of food-seeking behavior (Morely & Blundell, 1988; Nencini & Graziani, 1990). In addition to dose level, the time course of the drug may be important because studies of prolonged wheel-running (more than 6 hours) find suppression of running, whereas studies of shorter duration (2 to 3 hours) do not. Finally, it is possible that the level of food deprivation is involved in the differential response to opiate antagonists. Evidence suggest that body weight must fall to some relative fixed level (approximately 80% to 75% of a normal rats' ad libitum weight) during a fast before deprivation-induced running occurs (Sclafani & Rendel, 1978). Wheel-running at free-feeding weight may not have the same function and underlying neurobiology as food-restricted wheel-running or running induced by more severe starvation (e.g., chapter 7 shows that naloxone increased running and decreased food intake of anorectic rats).

Endogenous Opiates, Anorexia, and Food-Seeking.   ß-endorphin and the mu receptor appear to have some involvement in the relationship between increasing physical activity and reducing food intake in both rats and humans (e.g., Aravich, Rieg, Lauterio, & Doerries, 1993; Doerries, Aravich, Metcalf, Wall, & Lauterio, 1989; also see Epling & Pierce, 1991, for a review; and chapter 7, this volume, for evidence against this hypothesis).

Recently, Aravich et al. (1993) reported elevated levels of plasma ß-endorphin and anterior pituitary ß-endorphin in rats exposed to the activity anorexia procedure. Generally, declining food intake stimulates an increase in physical activity. Physical activity increases production of ß-endorphin (Colt, Wardlaw, & Frantz, 1981) and this neural opiate functions as reinforcement for exercise (see Shainberg, 1977, for runner's high; chapter 4, this volume). After reviewing the relevant evidence, Marrazzi and Luby (1986) suggested that anorexia results from addiction to opioids. In terms of activity anorexia, it is significant to note that anorectic patients show high plasma levels of ß-endorphin (Kaye, Picker, Naber, & Ebert, 1982). Also, ß-endorphin reduces the motivation to eat for patients with anorexia (Kaye, 1987; Moore, Mills, & Forster, 1981; Nakai, Kinoshita, Koh, Tsujii, & Tsukada, 1987) and for rats that are forced to exercise (Davis, Lamb, Yim, & Malvern, 1985).

Although ß-endorphin is implicated in the regulation of physical activity, other evidence points to dynorphin and the kappa receptor. Aravich et al. (1993) reported a reduction of supraoptic hypothalamic dynorphin-A in rats exposed to the activity anorexia procedure. Nencini and Graziani (1990) reported a result that is apparently at odds with the Aravich et al. experiment. They found that the kappa agonist U50 did not increase food intake, but accelerated running along a runway for food. This effect was blocked by a high dose of naloxone (5 mg/kg). Thus, in the context of food restriction and wheel-running, a reduction in kappa stimulation is associated with excessive running, whereas in a maze-learning experiment elevation of kappa stimulation leads to accelerated running for food. These findings on the kappa receptor and physical activity are not yet clarified, but the research does suggest involvement of dynorphin and kappa in the regulation of this behavior.

Dynorphin and the kappa receptor are also implicated in the regulation of food intake. In a review of the neurobiological basis of eating disorders, Morley and Blundell (1988) noted several studies in rats that pointed to the involvement of the kappa-opioid receptor in the regulation of feeding behavior (Morley, Levine, Plotka, & Seal, 1983). Recent evidence indicates that the kappa-opioid system plays a role in neuropeptide Y(NPY)-induced feeding. NPY and dynorphin have additive effects on food intake, suggesting that a component of NPY-induced feeding may be mediated by kappa-opioid system (Lambert, Wilding, al-Dokhayel, Gilbey, & Bloom, 1993).

Morley and Blundell (1988) speculated that opioids such as dynorphin and ß-endorphin were involved in the control of food-related behavior (i.e., food seeking) as well as feeding. One possibility is that deprivation-induced wheel-running (or exercise) functions as food-seeking behavior, which could be partially maintained through its effects on the ß-endorphin and the mu receptor. At the same time, changes in the level of physical activity may reduce the uptake of dynorphin by the kappa receptor. Together, the two opioid effects could, at least partially, account for increased travel or exercise during periods of food restriction and suppression of eating during the trek for a stable food supply or during exercise brought on by stringent dieting.

Endogenous Opiates and Fertility.   Disruption of the menstrual cycle is a major physical symptom of AN. Evidence suggests that increased levels of endorphins produced by physical activity disrupt hormones that regulate the menstrual cycle (Cumming & Rebar, 1983, 1985; Petraglia et al., 1986; Ropert, Quigley, & Yen, 1981; Warren, 1989) and testosterone production in males (Wheeler, Singh, Pierce, Epling, & Cumming, 1991). Simply stated, it makes sense that sexual reproduction should decrease during a time of food shortage and travel to a new food patch

In terms of fertility and anorexia, the issue is whether hyperactivty contributes directly to late onset of menstruation and amenorrhea (e.g., by altering endorphin, luteinizing hormone, and/or gonadotropin releasing hormone levels), or whether excessive physical activity works indirectly on body composition (i.e., fat to lean ratio) and/or nutrition (Frish, 1988; also see chapters 10 and 11, this volume, for more on fertility and anorexia). The role of exercise or physical activity in the regulation of menstrual cycle continues to be an important area of research related to activity anorexia.

Activity Anorexia and the Dopaminergic System

Although there is evidence implicating the endogenous opiates with activity anorexia, other research suggests an involvement of the dopaminergic system. More specifically, there is evidence that dopamine and its receptors in the hypothalamus play a role in the reward value of physical activity. In addition, research indicates that dopamine is an antagonist for NPY in the perifornical region of the hypothalamus. Neuropeptide Y elicits eating, and one hypothesis is that physical activity (induced by food restriction) causes a release of dopamine that blocks the effects of this neuropeptide. Thus suppression of eating based on excessive physical activity may be mediated by the interaction of dopamine with NPY.

Physical Activity, Dopamine, and Reinforcement.   Animal research also shows that dopamine, a neurotransmitter, is implicated in reinforcement processes and affects physical activity (see also chapter 4, this volume). Dopamine agonists (i.e., amphetamine, cocaine) increase running (Evans & Vaccarino, 1986; Glavin, Pare, Vincent, & Tsuda, 1981; Jakubczak & Gomer, 1973; Tainter, 1943), whereas dopamine antagonists (i.e., pimozide, chlorpromazine) reduce this behavior (Beninger & Freedman, 1982; Routtenberg, 1968; Routtenberg & Kuznesof, 1967). In terms of deprivation-induced wheel-running, Routtenberg and Kuznesof (1967) and Routtenberg (1968) found that 1 mg/kg or 2 mg/kg of chlorpromazine (CPZ) reduced wheel-running in rats. This effect presumably accounted for the increased survival of animals exposed to their self-starvation paradigm. Recently, Belke (1993) injected rats with amphetamine (.5, 1.0, and 2.0 mg/kg) and chlorpromazine (.5, 1.0, and 2.0 mg/kg) and measured the effects on lever-pressing for wheel-running reinforcement. His procedures separated the motoric effects of the drug from its effects on the reinforcement effectiveness of wheel-running (i.e., motivation). Results showed that both amphetamine and chlorpromazine reduced running. Further analysis showed that chlorpromazine reduced motivation to run, whereas amphetamine affected both motivation to run and motor performance. Considering both opioid and dopamine systems, the neurochemical basis for the reinforcing properties of running may be a function of either an opiate mechanism, a dopamine mechanism, or a mechanism involving both systems (see chapter 4, this volume).

Eating, Neuropeptide Y, and Dopamine.   The dopamine system may be implicated in the regulation of eating through its effects on hypothalamic NPY (Stanley & Gillard, 1994). Neuropeptide Y is the most abundant neurotransmitter in the human brain, and the peptide is highly concentrated in the hypothalamic nuclei (Adrian et al., 1983). When NPY is injected into hypothalamic sites, rats and other animals show excessive and prolonged eating (Stanley, in press). There is a dose response relationship between the level of the neurotransmitter and eating. Low doses of NPY elicit normal eating, whereas higher doses induce gorging (in 1 hour, rats may eat more than a half of their daily intake). Also, repeated injections of the peptide result in sustained overeating and weight gain without signs of tolerance. Generally, the evidence suggests that hypothalamic NPY is one of the most important neurochemicals in the regulation of eating.

Recent experiments have shown that NPY elicits eating through its effects on the perifornical hypothalamus region of the brain, the most sensitive site. In terms of anorexia, it is interesting to note that the perifornical hypothalamus is the primary site for the suppression of eating by endogenous dopamine and epinephrine (two catecholamine neurotransmitters) when activated by injections of amphetamine.

An important experiment by Gillard, Dang, and Stanley (1993) investigated whether these catecholamine neurotransmitters interact antagonistically with NPY-elicited eating. That is, would amphetamine activation of dopamine or epinephrine within the perifornical hypothalamic region suppress eating induced by NPY injections? Results indicated that amphetamine reduced or eliminated the eating response elicited by NPY, suggesting an antagonistic effect between these catecholamines and the NPY neurotransmitter. The suppression effects on NPY-elicted eating could be dopaminergic or adrenergic (i.e., via epinephrine). Further experiments with selective blockers of catecholamine receptors attempted to reverse the suppression of eating by amphetamine. Neither alpha- nor beta-adrenergic antagonists blocked the suppression of eating by amphetamine as would be expected if epinephrine were involved. In contrast, the dopamine antagonist haloperidol blocked the suppressive effects of the amphetamine. That is, the feeding response to NPY was restored by blocking the dompamine receptors. Thus the evidence indicates that dopamine and NPY interact antagonistically to control eating, especially in the perifornical hypothalamus.

In terms of activity anorexia, it is possible that physical activity induced by food restriction is strengthened or reinforced by an increase in dopamine (see also chapter 4, this volume). Gillard et al.'s (1993) experiments show that activation of the dopamine receptors would suppress eating by blocking the response to NPY in the perifornical hypothalamus. Thus the role of dopamine as a mediator of activity anorexia would be twofold: a neurotransmitter implicated in the reward value of physical activity and an antagonist for the eating response elicited by NPY. Finally, the perifornical hypothalamus is a major brain site implicated in both anorexia (suppression of eating) and obesity (excessive overeating). A reasonable hypothesis is that similar, but opposing, neurochemical processes are involved in the control of both anorexia and obesity.

CONCLUSIONS

The theory of activity anorexia continues to develop on the basis of new evidence from diverse areas of research. In Western culture, reinforcement contingencies (economic and social) strengthen and maintain the behavior of dieting and exercising to achieve the "thin-fit" standard of beauty. These contingencies are more concentrated in subgroups, such as athletes or ballet dancers, where the pursuit of thinness is a requisite for success. According to our theory, there is an increased risk of activity anorexia whenever strenuous exercise is combined with severe food restriction (the multiplier effect). The psychological factors emphasized by other perspectives are viewed as secondary, resulting from culture and social learning or from starvation itself.

This chapter has explored the behavioral and physiological basis of activity anorexia. Evidence indicates that eating and physical activity are motivationally interrelated. The reward value of physical activity is sensitive to changes in food supply. When food is reduced, animals work more for a bout of exercise than when food is abundant. An animal's daily travel within a location or patch is regulated by fluctuations in food supply, even when body weight remains relatively stable. As physical activity increases, the reward value of food declines. One implication is that excessive exercise or travel brought on by famine or food restriction ensures that animals become anorectic until the food supply is reinstated.

The motivational interrelations of feeding and physical activity are based on evolved neurophysiological processes. Current research points to the involvement of opioid and/or dopaminergic systems. ß-endorphin and the mu receptors could modulate the reinforcing effects of physical activity under conditions of food restriction. Also, physical activity would stimulate the release of opiates such as dynorphin and thereby contribute to anorexia through an effect on the kappa receptors. Alternatively, the dopamine system could modulate the reinforcing effects of physical activity, driving up the value of physical activity or travel in times of diminished food supply. An exercise-induced release of dopamine in the perifornical hypothalamus would produce anorexia by antagonizing the uptake of NPY. A reasonable hypothesis is that the activity anorexia cycle is maintained by an interplay of both the opioid and dopamine systems.

ACKNOWLEDGMENT

Preparation of this chapter was supported by research grant #51-25009 from the Alberta Health Research Council.

REFERENCES

Adrian, T. E., Allen, J. M., Bloom, S. R., Ghatei, M. A., Rosser, M. N., Crow, T. J., Tatemoto, K., & Polak, J. M. (1983). NeuropeptideY distribution in human brain. *Nature, 306*, 584–586.

American Psychiatric Association. (1994). *Diagnostic and statistical manual of mental disorders* (4th ed.). Washington, DC: Author.

Aravich, P. F., Rieg, T. S., Lauterio, T. J., & Doerries, L. E. (1993). Beta-endorphin and dynorphin abnormalities in rats subjected to exercise and restricted feeding: Relationship to anorexia nervosa? *Brain Research, 622*, 1–8.

Arnsten, A. T. & Segal, D. S. (1979). Naloxone alters locomotion and interaction with environmental stimuli. *Life Sciences, 25*, 1035–1042.

Babbini, M., & Davis, W. M., (1972). Time-dose relationships for locomotor activity effects of morphine after acute and repeated treatment. *British Journal of Pharmacology, 46*, 213–224.

Bandura, A. (1986). *Social Foundations of Thought and Action: A Social Cognitive Theory.* Englewood Cliffs, NJ: Prentice-Hall.

Beck, S. B., Ward-Hull, C. I., & McLear, P. M. (1976). Variables related to women's somatic preferences of the male and female body. *Journal of Personality and Social Psychology, 43*, 1200–1210.

Belke, T. W. (1993). *A matching law analysis of the effects of environmental and pharmacological agents on the reinforcing properties of wheel-running in rats.* Unpublished doctoral dissertation, Harvard University, Cambridge, MA.

Beninger, R. J., & Freedman, N. L. (1982). The use of two operants to examine the nature of pimozide-induced decreases in responding for brain stimulation. *Physiological Psychology, 10*, 409–412.

Beumont, A. L. (1991). Forward to solving the anorexia puzzle: A scientific approach. In W. F. Epling & W. D. Pierce (Eds.), *Solving the anorexia puzzle: A scientific approach* (pp. ix-xv). Toronto, ON: Hogrefe & Huber.

Beumont, A. L., Booth, S. F., Abraham, D. A., Griffiths, D. A., & Turner, T. R. (1983). Temporal sequence of symptoms in patients with anorexia nervosa: A preliminary report. In P. L. Darby, P. E. Garfinkel, D. M. Garner, & D. V. Coscina (Eds.), *Anorexia nervosa: Recent developments in research* (pp. 129–136). New York: Liss.

Boer, D. P. (1989). *Determinants of excessive activity in activity anorexia.* Unpublished doctoral dissertation, University of Alberta, Edmonton.

Boer, D. P., Epling, W. F., Pierce, W. D., & Russell, J. C. (1990). Suppression of food deprivation-induced high-rate wheel running in rats. *Physiology and Behavior, 48*, 339–342.

Brigham, J. C. (1980). Limiting conditions of the "physical attractiveness sterotype": Attributions about divorce. *Journal of Research in Personality, 14*, 365–375.

Bruch, H. (1978). *The golden cage.* Cambridge, MA: Harvard University Press.

Carey, M. P., Ross, J. A., & Enns, M. P. (1981). Naloxone suppresses feeding and drinking, but not wheel running in rats. *Pharmacology, Biochemistry, and Behavior, 14*, 569–571.

Collier, G. (1969). Body weight loss as a measure of motivation in hunger and thirst. *Annals of the New York Academy of Sciences, 157*, 594–609.

Colt, E. W. D., Wardlaw, S. L., & Frantz, A. G. (1981). The effect of running on plasma ß-endorphin. *Life Science, 28*, 1637–1640.

Cumming, D. C., & Rebar, R. W. (1983). Exercise and reproductive function in women. *American Journal of Industrial Medicine, 4*, 113–125.

Cumming, D. C., & Rebar, R. W. (1985). Hormonal changes with acute exercise and with training in women. *Seminars in Reproductive Endocrinology, 3*, 55–64.

Davies, E., & Furnham, A. (1986). The dieting and body shape concerns of adolescent females. *Journal of Child Psychology and Psychiatry, 27*, 417–428.

Davis, J. M., Lamb, D. R., Yim, G. K., & Malvern, P. V. (1985). Opioid modulation of feeding behavior following repeated exposure to forced swimming exercise in male rats. *Pharmacology and Biochemistry of Behavior, 23*, 709–714.

DeRossett, S. E., & Holtzman, S. G. (1982). Effects of naloxone and diprenorphine on spontaneous activity in rats and mice. *Pharmacology, Biochemistry, and Behavior, 17*, 347–351.

Devore, I., & Hall, K. R. L. (1985). *Baboon ecology*. In I. Devore (Ed.), *Primate behavior: Field studies of monkeys and apes* (pp. 20–52). New York: Holt, Rinehart & Winston.

Doerries, L. E., Aravich, P. F., Metcalf, V. A., Wall, J. D., & Lauterio, T. J. (1989). Beta endorphin and activity-based anorexia in the rat: Influence of simultaneously initiated dieting and exercise on weight loss and beta endorphin. *Annals of the New York Academy of Sciences, 575*, 609–610.

Dwyer, J. T., Feldman, J. J., & Mayer, J. (1970). The social psychology of dieting. *Journal of Health and Social Behavior, 11*, 269–287.

Epling, W. F., & Pierce, W. D. (1984). Activity-based anorexia in rats as a function of opportunity to run on an activity wheel. *Nutrition and Behavior, 2*, 37–49.

Epling, W. F., & Pierce, W. D. (1988). Activity-based anorexia: A biobehavioral perspective. *International Journal of Eating Disorders, 7*, 475–485.

Epling, W. F., & Pierce, W. D. (1989). Excessive activity and anorexia in rats. In K.M. Pirke, W. Wuttke, & U. Schweiger (Eds.), *The menstrual cycle and its disorders: Influences of nutrition, exercise and neurotransmitters* (pp. 79–87). New York: Springer-Verlag.

Epling, W. F., & Pierce, W. D. (1991). *Solving the anorexia puzzle: A scientific approach*. Toronto, ON: Hogrefe & Huber.

Epling, W. F., Pierce, W. D., & Stefan, L. (1983). A theory of activity-based anorexia. *International Journal of Eating Disorders, 3*, 27–46.

Evans, K. R., & Vaccarino, F. J. (1986). Intra-nucleus accumbens amphetamine: Dose-dependent effects on food intake. *Pharmacology, Biochemistry, and Behavior, 25*, 1149–1151.

Frisch, R. E. (1988). Fatness and fertility. *Scientific American, 258*, 88–95.

Garner, D. M., Rockert, W., Olmstead, M. P., Johnson, C., & Coscina, D. V. (1985). Psychoeducational principles in the treatment of bulimia and anorexia nervosa. In D. M. Garner & P. Garfinkel (Eds.), *Handbook of psychotherapy for anorexia nervosa and bulimia* (pp. 513–572). New York: Guilford Press.

Gillard, E. R., Dang, D. Q., & Stanley, B. G. (1993). Evidence that neuropeptide Y and dopamine in the perifornical hypothalamus interact antagonistically in the control of food intake. *Brain Research, 628*, 128–136.

Glavin, G. B., Pare, W. P., Vincent, G. P., & Tsuda, A. (1981). Effects of d-amphetamine on activity-stress ulcers in rats. *Kurume Medical Journal, 28*, 223–226.

Green, S. K., Buchanan, D. R., & Heuer, S. K. (1984). Winners, losers, and choosers: A field investigation of dating initiation. *Personality and Social Psychology Bulletin, 10*, 502–511.

Jakobovits, C., Halstead, P., Kelley, L., Roe, D. A., & Young, C. M. (1977). Eating habits and nutrient intakes of college women over a thirty-year period. *Journal of the American Dietetic Association, 71*, 405–411.

Jakubczak, L. F., & Gomer, F. E. (1973). Effects of food deprivation and initial levels on a wheel response to methamphetamine. *Bulletin of the Psychonomic Society, 1*, 343–345.

Jones, W. H., Hannson, R., & Philips, A. L. (1978). Physical attractiveness and judgments of psychotherapy, *Journal of Social Psychology, 105*, 79–84.

Kanarek, R. B., & Collier, G. H. (1983). Self-starvation: A problem of overriding the satiety signal? *Physiology and Behavior, 30*, 307–311.

Katz, J. L. (1986). Long distance running, anorexia nervosa, and bulimia: A report of two cases. *Comprehensive Psychiatry, 27*, 74–78.

Kaye, W. H. (1987). Opioid antagonist drugs in the treatment of anorexia nervosa. In P. E. Garfinkle & D. M. Garner (Eds.), *The role of drug treatments for eating disorders* (pp. 150–160). New York: Bruner/Mazel.

Kaye, W. H., Picker, D. M., Naber, D., & Ebert, M. H. (1982). Cerebrospinal fluid opioid activity in anorexia nervosa. *American Journal of Psychiatry, 139*, 643–645.

Keys, A., Brozek, J., Henschel, A., Mickelson, O., & Taylor, H. L. (1950). *The biology of human starvation*. Minneapolis: University of Minnesota Press.

Kurman, L. (1978). An analysis of messages concerning food, eating behaviors and ideal body image on prime-time American network television. *Dissertation Abstracts, 39*, 1907–1908.

Lakoff, R. T., & Scherr, R. L. (1984). *Face value: The politics of beauty*. Boston, MA: Routledge & Kegan Paul.

Lambert, P. D., Wilding, J. P., al-Dokhayel, A. A., Gilbey, S. G., & Bloom, S. R. (1993). The effect of central blockade of kappa-opioid receptors on neuropeptide Y-induced feeding in the rat. *Brain Research, 629*, 146–148.

Loy, J. (1970). Behavioral response of free-ranging rhesus monkeys to food shortage. *American Journal of Physical Anthropology, 33*, 263–272.

Marrazzi, M. A., & Luby, E. D. (1986). An auto-addiction opioid model of chronic anorexia nervosa. *International Journal of Eating Disorders, 5*, 191–208.

Mazur, A. (1986). U.S. trends in feminine beauty and overadaptation. *Journal of Sex Research, 22*, 281–303.

McMurray, R. G., Hardy, C. J., Roberts, S., & Forsythe, W. A. (1989). Neuroendocrine response of type A individuals to exercise. *Behavioural Medicine, 15*, 84–92.

Miller, T. M., Coffman, J. G., & Linke, R. A. (1980). Survey on body image, weight and diet of college students. *Journal of the American Dietetic Association, 77*, 561–566.

Moore, R., Mills, I. H., & Forster, A. (1981). Naloxone in the treatment of anorexia nervosa: Effect on weight gain and lipolysis. *Journal of the Royal Society of Medicine, 74*, 129–131.

Morley, J. E., & Blundell, J. E. (1988). The neurobiologicl basis of eating disorders: Some formulations. *Biological Psychiatry, 23*, 53–78.

Morley, J. E., Levine, A. S., Plotka, E. D., & Seal, U. S. (1983). The effects of nalaxone on feeding and spontaneous locomotion in the wolf. *Physiology and Behavior, 38*, 331–334.

Mrosovsky, N., & Barnes, D. S. (1974). Anorexia, food deprivation and hibernation. *Physiology and Behavior, 12*, 265–270.

Mrosovsky, N., & Sherry, D. F. (1980). Animal anorexias. *Science, 207*, 837–842.

Nakai, Y., Kinoshita, F., Koh, T., Tsujii, S., & Tsukada, T. (1987). Perception of hunger and satiety induced by 2-deoxy-D-glucose in anorexia nervosa and bulimia nervosa. *International Journal of Eating Disorders, 6*, 49–57.

Nencini, P., & Graziani, M. (1990). Opiatergic modulation of preparatory and consummatory components of feeding and drinking. *Pharmacology, Biochemistry, and Behavior, 37*, 531–537.

Petraglia, F., Porro, C., Facchinetti, F., Cicoli, C., Bertellini, E., Volpe, A., Barbieri, G. C., & Genazzani, A. R. (1986). Opioid control of LH secretion in humans: Menstrual cycle, menopause and aging reduce the effect of naloxone but not of morphine. *Life Sciences, 38*, 2103–2110.

Pierce, W. D., & Epling, W. F. (1994). Activity Anorexia: An interplay between basic and applied behavior analysis. *The Behavior Analyst, 17*, 7–23.

Pierce, W. D., Epling, W. F., & Boer, D. P. (1986). Deprivation and satiation: The interrelations between food and wheel running. *Journal of the Experimental Analysis of Behavior, 46*, 199–210.

Potter, C. D., Borer, K. T., & Katz, R. J. (1983). Opiate-receptor blockade reduces voluntary running but not self-stimulation in hamsters. *Pharmacology, Biochemistry, and Behavior, 18*, 217–223.

Radosevich, P. M., Nash, J. A., Lacy, D. B., O'Donovan, C., Williams, P. E., & Abumrad, N.N. (1989). Effects of low- and high-intensity exercise on plasma and cerebrospinal fluid levels of ß-endorphin, ACTH, cortisol, norepinephrine, and glucose in the conscious dog. *Brain Research, 498*, 89–98.

Rodgers, R. J., & Deacon, R. M. J. (1979). Effect of naloxone on the behavior of rats exposed to a novel environment. *Psychopharmacology, 65*, 103–105.

Routtenberg, A., & Kuznesof, A. W. (1967). Self-starvation of rats living in activity wheels on a restricted feeding schedule. *Journal of Comparative and Physiological Psychology, 64*, 414–421.

Russell, J. C., Epling, W. F., Pierce, W. D., Amy, R., & Boer, D. (1987). Induction of voluntary prolonged running by rats. *Journal of Applied Physiology, 63*, 2549–2553.

Schnur, P., & Barela, P. (1984). Locomotor activity and opiate effects in male and female hamsters. *Pharmacology, Biochemistry, and Behavior, 21*, 369–374.

Schnur, P., Bravo, F., & Trujillo, M. (1983). Tolerance and sensitization to the biphasic effects of low doses of morphine in hamsters. *Pharmacology, Biochemistry, and Behavior, 19*, 435–439.

Schnur, P., Bravo, F., Trujillo, M., & Rocha, S. (1983). Biphasic effects of morphine on locomotor activity in hamsters. *Pharmacology, Biochemistry, and Behavior, 18*, 357–361.

Schnur, P., Hang, D., & Stinchcomb, A. (1987). Naloxone antagonism of hyperactivity in morphine-treated hamsters. *Bulletin of the Psychonomic Society, 25*, 482–485.

Sclafani, A., & Rendel, A. (1978). Food deprivation-induced activity in dietary obese, dietary lean, and normal-weight rats. *Behavioral Biology, 24*, 220–228.

Shainberg, D. (1977). Long distance running as mediation. *Annals of the New York Academy of Science, 301*, 1002–1009.

Stanley, B. G. (in press). Neuropeptide Y in multiple hypothalamic sites controls eating behavior, endocrine, and autonomic systems for body energy balance. In W. F. Colmers & C. Wahlestedt (Eds.), *The biology of neuropeptideY and related peptides*. Totowa, NJ: Humana Press.

Stanley, G., & Gillard, E. R. (1994). Hypothalamic neuropeptide Y and the regulation of eating behavior and body weight. *Current Directions in Psychological Science, 3*, 9–15.

Tainter, M. L. (1943). Effects of certain analeptic drugs on spontaneous running activity of the white rat. *Journal of Comparative Psychology, 36*, 143–155.

Umberson, D., & Hughes, M. (1984, August). *The impact of physical attractiveness on achievement and psychological well-being.* Paper presented at the meetings of the American Sociological Association, San Antonio, TX.

Unger, R. K., Hilderbrand, M., & Madar, T. (1982). Physical attractivenss and assumptions about social deviance: Some sex-by-sex comparisons. *Personality and Social Psychology Bulletin, 8*, 293–301.

Warren, M. P. (1989). Reproductive function in the ballet dancer. In K. M. Pirke, W. Wuttke, & U. Schweiger (Eds.), *The menstrual cycle and its disorders: Influences of nutrition, exercise and neurotransmitters* (pp. 161–170). New York: Springer-Verlag.

Wheeler, G. D., Singh, M., Pierce, W. D., Epling, W. F., & Cumming, D. C. (1991). Endurance training decreases serum testosterone levels in men without change in luteinizing hormone pulsatile release. *Journal of Clinical Endocrinology and Metabolism, 72*, 422–425.

Wooley, O. W., Wooley, S. C., & Dyrenforth, S. R. (1979). Obesity in women. II. A neglected feminist topic. *Women's Studies International Quarterly, 2*, 67–79.

II

Behavioral Foundations of Activity Anorexia

4

Investigating the Reinforcing Properties of Running: Or, Running Is Its Own Reward

Terry William Belke
Mount Allison University

> Spontaneous activity has been studied longer, more persistently, and with less profit than any other single phenomenon in animal psychology. Its longevity of interest arises in part from its robustness and in part from its sensitivity to a number of easily manipulable, measurable, and inexpensive, independent variables, such as age, deprivation, temperature, time of day, and sex. The tidiness and reproducibility of spontaneous activity caused it to be a main structural member of most early theories of animal motivation. However, in spite of the attention it has received, spontaneous activity is still poorly understood. (Collier, 1970, p. 557)

As Collier stated, despite more than a century of research into spontaneous activity, it remains poorly understood. Recently, interest in activity has been reawakened by two phenomena, one of which is the runner's high. The phenomenon of the runner's high (Stamford, 1985; Wagemaker & Goldstein, 1980) suggests that endogenous opiates play a central role in the reinforcing effectiveness of running. Runners report experiencing the ability to run effortlessly without fatigue after the first several miles. Women with anorexia who are in constant motion seem elated, do not feel fatigue, and diet without experiencing hunger (Yates, Leehey, & Shisslak, 1983).

These effects have been attributed to the analgesic and euphoric effects of β-endorphins.

The second phenomenon is activity-based anorexia. Epling and Pierce (1991) proposed that the relationship between food intake, body weight, and activity plays a central role in an animal model of activity-based anorexia. According to this model, activity-based anorexia develops as a function of reciprocal effects of food intake on activity and activity on food intake. Activity suppresses food intake. The reduction in food intake leads to a decline in body weight and a correlated increase in activity. A cycle of increasing activity, decreasing food intake, and declining body weight results in emaciation associated with hyperactivity. The cycle appears to be initiated by a combination of restricted food consumption (i.e., dieting) and intense physical exercise.

The model does not imply that every individual who exercises and diets will develop activity anorexia. Development of the disorder depends on the rate of change in activity level and the pattern of food restriction. In addition, individuals appear to vary in vulnerability for developing the disorder (Epling & Pierce, 1984). However, the model readily accounts for the higher risk of anorexia observed in individuals engaging in activities that combine control of body weight by restriction of food consumption and high levels of physical activity.

This chapter is predicated on the supposition that our understanding of activity-based anorexia and the runner's high may be advanced by investigation of environmental and pharmacological factors that influence the reinforcing properties of running. In particular, a procedure based on a model of choice behavior is advocated as a starting point for such an investigation.

USING A MATCHING LAW ANALYSIS OF A RESPONSE-REINFORCEMENT RELATIONSHIP TO INVESTIGATE THE REINFORCING PROPERTIES OF RUNNING

One approach to investigating environmental and pharmacological factors that affect the reinforcing properties of running involves a model of choice developed by Herrnstein (1970) and generalized to the study of the behavioral effects of drugs by Heyman (Heyman, 1983, 1992; Heyman, Kinzie, & Seiden, 1986; Heyman & Monaghan, 1990). Herrnstein (1970) formulated an elementary matching law equation for the case where there is only a single measured source of reinforcement and a single measured response rate. The form of that equation is:

$$B_i = \frac{kR_1}{R_1 + R_e} \tag{1}$$

where B_1 is response rate, R_1 is reinforcement rate, and k and R_e are fitted constants. The structural or curve-fitting definitions of the constants reveal the relationship between response rate and reinforcement rate implied by equation 1. In the numerator, k is an estimate of the response rate asymptote. As reinforcement rate increases, response rate approaches but does not exceed k. The value of k is estimated in the same units as the measured behavior, for example, responses per minute. In the numerator, R_e is equal to the rate of reinforcement that maintains a one half asymptotic response rate. For example, when R_1 is equal to R_e, response rate must be equal to $k/2$. Thus R_e is estimated in the same units as the experimenter-controlled reinforcer, that is, reinforcers per hour. Figure 4.1 shows the equation fit to representative data along with the parameter definitions

On the basis of the matching law, Herrnstein (1970, 1974) provided empirical interpretations of the curve-fitting definitions of k and R_e. According to his account, k measures motoric aspects of responding, such as the topography of the response, and R_e measures background, uncontrolled sources of reinforcement, such as accrue from resting, exploring, the chamber, and so forth. However, because R_e is estimated in the units of the arranged reinforcer, the value of R_e can change either as a function of operations that directly affect the arranged reinforcer or, alternatively, of operations that directly affect the background reinforcers.

These interpretations have some empirical support. In a review of the literature, Heyman and Monaghan (1994) found that studies in which R_e changed but k did not, the experimenter varied either reinforcement magnitude, reinforcement quality, or deprivation level. For example, the value of R_e decreased when the body weight of subjects responding for sucrose reinforcement was reduced (Bradshaw, Szabadi, Ruddle, & Pears, 1983) or when the concentration of sucrose reinforcement was increased (Heyman & Monaghan, 1994). In essence, the value of R_e varied with changes in motivation to obtain the scheduled reinforcement. Specifically, as motivation to obtain the scheduled reinforcement increased, R_e decreased; as motivation decreased, R_e increased.

Figure 4.2 illustrates how the hyperbolic matching curve would change with a reduction in reinforcement amount, a reduction in reinforcement quality, or a reduction in deprivation. In Fig. 4.2, both curves have the same asymptotic level of responding (i.e., 65 responses per minute); however, the value of R_e for curve 2 is 200 reinforcers per hour compared with 132 reinforcers per hour for curve 1. This

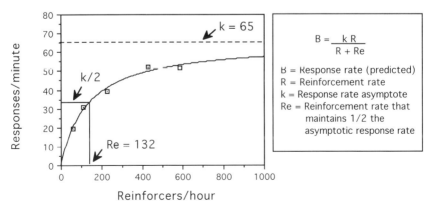

FIG. 4.1.   A hyperbolic curve fit to representative data to yield estimates of k and R_e. Parameter definitions are provided.

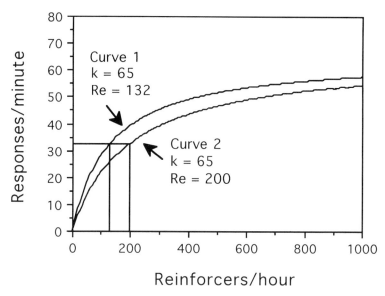

FIG. 4.2.   Curves illustrating a change in R_e whereas k remains constant.

increase in R_e reflects a reduction in the efficacy of the scheduled reinforcement to maintain behavior.

In their review, Heyman and Monaghan (1987) also noted that in studies where k changed but R_e did not, the experimenter manipulated the response requirement. For example, the value of k decreased when the response manipulandum was changed from a key to a treadle (McSweeney, 1978) or the force required to make a response was increased (Heyman & Monaghan, 1987). Based on this evidence, Heyman and Monaghan concluded that k indexes the response topography of reinforced responses, whereas R_e indexes the efficacy of the experimenter-controlled reinforcer relative to background reinforcement. In support of this idea, Porter and Villanueva (1988) found a relation between response duration and the value of the k parameter. Thus k varied with changes in motor performance.

Figure 4.3 illustrates how the hyperbolic matching curve would change if the force required to make a response were increased while motivation to obtain the scheduled reinforcement remained unchanged. In Fig. 4.3, the value for R_e for both curves is 132 reinforcers per hour; however, the asymptotic level of responding for curve 1 is 65 responses per minute compared with 35 responses per minute for curve 2. In both cases the efficacy of the scheduled reinforcement is equivalent, but much greater force is required to make a response in the situation illustrated by curve 2.

Based on empirical evidence about the nature of the manipulations that affect the k and R_e parameters, Heyman and Monaghan (1987) concluded that k indexes a motor component of the reinforced response, whereas R_e indexes a motivational component of the reinforced response. The ability of this procedure to discriminate motor and motivational aspects of reinforced responding makes this procedure a candidate for the investigation of pharmacological agents that affect the reinforcing efficacy of running.

Belke and Heyman (1994) extended the matching law approach to the study of the relationship between response and reinforcement rates when the opportunity to run was scheduled as the reinforcing consequence for lever-pressing. Manipulations of the force required to make a response and access to the wheel demonstrated that the empirical interpretations of the k and R_e parameters held when running functioned as a reinforcing consequence. When the force required to make a response was increased by 26 grams, the mean value of k decreased from 61 to 37 responses per minute, whereas R_e remained constant at approximately 93 reinforcers per hour. When access to the wheel was limited by placing the subjects in the locked wheel for 45 minutes prior to a session, the average value of R_e decreased from 73 to 51 reinforcers per hour, whereas k remained constant at 57 responses per minute.

PHARMACOLOGICAL BASIS OF THE REINFORCING PROPERTIES OF RUNNING

The two neurotransmitters or neurochemicals implicated in the biological basis of reinforcement are dopamine and endogenous opiates. The major dopamine pathway associated with reinforcement is the tegmentostriatal path from the ventral tegmental area (VTA) to the nucleus accumbens (NA). Evidence for involvement of dopamine in reinforcement processes comes from findings that animals learn to

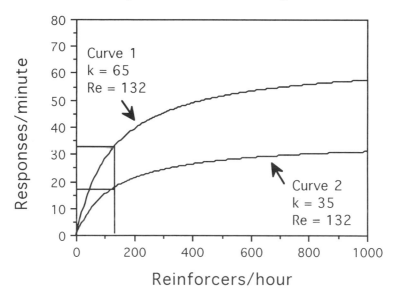

FIG. 4.3.   Curves illustrating a change in k whereas R_e remains constant.

self-administer dopamine agonists (i.e., amphetamine and cocaine), and that conditioned place preferences can be developed by prior exposure to these drugs in a particular location (Muchas, van der Kooy, O'Shaughnessy, & Bucenieks, 1982; Wise, 1978). Further evidence shows that destruction of the tegmentostriatal dopamine pathway or the administration of dopamine antagonists attenuates the efficacy of these drugs in self-administration and conditioned place preference paradigms (Lyness, Friedle, & Moore, 1979; Roberts, Corcoran, & Fibiger, 1977; Roberts & Koob, 1982; Wise, 1978). Thus activity in the tegmentostriatal pathway appears to be involved in reward processes and, as such, the reinforcing effect of wheel running may reflect activity in this pathway.

Opiates have also been implicated in reinforcement processes. As with dopaminergic agonists, animals will press a lever to self-administer opiate agonists (i.e., heroin, morphine) intravenously and will acquire a preference for a place associated with these drugs (Koob, Pettit, Ettenberg, & Bloom, 1984; Muchas et al., 1982). Intracranial self-administration studies have shown that animals will learn to administer opiate agonists in the lateral hypothalamus (Olds, 1979), ventral tegmental area (Bozarth & Wise, 1981), and nucleus accumbens (Goeders, Lane, & Smith, 1984; Olds, 1982). Furthermore, self-administration of these opiate agonists into the nucleus accumbens and the ventral tegmental area can be attenuated with opiate antagonists (Vaccarino, Bloom, & Koob, 1985). This evidence suggests that the reinforcing effect of opiates depends on the activation of the dopamine reward system by opiate receptors in the ventral tegmental area and the nucleus accumbens.

Not all evidence is consistent with this dependence on dopamine for reinforcing effects. For example, destruction of the tegmentostriatal dopamine system or blockade of dopamine receptors does not attenuate opiate self-administration, but does attenuate dopamine agonist self-administration (Pettit, Ettenberg, Bloom, & Koob, 1984). Further evidence showed that blockade of opiate receptors in the nucleus accumbens affected opiate self-administration, but not cocaine self-administration (Vaccarino et al., 1985). Thus the current view is that opiate receptors in the ventral tegmental area and in the nucleus accumbens are both involved in opiate reward. However, the rewarding effect of opiates in the ventral tegmental area is dependent on activation of the dopamine system, whereas the reinforcing effect of opiates in the nucleus accumbens is not dependent on the dopamine system (Vaccarino, Schiff, & Glickman, 1989).

In sum, previous research on the biological basis of reinforcement suggests that the reinforcing properties of wheel-running may be mediated by dopamine or endogenous opiates. In fact, hypotheses based on these neurotransmitters have been proposed. Most widely known is the endogenous opiate hypothesis, that running produces a release of endogenous opiates that produces euphoria or a positive mood. Despite widespread belief at this time, empirical evidence is insufficient to regard this hypothesis as validly established. First, exercise does produce powerful changes in emotional states; however, evidence implicating opiates as the basis for this exercise-induced euphoria remains elusive. Colt, Wardlaw, and Frantz (1981) suggest that increases in plasma ß-endorphins due to exercise are not sufficient to produce mood changes such as the runner's high. Second, evidence from attempts to block exercise-induced euphoria using opiate antagonists is equivocal. Janal, Colt, Clark, and Glusman (1984) found that intravenous injections of naloxone attenuated reports of euphoria in runners. However, Markoff, Ryan, and Young (1982) found no effects on reports of runner's high for the same dose administered subcutaneously. Even if the evidence were not contradictory, changes in behavior as a result of blockade of opiate receptors do not constitute sufficient evidence for involvement of opiate receptors.

A second hypothesis, proposed by Lambert (1992), suggests that excessive running observed in an activity–stress paradigm is sustained by reinforcement from increased levels of dopamine in the mesolimbic dopamine pathway. Evidence cited in support of this hypothesis is that dopamine agonists tend to increase activity levels, whereas dopamine antagonists produce reductions in locomotion. Changes in locomotion are interpreted as a function of changes in the rewarding value of running. For example, Glavin, Pare, Vincent, and Tsuda (1981) found that amphetamine significantly increased wheel-running activity, whereas Lambert and Porter (1992) showed that pimozide reduced wheel-running activity. Note that Lambert (1992) restricts his hypothesis to excessive running generated by the activity–stress paradigm and that the rewarding basis of running under other conditions may not be the same as that which underlies food deprivation-induced running.

Broocks, Liu, and Pirke (1990) offer a third approach to understanding the pharmacological basis for the reinforcing properties of running. Specifically, they speculated that the rewarding effects of running may result from compensation for the effects of starvation. They found that semistarvation reduced turnover rates of norepinephine and dopamine, whereas wheel-running increased norepinephine and dopamine turnover in rats. Consistent with this hypothesis, Tsuda et al. (1982) observed enhanced norepinephrine turnover extensively throughout the brain in hyperactive semistarved rats. Running appears to compensate for the effects of starvation on catecholamine levels.

This account, based on the opposite effects of starvation and running on catecholamine levels, may explain the relationship between body weight and activity levels. As catecholamine levels decrease with starvation, the reinforcing value of the compensatory increase in dopamine due to running may increase. In other words, as levels of catecholamines decline, the reinforcing value of behaviors that increase dopamine release should increase. Although this account is purely speculative, it frames the question appropriately in terms of examining the effects of hyperactivity in a context of starvation.

As previously stated, the matching law paradigm may prove useful in deciding between these accounts of the pharmacological basis of the reinforcing properties of running. For example, Belke (1993) investigated the effects of chlorpromazine on running and responding for the opportunity to run in rats. Seven male Wistar rats were trained to press a lever for the opportunity to run in a wheel for 30 seconds. In each session the rats were exposed to a series of variable interval schedules of reinforcement for running. Herrnstein's hyperbola was fit to the response and reinforcement rates generated from these schedules in each session. When the estimates of k and R_e appeared stable, drug testing was started. In the drug testing phase, three doses of chlorpromazine (.5, 1.0, and 2.0 mg/kg) were administered in a randomized order. Each dose was administered three times. Between drug administrations baseline and vehicle sessions were conducted.

Figure 4.4 shows a behavioral profile of the effects of chlorpromazine on revolutions, lever-presses, and cumulative latency to respond following reinforce-

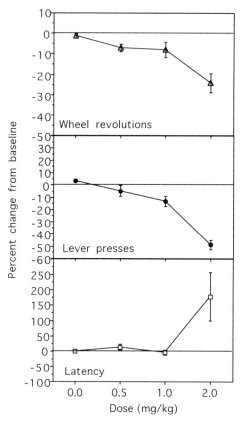

FIG. 4.4.   Effects of chlorpromazine on revolutions, lever presses, and cumulative latency to respond following reinforcement expressed as a percentage of baseline levels.

ment. With respect to total revolutions per session, chlorpromazine reduced running by 7%, 8%, and 24% relative to baseline levels at the .5, 1.0, and 2.0 mg/kg doses respectively, $F(3,18) = 13$, $p < .001$. Consistent with decrease in running, lever presses per session decreased by 5, 13, and 49% respectively across the dose series $F(3,18) = 42$, $p < .001$. Finally, mean cumulative latency to respond changed by 13%, -5%, and 178% relative to baseline level across the three doses, $F(3,18) = 5$, $p < .01$.

Figure 4.5 reveals the results of an analysis of the changes in k and R_e at different dose levels. Across chlorpromazine doses, average estimates of k remained relatively unchanged from baseline levels. On average, k changed by 7%, 5% and .6% across the three doses. In contrast, values of R_e increased with dose, $F(3,18) = 5$, $p < .01$. Mean changes from baseline were 48%, 100%, and 533% at the .5, 1.0, and 2.0 mg/kg dose levels respectively. Thus chlorpromazine increased R_e across doses, whereas k remained relatively stable.

In sum, at the session level total revolutions and lever presses for the opportunity to run decreased as the dose level of chlorpromazine increased. Within sessions,

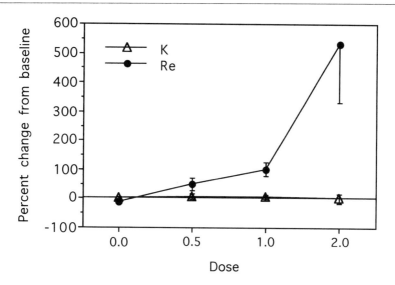

FIG. 4.5.   Mean estimates of k and R_e as a function of dose of chlorpromazine.

the pattern of responding as a function of rate of reinforcement changed in a manner consistent with the interpretation that chlorpromazine decreased motivation to respond for the opportunity to run. The lack of any systematic change in k suggests that the observed changes in response were a function of a change in motivational rather than motor aspects of responding. In conclusion, this result suggests that dopamine may be involved in the pharmacology of the reinforcing value of running. However, it is necessary to emphasize that this is a preliminary finding with a drug that has effects (e.g., sedation) other than blocking dopamine receptors. More conclusive statements must await a more extensive investigation across a series of dopamine and opiate agonists and antagonists.

ACKNOWLEDGMENT

Preparation of this chapter was supported by Research Grant 0GP0170022 from the Natural Sciences and Engineering Research Council of Canada.

REFERENCES

Belke, T. W. (1993). *A matching law analysis of the effects of environmental factors and pharmacological agents on the reinforcing properties of wheel-running in rats.* Unpublished doctoral dissertation, Harvard University, Cambridge, MA.

Belke, T. W., & Heyman, G. M. (1994). A matching law analysis of the reinforcing efficacy of wheel running in rats. *Animal Learning & Behavior, 22,* 267–274.

Bozarth, M. A., & Wise, R. A. (1981). Intracranial self-administration of morphine into the ventral tegmental area in rats. *Life Sciences, 28,* 551–555.

Bradshaw, C. M., Szabadi, E., Ruddle, H. V., & Pears, E. (1983). Herrnstein's equation: Effect of Deprivation level on performance in variable-interval schedule. *Behavior Analysis Letters, 3,* 93–100.

Broocks, A., Liu, J., & Pirke, K. M. (1990). Semistarvation-induced hyperactivity compensates for decreased norepinephrine and dopamine turnover in the mediobasal hypothalamus of the rat. *Journal of Neural Transmission, 79,* 113–124.

Collier, G. H. (1970). Work: A weak reinforcer. *Transactions of the New York Academy of Sciences, 32,* 557–576.

Colt, E. W. D., Wardlaw, S. L., & Frantz, A. G. (1981). The effect of running on plasma beta-endorphin. *Life Sciences, 28,* 1637–1640.

Epling, W. F., & Pierce, W. D. (1984). Activity-based anorexia in rats as a function of opportunity to run on an activity wheel. *Nutrition and Behavior, 2,* 37–49.

Epling, W. F., & Pierce, W. D. (1991). *Solving the anorexia puzzle: A scientific approach.* Toronto, ON: Hogrefe and Huber.

Glavin, G. B., Pare, W. P., Vincent, G. P., & Tsuda, A. (1981). Effects of d-amphetamine on activity-stress ulcers in rats. *Kurume Medical Journal, 28,* 223–226.

Goeders, N. E., Lane, J. D., & Smith, J. E. (1984). Self-administration of methionine enkephalin into the nucleus accumbens. *Pharmacology, Biochemistry, and Behavior, 20,* 451–455.

Herrnstein, R. J. (1970). On the law of effect. *Journal of the Experimental Analysis of Behavior, 13,* 243–266.

Herrnstein, R. J. (1974). Formal properties of the matching law. *Journal of the Experimental Analysis of Behavior, 21,* 159–164.

Heyman, G. M. (1983). A parametric evaluation of the hedonic and motoric effects of drugs: Pimozide and amphetamine. *Journal of the Experimental Analysis of Behavior, 40,* 113–122.

Heyman, G. M. (1992). Effects of methylphenidate on response rate and measures of motor performance and reinforcement efficacy. *Psychopharmacology, 109,* 145–152.

Heyman, G. M., Kinzie, D. L., & Seiden, L. S. (1986). Chlorpromazine and pimozide alter reinforcement efficacy and motor performance. *Psychopharmacology, 88,* 346–353.

Heyman, G. M., & Monaghan, M. M. (1987). Effects of changes in response requirement and deprivation on the parameters of the matching law equation: New data and review. *Journal of Experimental Psychology: Animal Behavior Processes, 13,* 384–394.

Heyman, G. M., & Monaghan, M. M. (1994). Reinforcer magnitude (sucrose concentration) and the matching law theory of response strength. *Journal of the Experimental Analysis of Behavior, 61,* 505–516.

Heyman, G. M., & Monaghan, M. M. (1990). Contributions of the matching law to the behavioral effects of drugs. In T. Thompson, P. B. Dews, & J. E. Barrett (Eds.), *Advances in behavioral pharmacology* (Vol. 7, pp. 39–77). Hillsdale, NJ: Lawrence Erlbaum Associates.

Janal, M. N. E., Colt, W. D., Clark, W. C., & Gusman, M. (1984). Pain sensitivity, mood, and plasma endocrine levels in man following long-distance running: Effects of naloxone. *Pain, 19,* 13–25.

Koob, G. F., Pettit, H. O., Ettenberg, A., & Bloom, F. E. (1984). Effects of opiate antagonists and their quaternary derivatives on heroin self-administration in the rat. *Journal of Pharmacology and Experimental Therapuetics, 229,* 481–486.

Lambert, K. G. (1992). The activity-stress paradigm: Possible mechanisms and applications. *Journal of General Psychology, 120,* 21–32.

Lambert, K. G., & Porter, J. H. (1992). Pimozide mitigates excessive running in activity-stress paradigm. *Physiology and Behavior, 52,* 299–304.

Lyness, W. H., Friedle, N. M., & Moore, K. E. (1979). Destruction of dopaminergic nerve terminals in nucleus accumbens: Effect on d-amphetamine self-administration. *Pharmacology, Biochemistry, and Behavior, 11,* 553–556.

Markoff, R. A., Ryan, P., & Young, T. (1982). Endorphins and mood changes in long-distance running. *Medicine and Science in Sports and Exercise, 14,* 11–15.

McSweeney, F. K. (1978). Prediction of concurrent keypeck and treadle-press responding from simple schedule performance. *Animal Learning and Behavior, 6,* 444–450.

Muchas, R. F., van der Kooy, D., O'Shaughnessy, M., & Bucenieks, P. (1982). Drug reinforcement studies by the use of place conditioning in rat. *Brain Research, 243,* 91–105.

Olds, M. E. (1979). Hypothalamic substrates for the reinforcing properties of morphine in the rat. *Brain Research, 168,* 351–360.

Olds, M. E. (1982). Reinforcing effects of morphine in the nucleus accumbens. *Brain Research, 237,* 429–440.

Pettit, H. O., Ettenberg, A., Bloom, F. E., & Koob, G. F. (1984). Destruction of the nucleus accumbens selectively attenuates cocaine but not heroin self-administration in rats. *Psychopharmacology, 84,* 167–173.

Porter, J. H., & Villanueva, H. F. (1988). Assessment of pimozide's motor and hedonic effects on operant behavior in rats. *Pharmacology, Biochemistry, and Behavior, 31,* 779–786.

Roberts, D. C. S., Corcoran, M. E., & Fibiger, H. C. (1977). On the role of ascending catecholaminergic systems in intravenous self-administration of cocaine. *Pharmacology, Biochemistry, and Behavior, 6,* 615–620.

Roberts, D. C. S., & Koob, G. F. (1982). Disruption of cocaine self-administration following 6-OHDA lesions of the VTA in rats. *Pharmacology, Biochemistry, and Behavior, 17,* 901–904.

Stamford, B. (1985). Runner's high. *Physician and Sportsmedicine, 13,* 166.

Tsuda, A., Tanaka, M., Kohno, Y., Nishikawa, T., Iimori, K., Nakagawa, R., Hoaki, Y., Ida, Y., & Nagasaki, N. (1982). Marked enhancement of noradrenaline turnover in extensive brain regions after activity-stress in rats. *Pharmacology, Biochemistry, and Behavior, 29,* 337–341.

Vaccarino, F. J., Bloom, F. E., & Koob, G. F. (1985). Blockade of nucleus accumbens opiate receptors attenuates intravenous heroin reward in the rat. *Psychopharmacology, 86,* 37–42.

Vaccarino, F. J., Schiff, B. B., & Glickman, S. E. (1989). Biological view of reinforcement. In S. B. Klein & R. R. Mowrer (Eds.), *Contemporary learning theories: Instrumental conditioning theory and the impact of biological constraints on learning* (pp. 111–144). Hillsdale, NJ: Lawrence Erlbaum Associates.

Wagemaker, H., & Goldstein, L. (1980). The runner's high. *Journal of Sports Medicine, 20,* 227–229.

Wise, R. A. (1978). Catecholamine theories of reward: A critical review. *Brain Research, 152,* 215–247.

Yates, A., Leehey, K., & Shisslak, C. M. (1983). Running—An analogue of anorexia? *New England Journal of Medicine, 308,* 251–255.

5

Effects of Dietary Protein and Food Restriction on Voluntary Running of Rats Living in Activity Wheels

William M. Beneke
Jerry G. Vander Tuig
Lincoln University of Missouri

Although the combination of food restriction and running wheel access is well established as necessary for the development of activity anorexia, the details of the causal relationships involved are not clearly understood. Noting that massive increases in wheel-running occur immediately before and after scheduled feeding, Epling and Pierce (1992) argued that this wheel-running was related to meal schedule and might be a schedule-induced behavior. Beneke, Schulte, and Vander Tuig (1995) explored this hypothesis by examining details of the temporal distribution of running. They found that disruptions produced by food restriction in the normal diurnal running pattern of rats, and the temporal distributions obtained, were inconsistent with a schedule-induced behavior hypothesis.

Food restriction and its effects on activity are important to the understanding of activity anorexia. Food restriction effects could be due to the resulting reduced body fat stores, total caloric restriction, or deprivation or relative deprivation of specific nutrients. The activity anorexia paradigm poses special difficulties for examining these details of food restriction. As running increases, so too do total caloric requirements. A fixed period of food availability does not allow careful experimental control of deprivation levels. The well documented reduction in food intake that accompanies excessive running further complicates this problem.

Limiting the amount of food provided to experimental animals as an alternative to limiting meal duration offers the advantage of eliminating some of the difficulties associated with the activity anorexia paradigm (Russell, Epling, Pierce, Amy, & Boer, 1987). Food intake can be titrated on a daily basis to maintain body weight at predetermined levels and the effects on daily running activity and running distributions observed. Experiment 1 was conducted to assess the effects of body weight on the distribution of running. We were also interested in determining the optimal levels of body weight restriction for use in future research. As in the activity anorexia paradigm, rats were maintained throughout the day in activity wheels.

EXPERIMENT 1

Methods

Subjects.   Subjects were 10 male Sprague-Dawley rats obtained from Lincoln University's breeding colony. At the start of the study, the rats were approximately 75 days old with weights ranging from 315 to 384 grams.

Apparatus.   Ten standard Wahmann activity wheels equipped with side cages and revolution counters were used. The wheels had a circumference of 1.125 meters. Wheels were modified with the addition of a microswitch to enable electronic recording of wheel revolutions. Data were recorded with an IBM-compatible microcomputer and Med-Associates interface. Med-PC software was programmed to record wheel revolutions for individual rats in 30-minute intervals.

Procedure.   A repeated measures design was used consisting of four conditions: 100%, 90%, 80%, and 70% of ad libitum body weight. In the 100% condition, animals were fed ad libitum throughout treatment. In the remaining conditions, a target weight for each animal was calculated by multiplying the animal's weight on the last day of the baseline prior to treatment by the required percentage. Animals were weighed daily, and their food ration was titrated to hold them as close to their target weights as possible.

During treatment conditions, animals had free access to both activity wheels and side cages for 23 hours per day. During the remaining hour, all animals were locked out of their wheels; this hour was used for weighing and feeding animals, saving recorded wheel revolutions to a permanent file, and general animal care.

Treatment continued until both body weight and running stabilized over a 4-day period. Stable weight was defined as within 5 grams of target weight. Running was considered stable when visual inspection of individual data indicated a reduction in variability and no increasing or decreasing trends. When both criteria were met, the treatment condition was concluded; the animal was placed in a home cage and fed ad libitum for another 5-day baseline period. At the end of the baseline, the animal entered the next treatment condition. This procedure was followed until each animal had been in each condition. All animals progressed through the conditions in the same order 100%, 90%, 80%, 70%, [100]%. However, in order to rule out proactive interference effects, individual animals were started at different points in the sequence: 3 rats began at 100%, 2 began at 90% (ending at 100%), 2 began at 80% (ending at 90%), and the remaining 3 began at 70% (ending at 80%).

Because the stability criteria were based on individual performance, some animals progressed through the protocol more rapidly than others. We were able to replicate some of the initial treatment conditions for those animals that completed the protocol more rapidly to further rule out sequential effects.

Results and Discussion

All data for 1 rat were discarded because this animal failed to stabilize at all four deprivation levels. For the remaining rats, mean daily wheel revolutions were computed for each over the final 4 days in each deprivation condition. Where conditions were replicated for an animal, mean daily wheel revolutions were based on the average of the replications. Large individual differences in running rates were observed. To remove individual differences from the group data, relative wheel revolutions were calculated for each animal by dividing mean daily revolutions at each deprivation level by the mean daily revolutions in the 100% condition for that animal. Relative wheel revolutions averaged across animals are shown in the left panel of Fig. 5.1. The calculations resulted in a value of 1.00 with 0 standard error of the mean (*SEM*) for the 100% condition and a multiple of the 100% running at other deprivation levels. Relative wheel revolutions increased with decreasing percent ad libitum weights, $F(2,26) = 4.92$, $p \leq .0216$, to more than three times ($x3.43 \pm .71$ [mean $\pm$ *SEM*]) in the 70% condition.

The effects of deprivation on running were not uniform over the 23 hours of daily wheel access. Temporal distributions of mean wheel revolutions in successive 30-minute intervals are shown in the right panel of Fig. 5.1. These distributions clearly indicate that the running differences were produced by running in the light periods. Nocturnal running showed a small deprivation effect for the first 90 minutes of darkness, but after that, effects of deprivation were either nonsystematic or negligible. Peak running occurred in the light intervals immediately preceding the animal care and feeding period.

Large individual differences in overall running suggest that there may be merit in examining data for individual animals. Data from rat A11 is typical and further illustrates the relationships among running, weight restriction, and food intake. Treatment conditions are separated by vertical lines and labeled according to percent ad libitum weight. Separation of treatment and baseline phases of each treatment are readily apparent. Because running wheels were not available during

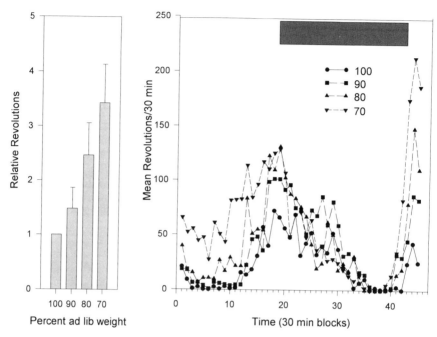

FIG. 5.1.   Effects of weight restriction on activity. Left panel shows mean relative revolutions with standard error of the mean. Relative revolutions were calculated by dividing revolutions at each deprivation level by the revolutions made by that animal in the 100% condition. Right panel shows the temporal distribution of running over the 23-hour wheel access. The shaded bar at top indicates the 12-hour dark period. Feeding/care occurred prior to period 1 and after period 46.

baselines, those phases are the portion of the figure where the breaks in wheel revolutions occur. Rat A11 began in the 100% condition. Although there was no difference between stable running rates in the 100% and 90% conditions, running increased to an average of 1,307 revolutions per day by the end of the 80% treatment condition and rose rather sharply to an average of 3,626 revolutions per day at 70%. Time permitted replicating the 100%, 70%, and 80% conditions, and in each case initial performance was recovered.

Examination of the food intakes in Fig. 5.2 suggests that the intake required to maintain stable body weights differed little in the 90%, 80%, and 70% conditions. Our ability to maintain various reduced body weights with comparable rations is probably the result of the energy costs of running. Once high running rates were established, gradually increasing food rations needed to hold body weight constant did not result in reduced running. Absolute food intake appeared to be less important than body weight reduction in determining the amount of excessive activity. The data are consistent with either body weight reduction or food intake restriction relative to increased needs as responsible for the running effect.

EXPERIMENT 2

Experiment 1 produced results inconsistent with absolute daily rations controlling the level of running. Other research (Russell et al., 1987; Boer, 1989) suggests that daily food ration and not weight restriction affect running levels. One possibility is that food rations exert an effect relative to need of either energy (total calories) or of a specific energy source. The three energy sources in food are protein, carbohydrate, and fat. Commercial cereal-based diets for laboratory rats are formulated to provide approximately 20% to 25% of metabolizable energy from protein, 65% to 70% from carbohydrate, and the remaining 10% to 12% from fat. Restricting food intake relative to caloric need produces proportionate restrictions in all three energy sources. It is possible that excessive running in activity anorexia is mediated by only one of these energy sources.

Protein is an interesting and perhaps most likely candidate. Proteins provide amino acid precursors for the biosynthesis of certain neurotransmitters. For example, tyrosine is an amino acid that is a precursor in the synthesis of dopamine and norepinephrine. These catecholamines have already been implicated in activity

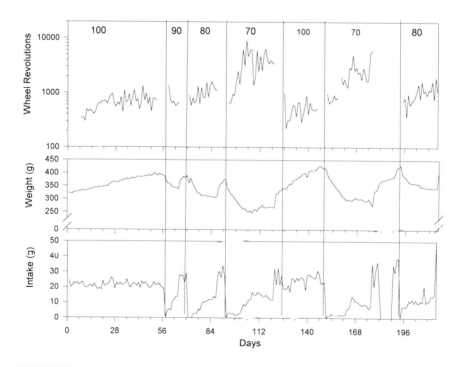

FIG. 5.2. Data for Rat A11. Upper panel shows total daily wheel revolutions plotted on a log scale, middle panel shows daily animal weights, and lower panel shows daily food intake. Weight restriction conditions are shown at top. Abscissa for all plots is consecutive days of the experiment.

anorexia (Broocks, Liu, & Pirke, 1990) and in human anorexia (Heufelder, Warn-hoff, & Pirke, 1985).

The second experiment was designed to examine the effects of diet composition and weight restriction on running. Data from the first experiment suggested that a comparison of an ad libitum feeding condition either with 70% or 80% body weight would reveal any effect of weight restriction. We opted to compare the 100% condition of Experiment 1 with a 75% condition. That the current weight criteria in the diagnosis of anorexia nervosa (AN) had shifted to 75% did not go unnoticed. The study used two formulated diets in which protein constituted either 20% or 5% of metabolizable energy.

Methods

Subjects and Diets.   Twelve male Sprague Dawley rats weighing 117 ± 1 g (mean $\pm$ *SEM*) were obtained from Small Animal Supply Company, Inc., Omaha, NE, and given unlimited access to a commercial laboratory pellet diet for 7 days before the start of the experiment. The rats were housed in individual cages under controlled temperature (21 ± 1 $^{\circ}$C) and lighting (12 hours light; 12 hours dark) conditions and had unlimited access to water at all times. Composition of the 2 semipurified diets used in this study are summarized in Table 5.1. Diets were designed to provide protein at 5% or 20% of total metabolizable energy. Carbohy-

TABLE 5.1

Diet Formulation and Composition

Ingredient	Diet	
	5% Protein	20% Protein
Mineral Mix	418 g	418 g
Vitamin Mix	119 g	119 g
Cellulose	478 g	478 g
Choline Chloride	24 g	24 g
Casein	597 g	2389 g
Glucose	6450 g	4679 g
Corn Oil	597 g	597 g
Beef Tallow	1296 g	1296 g
Total	9979 g	10000 g
Kilocalories/gram	4.275 kcal/g	4.267 kcal/g
Protein: % of kcal	5	20
Carbohydrate: % of kcal	55	40
Fat: % of kcal	40	40

drate was substituted for protein on an equal energy basis, and fat was kept constant at 40% of total metabolizable energy.

Apparatus.   Twelve NalgeneTM activity wheel cages (Mini Mitter, Sunriver, OR) with wheel circumference of 1.07 meters were interfaced with a computer to record running activity using two switches mounted approximately 135 degrees apart to rule out counting wheel-rocking with running. Activity wheel cages were located in individual sound-attenuating isolation cubicles (Coulbourn Instruments, Allentown, PA). A lamp inside each cubicle was programmed to provide a 12/12 light–dark cycle. The lamp was illuminated for the first five hours after animal care, then was turned off for 12 hours, and illuminated for the remaining 6 hours of the daily cycle.

Procedure.   Rats were divided into two groups on a weight-matched basis and exposed to the within-subjects design described in the next paragraph. As in Experiment 1, wheel revolutions were recorded in 30-minute intervals; food intakes and body weights were recorded daily.

Six rats were placed on the 5% protein diet. After eating this diet for a 3-day adaptation period, rats were housed in activity apparatus for a 7-day period with food available ad libitum. Rats were then returned to individual metabolism cages for a 3-day period. They were then placed back in the activity treatment cages, and intake of the 5% protein diet was limited to reduce body weight to 75% of body weight recorded on the final day of the unrestricted feeding period. The 75% target weight was maintained for 10 days by titrating food rations in the activity treatment cages (7 days) and in the metabolism cages (3 days). Each rat was then fed a commercial laboratory pellet diet for 7 days, and the above procedures were repeated with the 20% protein diet. The remaining 6 rats went through the same procedures, but began with the 20% protein diet followed by the 5% protein diet.

Results and Discussion

Food Intake and Weight Change.   Each animal was exposed to all treatment conditions. Half of the rats experienced the 20% diet first and the remainder experienced the 5% diet first. Food was provided ad libitum during the first 13 days on a diet (3 days adaptation + 3 days in metabolism cages + 7 days baseline). During the initial ad libitum feeding, significantly more of the 20% protein diet was consumed (557 ± 23 vs. 412 ± 15 kcal/7 days). This resulted in significant gain in animal weights of about 100 grams with the 20% protein diet, whereas the 5% diet produced stable weights. By the beginning of ad libitum feeding of the second diet, body weights were again equivalent. Intakes of the second diets did not differ, and weight differences were not significant.

Total Daily Running.   Average wheel revolutions over the final 7 days in each condition were computed for each animal. Individual data along with means and standard errors for each condition are shown in Table 5.2. Significant sequence

TABLE 5.2

Mean Daily Wheel Revolutions by Condition

Rat	Mean Wheel Revolutions			
	20% AL	20% Dep	5% AL	5% Dep
7	570	3078	1514	7561
8	281	1479	453	1349
9	503	6319	824	8847
10	944	12483	3871	11451
11	673	6337	2542	5407
12	754	8797	5669	9052
M	621	6416	2479	7278
SE	93	1312	814	1435

Rat	Mean Wheel Revolutions			
	5% AL	5% Dep	20% AL	20% Dep
19	1011	7155	698	6267
20	3639	5174	712	8002
21	4620	10186	1246	11834
22	3197	11205	569	10580
23	5384	4197	1545	9274
24	5443	9715	1356	13476
M	3882	7939	1021	9906
SE	683	1171	168	1067

Note. Rats 7–12 began with the 20% protein diet; rats 19–24 began with the 5% protein diets. Wheel revolutions are shown in the sequence animals experienced the conditions.

effects were noted, $F(1,30) = 7.44$, $p \leq .0106$, and considerable individual differences between animals were again observed. The data in Table 5.2 are therefore separated by sequence. Regardless of diet or sequence, deprivation produced significantly more running than ad libitum feeding, $F(1,30) = 116.26$, $p \leq .0001$. Interestingly, a significant diet times deprivation interaction was observed, $F(1,30) = 7.12$, $p \leq .0122$, in which ad libitum feeding of the 5% protein diet produced significantly more running ($p \leq .05$) than did ad libitum feeding of the 20% protein diet. Ad libitum feeding of the 5% protein diet produced increased running in every animal and more than tripled group mean running rates. Deprivation resulted in large increases in individual running relative to both ad libitum conditions in every animal. It produced a more than ninefold increase in mean group running. As with absolute measures, the two deprivation conditions did not differ significantly. Comparisons of running in the two deprivation conditions for individual animals showed mixed results.

Temporal Running Distributions.   Figure 5.3 shows that the differences in total daily running observed were primarily the result of differences in running in the light portion of the 12/12 light–dark cycle. Running in the 20% protein ad libitum condition remained substantially below deprivation conditions for the first eight hours of the dark phase (periods 10–26). Very little running occurred in any period in that condition. Dark-phase running in the 5% protein ad libitum condition looked more like running in the deprived condition for animals that began with the 5% diet

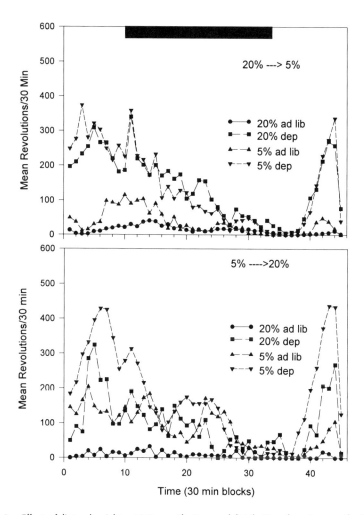

FIG. 5.3.   Effects of diet and weight restriction on the temporal distribution of running over the 23-hour wheel access period. The shaded bar at top indicates the 12-hour dark period. Feeding and care occurred prior to period 1 and after period 46. The group that began with the 20% protein diet is shown in the upper panel and the group that began on the 5% protein diet in the lower panel.

(lower panel). For animals that began on the 20% protein diet (upper panel), running dropped to the level of the 20% ad libitum running after the first three hours of the dark phase.

That 5% protein animals fed ad libitum shown in the lower panel more closely resemble deprived animals is not surprising. Animals that began on the 5% protein diet showed reduced food consumption compared with animals that began on 20% protein. The 5% protein animals also did not gain weight during ad libitum feeding. In effect, they appeared to be slightly deprived. These feeding and weight effects were not in evidence when the 5% protein diet was fed second. Perhaps as a result, the 5% protein ad libitum condition was more similar to the 20% ad libitum condition in the upper panel.

GENERAL DISCUSSION

Experiment 1 showed that voluntary activity was parametrically related to body weight restriction, at least between 100% and 70% of ad libitum weights. Analysis of temporal distributions indicated that this effect was primarily the result of running in the light portions of a 12/12 light–dark cycle. Studies that use short experimental sessions to investigate deprivation effects in other contexts should be aware of temporal distributions of activity. Our distribution data suggest that results of such studies could vary wildly depending on when experimental sessions occurred relative to the feeding and care period and light–dark cycle.

Experiment 2 extended these effects to formulated diets. The commercial laboratory diet fed in experiment one was approximately 25% of energy from protein, 10% from fat, and 65% from carbohydrate. The two diets utilized in experiment 2 were 20%, 40%, 40% and 5%, 40%, 55%, protein, fat, and carbohydrate respectively. Relative to standard commercial diets, both formulated diets were high in fat. In spite of dietary differences, the effects of food restriction were comparable to that shown in Experiment 1.

Although the increase was smaller than in the deprivation conditions, the significant running increase produced by the 5% protein diet fed ad libitum (see Table 5.2) suggests that dietary protein restriction may be implicated as a causal factor in activity anorexia. Tyrosine represents one specific possibility. Tyrosine is the amino acid precursor to both norepinephrine and dopamine in catecholamine biosynthesis. Diets deficient in tyrosine because of low protein content or food restriction might reduce catecholamine synthesis. This is consistent with a report by Broocks, Liu, and Pirke (1990) that semistarvation reduced norepinephrine and dopamine turnover in the mediobasal hypothalamus.

In the formulation of the two diets used in Experiment 2, protein was exchanged for carbohydrate: the 5% protein diet contained 55% carbohydrate, and the 20% protein diet contained 40% carbohydrate. The effects we believe are attributable to lower levels of protein could also have resulted from elevated carbohydrate levels. Although we are unaware of an explanation for a carbohydrate effect, we are presently ruling out that possibility by systematically replicating experiment 2 with diets in which protein is exchanged for fat. If we can replicate the dietary effect, then selectively manipulating individual amino acids in the diet is a logical next step in understanding the role of food restriction in activity anorexia.

ACKNOWLEDGMENTS

This research was supported by USDA/CSREES project MO.X-OH90-519. The authors wish to acknowledge Vevia Newberry for her contributions to animal handling and care, data collection, and data entry in experiment 1 and Traci Richmond for her animal handling and care and data collection assistance in experiment 2.

REFERENCES

Beneke, W. M., Schulte, S. E., & Vander Tuig, J. G. (1995). An analysis of excessive running in the development of activity anorexia. *Physiology and Behavior, 58*, 451–457.

Boer, D. P. (1989). *Determinants of excessive running in activity anorexia.* Unpublished doctoral dissertation, University of Alberta, Edmonton.

Broocks, A., Liu, J., & Pirke, K. M. (1990). Semistarvation-induced hyperactivity compensates for decreased norepinephrine and dopamine turnover in the mediobasal hypothalamus of the rat. *Journal of Neural Transmission, 79*, 113–124.

Epling, W. F., & Pierce, W. D. (1992). *Solving the anorexia puzzle: A scientific approach.* Toronto, ON: Hogrefe and Huber.

Heufelder, A., Warnhoff, M., & Pirke, K. M. (1985). Platelet α2-adrenoceptor and adenylate cyclase in patients with anorexia nervosa and bulimia. *Journal of Clinical Endocrinology and Metabolism, 61*, 1053–1060.

Russell, J. C., Epling, W. F., Pierce, W. D., Amy, R. M., & Boer, D. P. (1987). Induction of voluntary prolonged running by rats. *Journal of Applied Physiology, 63*, 2549–2553.

6

Gender Differences in Activity Anorexia: Predictable, Paradoxical, or Enigmatic

Lee E. Doerries
Christopher Newport University

Activity anorexia (Epling & Pierce, 1988; Epling, Pierce, & Stefan, 1983), activity-stress ulcer (Pare & Houser, 1973), and self-starvation (Routtenberg & Kuznesof, 1967) each refer to paradigms in which rats are simultaneously introduced to restricted feeding (30–90 minutes daily) and provided access to running wheels (22.5–24 hours daily). The weight loss criterion used to define each paradigm varies between 75% of original body weight for activity-based anorexia and 70% or more of original body weight for the activity-stress ulcer (Doerries, Stanley, & Aravich, 1991). Other than this distinction, the basic paradigms are similar.

The simultaneous introduction of food restriction and exercise results in highly reliable consequences—increases in activity levels and weight loss with concomitant reductions in food intake (compared with nonexercising but food-restricted control animals). Manipulations of the paradigm conducted in our laboratory[1] that

---

[1]Medical Research Service, Veterans Affairs Medical Center, Hampton, VA 23667; laboratory of Paul F. Aravich, Lee E. Doerries, and Thomas S. Rieg.

exacerbate weight loss include changes in circadian rhythm disruption (Aravich, Goduti, & Rieg, 1992; Aravich, Stanley, Downing, Rieg & Doerries, 1991), chronic alpha adrenergic injection into the paraventricular hypothalamic nucleus (Rieg & Aravich, 1992), administration of anabolic steroids (Aravich, Choi, & Rieg, 1993), and serotonin depletion (Rieg, Burt, Contakes, Chiou, & Aravich, 1994). Manipulations identified as having a protective effect against weight loss include dietary tryptophan loading (Aravich, Kaminski, & Rieg, 1994), the administration of the serotonin agonist fenfluramine (Rieg, Maestrello, & Aravich, 1994), and neonatal injection of monosodium glutamate (Rieg, Woynicz, Fulton, Downing, & Aravich, 1993).

Compared with the manipulations already cited, several variables deserve special mention because of their relatively stronger effects in protecting against the weight loss associated with activity anorexia. Habituation of animals to the running wheel can prevent or retard the occurrence of the phenomenon, depending on the length of the habituation period (Epling & Pierce, 1984). The timing of the introduction of restricted feeding and opportunity to exercise, although not preventing the phenomenon totally, has a significant effect in retarding weight loss. Rats allowed to exercise in running wheels while being fed ad libitum are better protected against weight loss than are rats that are simultaneously introduced to the food restricted and exercise manipulations (Rolls & Rowe, 1979). Finally, gender, age, starting weight, and carcass composition are interrelated variables that, depending on whether animals are male or female, young or old, fat or lean, may provide them significant protection against weight loss associated with the activity anorexia paradigm.

This chapter explores the relationships among gender, age, starting weight, and carcass composition and attempts to determine whether their effects on the activity paradigm are predictable, paradoxical, or enigmatic. First, however, it is important to note a fundamental distinction between anorectic rats and anorectic humans, one that presents investigators of the animal model of anorexia with a fundamental paradox.

ANORECTIC RATS AND ANORECTIC HUMANS

Nearly all people, from patients to practitioners, from physicians to the general public, characterize human anorexia as largely a female disorder. Not surprisingly, 90% of the reported incidence occurs in women (Yates, 1989). This statistic, nonetheless, may mask the frequency with which anorexia occurs among men. For various reasons, men who weigh 15% to 25% below their normal body weight may not be diagnosed formally as having anorexia. Yates, Leehey, and Shisslak (1983) described marathon runner Alberto Salizar as exhibiting quintessentially anorectic characteristics. Weightlifters, wrestlers, and gymnasts are examples of other types of athletes who may experience extreme weight loss without being diagnosed as having anorexia (Smith, 1980). From a purely speculative point of view, it would appear that individuals who lose weight to achieve some standard of professional or athletic performance individuals (e.g. models, professional dancers, athletes) are more likely to remain undiagnosed than are individuals who lose weight for more personal or aesthetic reasons. Contradictory evidence reported by Garner and Garfinkel (1988) indicates that the reasons for food restriction given by males with anorexia are largely the same as those given by females. Regardless of the validity of this hypothesis, there is some agreement that statistics underrepresent the actual number of males with this disease (Garner & Garfinkel, 1977; Gilbert, 1986).

Studies that directly compare the susceptibility of male and female rats to activity anorexia are rare, and, in those that do exist, gender is likely to be confounded with age, starting weight, and carcass composition. Like most other investigators, we have chosen to use either male or female rats in individual studies, and only in rare cases have we tested both males and females to determine whether gender is associated with differences in activity level, food intake, and days required to reach the weight loss criterion (Doerries et al., 1991). I recall my initial experience running four 675-gram female retired breeders that, in contrast to the predictions of Epling et al. (1983), behaved similarly to older, heavier humans. In other words, they exercised minimally—approximately 50 wheel turns in a 22.5-hour period following 10 or more days of restricted feeding and access to a running wheel—while continuing to eat proportionately large amounts of food. Not until I began using preadolescent rats weighing between 150 and 250 grams was I able to observe reliably the diet and exercise induced weight loss phenomenon described by Epling and Pierce (1988). Early research by Routtenberg and Kuznesof (1967) suggests that rats weighing significantly more than 140 grams are highly susceptible to the weight loss phenomenon. However, our own research (Rieg et al., 1994) suggests a weight level (350 grams) beyond which animals are significantly less likely to reach the 25% weight loss criterion that we use to define activity anorexia. Do old, fat rats behave like human couch potatoes? It would seem they do.

Despite this predictable similarity in behavior between heavier rats and humans subjected to restricted feeding and exercise, in order to validate the animal paradigm as a model for human anorexia, one must reconcile the paradoxical evidence showing male rats more susceptible than female rats to the manipulations of restricted feeding and exercise (Rolls & Rowe, 1979).

A PROTOTYPE EXPERIMENT

In order to illustrate the interdependence of gender, age, starting weight, and carcass composition, a prototype experiment is presented. Part 1 of the experiment found that male rats were more susceptible to the activity anorexia paradigm than were female rats, despite the fact that the female rats weighed less than the males at the start of the experiment and that the female rats ran and ate more than the males.[2] Part 2 of the experiment confirms the hypothesis that differential changes in carcass

---

[2]Experimental animals included in this study are from Doerries et al. (1991).

lipid composition are related to this sexually dimorphic effect.[3] The discussion that follows relates critical choices that I made in designing the experiment to the literature identifying gender differences in age, body weight, and carcass composition.

Methodology for Part 1

The subjects included 16 male and 16 female Holtzman Sprague-Dawley rats, 41 to 44 days old at the start of the experiment. Male and female rats were housed and run independently of each other. Rats were habituated for 7 days to Whamann-type running wheels with connecting side cages. During the habituation period, rats had free access to Purina Lab Chow number 5001; passage between the running wheel and the side cage was controlled by a sliding door that remained closed throughout this period. The animals were maintained on a 12/12 hour light–dark cycle in a room in which temperature was held constant at 72°F.

The experiment began at 12:30 hours when the animals were weighed, the food was removed from the side cages, and the rats were given access to the running wheels for the next 22.5 hours. At 11:00 hours on the following day the animals were weighed to determine their percentage of original body weight loss and given a measured amount of food in the side cages. The number of wheel revolutions was recorded to determine the total activity for that day. Access to the running wheel was blocked during feeding. After 1.5 hours of food access (midway through the 12-hour light phase of the cycle), the remaining food and spillage were collected and weighed. The door to the wheel was then opened to allow the rat access to the wheel for the next 22.5 hours. This procedure was followed daily until the rats lost 25 ± 1.5% of original body weight.

Methodology for Part 2

Body Composition.   The gut was removed, opened, rinsed, blotted dry, and returned to the carcass. The carcass weight was recorded and the rats frozen at -20°C until assay. The carcasses were autoclaved for 24 hours in large beakers with covered tops, then homogenized with a large-bore Polyton. After weighing, aliquots (in triplicate) were dried to stable weight to determine water content. Triplicate samples were ashed at 600°C in a muffle furnace for mineral content. Other aliquots were assayed for lipid by the Folch methods (Forbes, Swift, Elliott, & James, 1946). From these measurements, fat mass, fat-free body mass, and water content were calculated.

Results

The results of a *t* test for independent samples performed on the data reveal that despite an attempt to match the rats for body weight at the beginning of the

---

[3]Preliminary data from this portion of the study were presented at the 1992 Annual Meeting of the Eastern Psychological Association, Boston, MA.

experiment, there were significant differences between the starting weights of the male and female rats in the restricted feeding and exercise conditions (males = 159.88 g, $SE = \pm 2.10$ vs. females = 151.63 g, $SE = \pm 1.85$, $p < .05$). Starting body weights of male and female ad libitum-fed control rats were matched to the starting weights of male and female rats in the experimental condition.

Although male rats began the experiment weighing more than female rats, they reached the weight loss criterion in 3.125 ($SE = .35$) days compared with 4.75 ($SE = \pm .31$) days for the female rats, $t(14) = -3.45$, $p < .001$.

Significant gender differences relative to both food intake and activity were also observed. Cumulative food intake was greater for females ($M = 17.4$ g, $SE = \pm 2.47$) compared with males ($M = 8.91$, g $SE = \pm 1.98$), $t(14) = 2.68$, $p < .02$. A similar difference was observed relative to food intake 24 hours prior to sacrifice.

The cumulative wheel activity for the females ($M = 10829.25$ revolutions, $SE = \pm 1169.7$) was significantly greater then that of the males ($M = 6641.75$ revolutions $SE = \pm 1005.01$), $t(14) = 2.72$, $p < .02$). During the 24-hour period preceding sacrifice, wheel activity did not differ significantly between female and male experimental rats.

Carcass composition analyses indicated no differences in percent lipid content of ad libitum-fed male (5.2%, $SE = \pm .4\%$) and female (4.8%, $SE = \pm .4\%$, $p > .05$, rats. As predicted, males subjected to the activity anorexia paradigm lost a significantly higher percentage of lipid content (3.32, $SE = \pm .04$) than did females (2.1, $SE \pm .4$; $p < .05$).

CHOICES AND IMPLICATIONS
FOR RESEARCHERS
OF ACTIVITY ANOREXIA

Once it had been decided to commit resources to a parametric study of possible gender differences in susceptibility to activity anorexia, the first decision that had to be made involved which strain of rat to test in the experiment. Because a majority of researchers investigating activity anorexia use Sprague-Dawley rats, and because their data are readily available for comparison purposes, we elected to use Sprague-Dawley animals in the reference study.

A second critical decision involved the starting age and starting weight of the animals to be tested. Because a collateral goal of the research was to validate activity anorexia as a model for human anorexia, and given that human anorexia is primarily associated with adolescent and younger women (Yates, 1989), it seemed prudent to run younger rather than older animals. Although we were aware that anorexia can occur among middle aged and even geriatric populations, we believe that the weight loss associated with changes in metabolism, brain function, and reproductive physiology that occur with increasing age may not be comparable with those seen in younger individuals. Therefore, to extend the external validity of the animal model, younger rather than older rats became the focus of our study.

A related decision we faced regarded the starting weights of the animals in the study. Anyone who has ordered rats from a breeder knows that the differences in weights between male and female rats can vary by as much as 25% to 30%, depending on the age of the animals. In the study just described that tested 41- to 44-day-old animals, the starting weights of males and females differed significantly, but by less than 10 grams. However, as male and female animals age, differences in their respective weights increase, thereby introducing a third major factor for decision of whether or not to match the starting weights of the males and females. Except for the youngest of rats, matching starting weights will inevitably involve a confounding with age. Because it was possible to match age and weight fairly closely in the male and female animals used in the reference study, this decision was made easier. Nevertheless, the investigators were not unmindful that in controlling for age and starting weight, they were introducing a possible threat to external validity due to the larger differences in weight between older male and female rats and humans.

The decision regarding at what age and weight to begin testing the animals was also informed by differences in activity levels observed in younger and older rats. In studies using older, heavier animals, activity levels are significantly lower. In certain cases they vary by more than 50% (Rieg et al., 1994). This may not be critical when the difference is between 6,000 and 10,000 wheel turns as it is in the reference study. However, it may be of greater concern when differences are between 300 and 1,500 wheel turns in a 24-hour period. At some point, one must ask whether a 500- to 600-gram rat running between 300 and 1500 wheel turns a day adequately characterizes the rigorous or strenuous exercise used to define activity-based anorexia. Epling and Pierce (1984) noted that the onset of strong anorexia is characterized by an accelerating activity curve. This suggests that it is the change in the level of activity, not activity per se, that is responsible for the phenomenon.

Because younger animals introduced to the paradigm survive a fewer number of days than do older and heavier animals, investigators often face a trade-off: whether to use animals that more closely match dimensions of human anorexia in terms of age and relative weight, or to use older animals that survive longer under food restriction and exercise conditions, thereby allowing the investigator the opportunity to observe differences in susceptibility between male and female rats. One way to solve this dilemma is to use a measure other than number of days as the criterion determining susceptibility. By employing a repeated-measures design, it is possible to determine differences in the daily percentage of weight loss associated with different groups of animals. A recent investigation conducted in our lab showed significant differences in percentages of weight loss between two groups of animals despite the fact that the rats reached the weight loss criterion in the same number of days (Ness, Marshall, & Aravich, 1995).

A fourth decision faced by the authors of the reference study regarded how to determine changes in carcass composition that occur as a consequence of the food restriction and exercise conditions. It is generally agreed that male and female rats reflect approximately the same ratios of fat to lean body mass as do male and female humans. Characteristically, normal weight males and females differ in the number of body fat cells by up to 50%, with females having a larger fat mass (Bjorntorp, 1989) and the larger percentage of fat cells (Bjorntorp, 1974). Data on male and female runners indicate that, while in training, male distance runners may reduce body fat to as low as 5% of their total body weight. Female runners experience similar but less severe reductions in body fat to between 15% and 18% of their total body weight (Gadpaille, Sanborn, & Wagner, 1987).

Although studies have been conducted to measure the percentage change in body fat among exercising and nonexercising adult male and female rats, such studies fail to confirm the existence of differences in body fat in younger male and female animals (Pitts, 1984). Pitts' summary of the data from the available studies indicates that, with one exception in which body fat was unchanged, both voluntary (wheel-running) and involuntary (treadmill) exercise modes reduced body fat in both sexes at all ages. All exercise modes changed free fat body mass (FFBM) if initiated at 7 weeks of age or earlier; however, exercising males evidenced a smaller FFBM than control animals. Females that ran in activity wheels or experienced forced swimming showed a FFBM larger than controls did. The significance of these findings is that investigators must not only decide at what age and weight to run their animals, they must also consider differences in initial carcass composition and differential changes in the ratio of fat to lean body mass that occur in male and female rats as a function of continued exposure to restricted feeding and exercise.

Gross examination of the carcasses of younger and older animals suggests that the ratios reported for older rats do not accurately describe what would be found in 140- to 160-gram animals. In the absence of comparison data, we elected to match the starting weights of male and female controls to the respective starting weights of male and female experimental animals and to determine, following sacrifice, their relative proportions of lean FFBM. An empirical investigation reporting the ratios of body fat to lean body mass in younger age (40- to 60-day-old) animals is clearly needed.

Finally, investigators must choose the method for determining carcass composition following sacrifice. The reference study used a procedure that may provide an incomplete picture of changes associated with the paradigm (Forbes et al., 1946). Pitts (1984) hypothesized that the growth period between 7 and 11 weeks is a time when mechanisms regulating the FFBM and its growth have not matured. The validity of this hypothesis should be of concern to all researchers of activity anorexia who work with rats 80 days old or younger.

Following weaning, FFBM develops more slowly in exercising males than in exercising females. For animals less than 42 days old that were introduced to exercise, the exercise increased FFBM in females and reduced it in males (Pitts, 1984).

Although exercise has a marked effect on reducing weight gains in male rats, it has little effect on females (Rolls & Rowe, 1979). Data from the reference study support a body of reliable evidence showing that male rats eat less than female rats both ad libitum and in exercising conditions. These data suggest that as females exercise more, they compensate for the additional energy expenditure by increasing their food intake. Nonobese male rats, and perhaps non-obese male humans (Bjorntorp, 1989), are more vulnerable to the effects of severe exercise, the consequence of which is a more rapid depletion of limited fat reserves.

More research regarding changes in metabolism and variation in mass, topography, morphology, and function of adipose tissue relative to lean body mass is needed. To better understand the complex relationship between gender, age, carcass composition, and energy expenditure, calorimetry studies on animals tested at various stages of the activity anorexia protocol should be conducted.

Two potentially relevant issues were not addressed in the reference study. Male and female animals were housed and run independently of each other. Investigators who run male and female rats together may not observe similar effects. Preliminary data from our laboratory indicated that 41-day-old rats with 15% body weight loss were menarcheal. However, similar measures were not taken on animals in the reference study. To control for the effects of estrus on activity levels and food intake, investigators should monitor the reproductive cycle in female animals.

CONCLUSIONS

In a prototype investigation of the susceptibility of male and female rats to activity-based anorexia, significant sex differences were observed. In designing the study the authors confronted several choices of potential concern to all investigators of activity anorexia. These choices included what strain of rat to use in the study, at what age and at what weight to begin testing animals and whether or not to match male and female rats by age and/or weight at the start of the experiment. In turn, each of these choices was informed by differences in activity levels, food intake, and carcass composition used to define anorexia in humans.

REFERENCES

Aravich, P. F., Choi, J. J., & Rieg, T. S. (1993, November). *Anabolic steroid administration increases vulnerability to an animal model of anorexia nervosa.* Paper presented at the Annual Meeting of the Society for Neuroscience, Washington, DC.

Aravich, P. F., Goduti, M., & Rieg, T. S. (1992). Rostral hypothalamic fetal transplants reduce activity-based anorexia in rats with lesions aimed at the suprachiasmatic nucleus. *Journal of Neural Transplantation and Plasticity, 3,* 299–300.

Aravich, P. F., Kaminski, L. A., & Rieg, T. S. (November, 1994). *Dietary tryptophan: Beneficial effects on an animal model of anorexia nervosa.* Paper presented at the Annual Meeting of the Society for Neuroscience, Miami Beach, FL.

Aravich, P. F., Stanley, E. Z., Downing, S., Rieg, T. S., & Doerries, L. E. (1991, June). *Circadian rhythms and activity-based anorexia in the rat: Relationship to suprachiasmatic but not supraoptic dynorphin.* Paper presented at the Annual Meeting of the Endocrine Society, Washington, DC.

Bjorntorp, P. A. (1974). Effects of age, sex and clinical conditions on adipose tissue cellularity in man. *Metabolism, 23,* 1091–1102.

Bjorntorp, P. A. (1989). Sex differences in the regulation of energy balance with exercise. *American Journal of Clinical Nutrition, 49,* 958–961.

Doerries, L. E., Stanley, E. Z., & Aravich, P. F. (1991). Activity-based anorexia: Relationship to gender and activity–stress ulcers. *Physiology & Behavior, 50,* 945–949.

Epling, W. F., Pierce, W. D., & Stefan, L. (1983). A theory of activity-based anorexia. *International Journal of Eating Disorders, 3,* 27–46.

Epling, W. F., & Pierce, W. D. (1984). Activity-based anorexia in rats as a function of opportunity to run on an activity wheel. *Nutrition and Behavior, 2,* 37–49.

Epling, W. F., & Pierce, W. D. (1988). Activity-based anorexia: A biobehavioral perspective. *International Journal of Eating Disorders, 7*, 475–485.

Forbes, E. B., Swift, R. W., Elliott, R. F., James, W. J. (1946). Relation of fat to economy and food utilization by the growing albino rat. *Journal of Nutrition, 31*, 203–212.

Gadpaille, W. J., Sanborn, C. F., & Wagner, W. E. W. (1987). Athletic amenorrhea, major affective disorders, and eating disorders. *American Journal of Psychiatry, 144*, 939–942.

Garner, D. M., & Garfinkel, P. E. (1977). The role of behavior modification in the treatment of anorexia nervosa. *Journal of Pediatric Psychology, 2*, 113–121.

Garner, D. M., & Garfinkel, P. E. (1988). *Diagnostic issues in anorexia nervosa and bulimia nervosa.* New York: Brunner/Mazel.

Gilbert, S. (1986). *Pathology of eating: Psychology and treatment.* New York: Routledge & Kegan Paul.

Ness, J. W., Marshall, T. R., & Aravich, P. F. (1995). Effects of rearing condition on restricted feeding and activity induced weight loss. *Developmental Psychobiology, 28*, 165–173..

Pare, W. P., & Houser, V. P. (1973). Activity and food-restriction effects on gastric glandular lesions in the rat: The activity–stress ulcer. *Bulletin of the Psychonomic Society, 2*, 213–224.

Pitts, G. C. (1984). Body composition in the rat: Interactions of exercise, age, sex, and diet. *American Journal of Physiology, 246*, R495–R501.

Rieg, T. S., & Aravich, P. F. (1992). Paraventricular hypothalamic clonidine increases rather than decreases susceptibility to activity-based anorexia in the rat. *Behavioral Neuroscience, 106*, 1015–1022.

Rieg, T. S., Burt, J. L., Contakes, L. M., Chiou, A. L., & Aravich, P. F. (1994, April). *Central serotonergic depletion exacerbates activity-based anorexia.* Paper presented at the Annual Meeting of the Eastern Psychological Association, Providence, RI.

Rieg, T. S., Maestrello, A. M., & Aravich, P. F. (1994). Weight cycling alters the effects of d-fenfluramine on susceptibility to activity-based anorexia. *American Journal of Clinical Nutrition, 60*, 494–500.

Rieg, T. S., Woynicz, B. A., Fulton, K. F., Downing, S. N., & Aravich, P. F. (1993, November). *Neonatal monosodium glutamate (MSG) decreases vulnerability to the weight-loss syndrome produced in adult rats by voluntary exercise and food restriction.* Paper presented at the Annual Meeting of the Society for Neuroscience, Washington, DC.

Rolls, B. J., & Rowe, E. A. (1979). Exercise and development and persistence of dietary obesity in male and female rats. *Physiology & Behavior, 23*, 241–247.

Routtenberg, A., & Kuznesof, A. W. (1967). Self-starvation of rats living in activity wheels on a restricted feeding schedule. *Journal of Comparative and Physiological Psychology, 64*, 414–421.

Smith, N. J. (1980). Excessive weight loss and food aversions in athletes simulating anorexia nervosa. *Pediatrics, 66*, 139–142.

Yates, A. (1989). Current perspectives on the eating disorders: I. History, psychological and biological aspects. *Journal of the American Academy of Child and Adolescent Psychiatry, 28*, 813–828.

Yates, A., Leehey, K., & Shisslak, C. M. (1983). Running—An analogue of anorexia? *New England Journal of Medicine, 408*, 251–255.

III

Physiological Foundations
of Activity Anorexia

7

Adverse Effects of Exercise Stress and Restricted Feeding in the Rat: Theoretical and Neurobiological Considerations

Paul F. Aravich
*Eastern Virginia Medical School
and Hampton Veterans Affairs Medical Center*

The benefits of exercise in normal weight and obese people are well known. However, less attention has focused on exercise in the malnourished. This is an important public health consideration because of nutritional ignorance and the preoccupation with body weight in Western cultures, because of anorexia nervosa (AN), which is a relatively intractable disorder highly correlated with hyperactivity and malnutrition, and because of growing interest in exercise for the treatment and prevention of disease. Further research is clearly needed to determine the effects of exercise stress in malnourished people.

We have been exploring an exercise-stress syndrome produced when otherwise normal rats are placed on a moderate food deprivation schedule and given free access to running wheels (Spear & Hill, 1962). Under these conditions, rats, mice (Epling, Pierce, & Stefan, 1983), hamsters (Vincent & Pare, 1976a), chipmunks

(Vincent, Pare, Isom, & Reeves, 1977), gerbils, and guinea pigs (Vincent & Pare, 1976b) progressively increase running and decrease body weight compared to animals simply given restricted feeding. This chapter addresses theoretical issues related to the syndrome and summarize our research program on it. Specific issues include the clinical relevancy of the syndrome, the anorexia of activity anorexia, paradigmatic considerations, the respective roles of the endogenous opioids and serotonin, risk factors for the syndrome, physiological changes specific to it, and other variables we manipulated. In the spirit of the free and open exchange of information that is vital to science, unpublished as well as published experiments are summarized.

CLINICAL RELEVANCY
OF THE EXERCISE-STRESS SYNDROME

The issue of animal modeling has been discussed by a variety of investigators (chapter 2, this volume). McKinney (1988) stresses the need to determine whether the modeling is for a specific clinical disorder, or for a fundamental feature applicable to many types of pathology. Our publications, as well as those of others, stressed the relationship between the exercise syndrome and a specific clinical entity: AN. However, the syndrome has broader applications: It is relevant to the adverse effects of voluntary exercise stress in malnourished people. This makes it especially pertinent to the health care needs of women who are preoccupied with weight loss and, unlike men, combine intense exercise with dieting (Drewnowski, Kurth, & Krahn, 1994); to AN, which is associated with hyperactivity (chapter 14, this volume) and has one of the highest mortality rates of any psychiatric disorder; and to the increasing use of exercise regimens for the treatment and prevention of disease. Others showed that it is also relevant to obsessive–compulsive disorders because individuals with AN exhibit relentless running and sensitivity to a drug used in the treatment of these disorders (viz., fluoxetine). A broader view of the syndrome is needed to identify novel intervention strategies and stimulate further research on its neurobiological and environmental determinants.

ACTIVITY ANOREXIA NOMENCLATURE

The syndrome has various names, including *self-starvation* (Routtenberg & Kuznesof, 1967), *activity stress* (Pare & Houser, 1973), and *activity-based anorexia* (chapter 1). It is clear that animals subject to it eat less than rats placed on a similar food deprivation schedule without exercise (Routtenberg & Kuznesof, 1967). However, several lines of evidence suggest that this effect should not be described as a self-starvation or anorexia phenomenon.

For example, Kanarek & Collier (1983) assessed the syndrome with respect to the impact of wheel-running on adaptation to suddenly imposed time restricted feeding schedules. They found that it is more difficult to adapt rats to a limited frequency but longer duration restricted feeding schedule (e.g., one 60-minute feeding period per day) than to a more frequent but shorter duration restricted-feeding schedule (e.g., four 15-minute feeding periods per day). They also found that running wheel access retards adaptation to suddenly imposed restricted-feeding schedules, irrespective of the type of schedule. Finally, they found that the adverse impact of wheel-running synergizes with a limited frequency feeding schedule to retard substantially adaptation to the sudden imposition of that schedule. They concluded that wheel-running does not actually suppress food intake under these conditions. Rather, it primarily retards recovery of intake following the imposition of the feeding schedule. Thus, wheel-running does not suppress hunger (i.e., the drive to eat) and the effect should not be referred to as self-starvation or anorexia. Kanarek and Collier (1983) also noted that wheel-running is not unique in this respect and that a similar effect occurs when sucrose or saccharin is given coincident with restricted feeding schedules. The view that exercise interferes with the ability to adapt to a restricted feeding schedule explains the observation that the syndrome can be retarded by previous adaptation to that schedule (Routtenberg, 1968).

In addition, we generated data that challenged the self-starvation–anorexia nomenclature (Aravich, Stanley, & Doerries, 1995). Animals subjected to the syndrome were compared to control rats sustaining the same degree of weight loss by food deprivation without exercise. Once comparable weight losses were established, all animals were fed for 6 hours. It was found that syndrome animals were not anorexic compared to the weight-reduced controls during the 6-hour refeeding period. Indeed, both groups ate the same amount (Fig. 7.1). This is not consistent

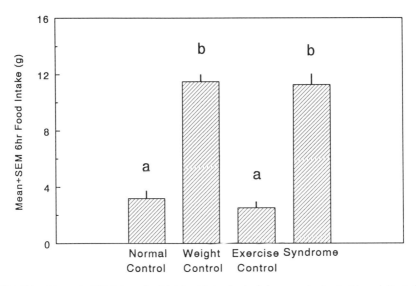

FIG. 7.1. Mean + SEM 6-hour food intake (g) for freely fed unexercised rats (Normal Control), weight-reduced rats (Weight Control), freely fed exercised rats (Exercise Control), and rats simultaneously subjected to exercise and weight reduction (Syndrome). Different letters refer to differences at the .05 level of significance.

with an anorexia view, nor with the view that the syndrome reduces the reinforcing value of food (Routtenberg & Kuznesof, 1967; Pierce & Epling, 1991). If anything, the reinforcing value of food was increased because syndrome animals ate more than freely fed–exercised and freely fed–unexercised controls (Fig. 7.1). This increased food intake, relative to the freely fed groups, was attributed to the secondary consequence of weight loss, because weight-reduced control rats were similarly elevated (Fig. 7.1). Animals subjected to the syndrome were also not anorectic compared with weight-reduced controls when subjected to acute glucose insufficiency (by the glucose antimetabolite, 2-deoxy-D-glucose), which normally stimulates food intake (Aravich et al., 1995). Syndrome animals injected with the drug did, however, paradoxically reduce food intake compared to syndrome animals injected with placebo (Aravich et al., 1995). This paradoxical effect is consistent with similar data obtained in AN, which further validates the syndrome as a model of the disorder (Aravich et al., 1995). Because this effect also occurred in weight-reduced controls, it was attributed to the secondary consequences of weight loss.

It should be noted that food intake progressively increases as the syndrome develops (i.e., the anorexia attenuates); it is only at its terminal stages that intake falls again (see Aravich et al., 1995; Epling & Pierce, 1984). The animals in our protocol were not allowed to reach this stage to control for the nonspecific complications of starvation-induced morbidity. According to the nomenclature of Epling and Pierce (1984), we produced a weak anorexia syndrome to examine the self-starvation–anorexia issue. However, others argue that, even when the terminal reduction in food intake is allowed, it is actually an example of so-called starvation-induced anorexia (Spatz & Jones, 1971). This is the well established reduction in food intake that occurs when prolonged food deprivation produces a critical level of energy depletion. According to this view, activity anorexia is not a unique form of anorexia but an example of a rapidly induced starvation anorexia. Thus, the anorexia is not activity-based but starvation-based. In addition to these concerns, a final difficulty with the self-starvation–anorexia nomenclature is that the reduction in food intake is, in part, experimenter imposed (Aravich, Doerries, et al., 1994; Watanabe, Hara, & Ogawa, 1992).

We conclude that the syndrome is not a general self-starvation or anorexia syndrome. Although AN itself is not a true anorexia syndrome, because hunger sensations are maintained well into the disease process (Devlin & Walsh, 1992), the self-starvation–anorexia nomenclature is debatable and detracts from the syndrome's overall clinical relevance. The nomenclature also detracts from two more fundamental features of the syndrome. These are the freely induced hyperactivity and profound weight loss (Aravich, Doerries, et al., 1994), which are indisputably related to AN. Another clinically relevant feature of the syndrome is the so-called morphological stress triad (relative adrenal hypertrophy, thymus atrophy, and spleen atrophy; Hara, Manabe, & Ogawa, 1981), because glucocorticoid and immunological changes occur in AN. As a result of these considerations, we suggest that the syndrome be described more empirically to avoid debatable theoretical constructs (Aravich et al., 1995). If theoretical constructs are used, it is proposed that the activity-stress (or exercise-stress) nomenclature has historical precedence (Pare & Houser, 1973) and greater heuristic value. Authors should use the following key words to follow the syndrome more closely in the literature: *exercise, weight loss, AN,* and *rat* (Aravich et al., 1995).

PARADIGMATIC CONSIDERATIONS

Several procedural issues are related to the implementation and interpretation of the model. These include the types of behavioral controls used, the acute and chronic variants of the model, the severity of weight loss allowed, housing conditions, and the age and sex used.

It is important to control for the general effects of exercise and weight loss if the combined effects of exercise stress and weight loss are to be determined. We showed early in our program that the rate and degree of weight loss can be readily controlled by weight-reduced controls' losing body weight with simple food restriction (Aravich, Doerries, Stanley, Metcalf, & Lauterio, 1989). This is achieved by adjusting the time food is available on a daily basis, starting with the full 1.5-hour period used by the exercise-stress rats and then progressively reducing food access in 10-minute blocks according to the rate of weight loss in the exercise-stress group. The ability to expressly control for the general effects of weight loss is one of the most significant benefits of the syndrome, especially as it relates to the study of AN, which lacks explicit weight-loss controls (Aravich et al., 1995).

One weakness of the syndrome is the inability to control for the general effects of excessive exercise. Freely fed rats given access to running wheels run substantially less than food deprived rats. As stated previously (Aravich, Rieg, Ahmed, & Lauterio, 1993), we know of no way to stimulate normal weight, nutritionally replete rats to run to the same extent as animals subjected to the syndrome except by the stress of electric shock or the stress of forced running, each of which elicit additional intervening variables. Although this provides further evidence for the view that wheel-running and the sudden imposition of a food restriction schedule are inherently interactive (Kanarek & Collier, 1983), conclusions regarding the relative contribution of exercise are restricted to effects obtained from moderately exercised controls (Aravich, Rieg, Ahmed, et al., 1993).

One alternative is the sustained wheel-running procedure used by the Canadian group (chapter 9, this volume) and modified by the German group (chapter 8). It involves giving wheel-running animals a limited and fixed amount of food each day to induce running. Once the desired level of running is achieved, sufficient food is provided thereafter to maintain running and stabilize body weight.

This is a significantly different protocol from the original one. First, it is a more chronic model. Changes that occur under one condition may, therefore, not occur under the other. Stated differently, factors that play a role in precipitating the hyperactivity may differ from those that maintain it. The results of three drug manipulations illustrate this point: in the acute variant of the syndrome, mianserin, which blocks certain serotonin receptors (i.e., the 5HT1C and 5HT2 serotonin receptor subtypes, which are now called the 5HT2C and 5HT2A subtypes), reduced running (Rieg, Jenkins, & Aravich, 1994); naloxone, a general opioid blocker, increased running and decreased food intake (Aravich, Rieg, & Doerries, 1991); and clonidine, an $\alpha2$-adrenergic agonist, markedly increased wheel-running (Rieg & Aravich, 1994). All these running effects are in direct opposition to those obtained in chronic variants of the model (Wilckens, Schweiger, & Pirke, 1992a; Boer, Epling, Pierce, & Russell, 1990; Wilckens, Schweiger, & Pirke, 1992b).

A second distinction is that the primary dependent variable in the chronic hyperactivity protocol is, by definition, wheel-running. By implication, a reduction in wheel-running should mitigate the adverse effects of exercise stress on, for example, weight loss. However, several examples show that changes in running behavior can be dissociated from changes in body weight, at least in the acute model. First, one variable (a disruption of circadian rhythms) decreased wheel-running but increased rate of weight loss in the syndrome, without affecting food intake (presumably by altering metabolic efficiency; Stanley, Doerries, Rieg, & Aravich, 1992). Second, other variables (injection of mianserin after the daily feeding period; neonatal morphine exposure) decreased wheel-running but had no effect on days to reach a weight loss criterion (or food intake; Aravich, Howell, Downing, Rieg, & Doerries, 1992; Rieg, Jenkins, et al., 1994). Last, still other variables (i.e., introduction to the syndrome after lactation; chronic anabolic steroid administration) had no effect on running or food intake but increased rate of weight loss (Aravich, Choi, & Rieg, 1993; Downing, et al., 1992). It was shown that changes in the rate of running reliably predict declining weight loss in the syndrome in the absence of other variables (Epling & Pierce, 1984). However, our data suggest this may not be true under other circumstances. A fundamental difference between our work and that of others is the focus on weight loss as the primary clinically relevant dependent variable. This allows factors to be considered that affect overall energy expenditure rather than those that simply maintain excessive running. A recognition of the strengths and weaknesses of the acute versus chronic variants of the model, as well as wheel-running versus weight loss as the primary dependent variables, is clearly needed.

Another paradigmatic issue relates to the severity of weight loss that is allowed. It has been argued that a restricted-feeding period of three to four hours for three weeks in young female rats is the best way to model AN since it causes a progressive weight loss and disrupts ovarian function without producing activity-stress ulcers or immune organ atrophy (Watanabe et al., 1992). Others routinely use 30% (Epling & Pierce, 1984) or 25% (Aravich et al., 1995) weight-loss criteria in 1.5-hour fed animals. We use the later criterion because it avoids the nonspecific complications of activity-stress ulcers and starvation-induced morbidity and produces reasonably high levels of running (Doerries, Stanley, & Aravich, 1991). However, the animals run less than those sustaining a 30% weight loss (Doerries et al., 1991), which has the effect of producing a weaker overall syndrome (Epling & Pierce, 1984).

Other procedural variables affecting the severity of the syndrome are the social facilitation of running and isolation housing prior to the syndrome. Social facilitation is relevant because placing the wheels in individual sound-attenuating chambers prevents the syndrome (Spatz & Jones, 1971). Isolation housing prior to the syndrome, as opposed to group housing, is relevant because it increases rate of weight loss (Ness, Marshall, & Aravich, 1995). Accordingly, greater running levels will be produced by individually housing the rats before the syndrome and by placing their wheels in the presence of several other wheels during the syndrome.

Age is another pertinent variable. Younger animals, which weigh less than older animals, are more active and lose weight more quickly than older heavier animals (Jakubczak, 1967; Woods & Routtenberg, 1971). One difficulty with the rapid and profound induction of the syndrome in younger animals is that this may mask the ability to mitigate it by various experimental treatments (i.e., because of a floor effect problem). To avoid this, we now prefer to use 250g to 275g female Sprague-Dawley rats. They take about 10 days to reach a 25% weight-loss criterion on a 1.5 hours per day feeding schedule. This is sufficient time to reveal the effects of a variety of manipulations. Clearly, there is no standardized protocol for the syndrome and conclusions based on one variant may or may not generalize to another.

A final paradigmatic issue concerns the sex of the subjects. Males are typically used in behavioral, neuroendocrine, and immunological studies to control for cyclic changes in reproductive hormone status. However, to the extent that the syndrome is a model for an important women's health care issue in general and for AN in particular, female subjects should be used. It is clear that males differ from females in their responses to a number of variables. It is also possible that sexually dimorphic differences (e.g., receptor and body composition changes) persist even when a stable hormonal environment is imposed by ovariectomy and hormone replacement therapy. The use of males may, therefore, obscure or exaggerate effects that occur in females. If females are used, how can cyclic reproductive cycle effects be controlled? One way is to recognize that the exercise-stress syndrome induces anestrous (Watanabe et al., 1992) and that cyclic changes no longer occur thereafter. More direct experimental control can be achieved, as previously indicated, by using gonadectomized, hormonally replaced females. We have used females in some of our studies and males in others. We believe that female subjects should be used unless compelling experimental reasons dictate otherwise.

One final comment regarding gender and the exercise-stress syndrome is that females defend against it better than males (chapter 6, this volume). This is consistent with the well established literature that females defend body weight better than males under a variety of other conditions. The greater rate of weight loss by males does do not negate the syndrome as an animal model of AN. Rather, it confirms that females need to combine more strenuous exercising and dieting to lose body weight compared to males, and that the syndrome is uniquely positioned to model the interaction of these clinically relevant variables for women's health.

ENDOGENOUS OPIOIDS
AND THE SYNDROME

There are several independent opioid systems (see Aravich, Rieg, Lauterio, & Doerries, 1993), including the circulating ß-endorphin system, which emanates from the anterior pituitary gland; the brain ß-endorphin system, which primarily originates from the arcuate hypothalamic nucleus; and various central dynorphin systems, one of which is the neurohypophyseal system originating in part from the supraoptic hypothalamic nucleus.

As reviewed elsewhere (Aravich, Rieg, Lauterio, et al., 1993), it is well known that exercise elevates circulating ß-endorphin levels, which return to baseline during rest. Contrary to popular belief, much less is known about the effects of exercise on central opioid function. There is, however, evidence linking opioid changes to AN (see Aravich, Rieg, Lauterio, et al., 1993). In fact, it has been proposed that an exercise-induced increase in ß-endorphin perpetuates AN by promoting hyperactivity and reducing food intake (Epling & Pierce, 1988). It has also been proposed that AN is due to an autoaddiction to the endogenous opioids, which maintains the maladaptive behavior (Marrazzi & Luby, 1986).

As a result of these considerations, the endogenous opioids were evaluated in the acute version of the exercise-stress syndrome. We found peripheral and central abnormalities in animals tested under resting-fed conditions (i.e., fed and rested for 6 hours; Aravich, Rieg, Lauterio, et al., 1993). The abnormalities included a marked elevation in resting plasma ß-endorphin, which did not occur in weight-reduced or exercised controls (Fig. 7.2). Arcuate hypothalamic ß-endorphin content, on the other hand, was normal under basal conditions, but abnormally increased following the stress of acute glucose insufficiency (by the glucose antimetabolite, 2-deoxy-D-glucose, Aravich, Rieg, Lauterio, et al., 1993). Finally, supraoptic hypothalamic dynorphin A content had a response profile that was similar to arcuate ß-endorphin (Aravich, Rieg, Lauterio, et al., 1993).

These data are consistent with the possibility that opioid perturbations are causally related to the syndrome. However, a number of experiments failed to support this hypothesis. For example, if central ß-endorphin is important, its destruction should protect against the syndrome. We found that systemic neonatal glutamic acid exposure, which damages the arcuate hypothalamic ß-endorphin system, protects against weight-loss in the syndrome even though it actually caused the rats to eat less during the protocol; running was unaffected (Rieg, Woynicz, Fulton, Downing, & Aravich, 1993). However, neonatal glutamic acid produces, among other things, animals that are obese but underweight due to a loss of lean body mass. Evidence generated from carcass composition studies in male versus female rats (chapter 6, this volume) and studies on deprivation-induced wheel-run-

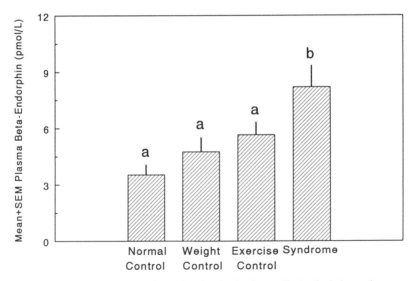

FIG. 7.2.   Mean + *SEM* resting, fed plasma ß-endorphin levels (pmol/L) for the behavioral treatment conditions described in Fig. 7.1. Different letters refer to differences at the .05 level of significance.

ning in obese animals (Sclafani & Rendel, 1978) argued that it is the increased relative adiposity that protects against the syndrome rather than a depletion of brain ß-endorphin.

Other data also fail to implicate increased opioid function in the syndrome. As noted before, continuous systemic infusion of the general opioid antagonist, naloxone (via osmotic minipumps), did not protect against the weight loss effect; rather, it actually increased running and decreased food intake (Aravich et al., 1991). Finally, another experiment indicates that perturbation of the supraoptic dynorphin A system, which we found can occur following neonatal morphine exposure, did not alter weight loss in the syndrome (Aravich, Howell, et al., 1992). Collectively, our data fail to support a causal role for the endogenous opioids in the acute version of the syndrome.

SEROTONIN AND THE EXERCISE-STRESS SYNDROME

A more promising line of research involves serotonin. This effort is a good example of the benefits of animal modeling for complex clinical disorders. The serotonin studies were stimulated by the proposal that AN should be treated with serotonin agonists, because individuals with anorexia may also suffer from obsessive-compulsive disorders, which are treatable with these drugs (Hsu, Kaye, & Weltzin, 1993). However, serotonin agonists are also appetite suppressants, which would seem contraindicated in AN. Animal modeling was, therefore, needed to provide further evidence for beneficial or adverse treatment effects.

Our first experiment provided evidence for serotonin abnormalities using the indirect-acting serotonin agonist, fluoxetine, as a pharmacological probe (Aravich, Rieg, Ahmed, et al., 1993). It was found that animals subjected to the exercise-stress syndrome had region-specific vasopressin, oxytocin and dynorphin-A abnormalities following the fluoxetine challenge (Aravich et al., 1993). These data are consistent with other data indicating regional brain serotonin dysfunction in both the acute (Hellhammer, Hingtgen, Wade, Shea, & Aprison, 1983) and chronic variants of the syndrome (Broocks, Schweiger, & Pirke, 1991). We then assessed the functional significance of serotonin in the acute version of the syndrome. If serotonin is protective, its depletion should have an adverse effect and its promotion should have a beneficial effect. Several observations support these predictions. First, intracerebroventricular administration of the neurotoxin, 5,7-dihydroxytryptamine (5,7-DHT), which selectively depletes brain serotonin, increased rate of weight loss in the syndrome (Rieg, Burt, Contakes, Chiou, & Aravich, 1994). This effect occurred without changes in food intake or running and was attributed to an increase in the metabolic cost of running.

Second, the indirect-acting serotonin agonist, D-fenfluramine, protected against weight loss in the syndrome (Rieg, Maestrello, et al., 1994). However, this effect required tolerance to the appetite suppressant effects of the drug prior to imposition of the syndrome and a previous history of weight cycling (which typically occurs in AN); neither weight cycling or fenfluramine alone were protective (Rieg,

Maestrello, & Aravich, 1994). The beneficial effect occurred without changes in food intake or running. We proposed that weight cycling reversed the well known effects of D-fenfluramine on energy expenditure, which reduced the metabolic cost of running. This proposed mechanism differs from the substrate mediating the protective effect of the indirect-acting serotonin agonist, fluoxetine, on the syndrome, which others showed is due to decreased running and increased food intake. The differences between the two drugs may be due to differences in their mechanisms of action (Garattini, Bizzi, Codegoni, Caccia, & Mennini, 1992).

Finally, dietary L-tryptophan loading, which is a well established way to increase brain serotonin synthesis in normal weight sedentary animals, also protected against weight loss in the syndrome (Aravich, Kaminski, & Rieg, 1994). Unlike D-fenfluramine, this effect was related to increased food intake when the data were expressed relative to the weight-loss criterion day (i.e., when the syndrome was at its maximum). The different effects of D-fenfluramine and L-tryptophan on food intake suggest that different serotonin substrates mediate their protective actions.

Collectively, our data support the hypothesis that brain serotonin protects against the adverse effect of the exercise-stress syndrome on body weight loss. This is a novel view considering the well established role of serotonin as an appetite suppressant. Because exercise increases brain serotonin (Dey, Singh, & Dey, 1992), we believe that wheel-running is an attempt to protect brain serotonin from the depletion that otherwise occurs with weight loss (Thibault & Roberge, 1989). Regardless of this proposal, our data justify more studies on serotonin agonists in clinical disorders associated with hyperactivity and caloric restriction such as AN.

RISK FACTORS FOR
THE EXERCISE-STRESS SYNDROME

If the syndrome is relevant to the adverse effects of exercise stress and dieting in malnourished people and to AN, the identification of factors that increase its risk has considerable clinical significance. We determined that a disruption of circadian rhythms with suprachiasmatic hypothalamic lesions or constant bright light increases vulnerability to the syndrome, even though running was decreased and food intake unchanged (Stanley et al., 1992). This effect was prevented in brain-damaged animals by fetal hypothalamic neural transplants containing the suprachiasmatic nucleus (Aravich, Goduti, & Rieg, 1992). These data raise the possibility that a disruption of circadian rhythms is a potential risk factor for anorexia nervosa and other disorders related to exercise stress and malnutrition.

Various other risk factors were also identified. For example, when the restricted feeding period was in the resting phase of the circadian cycle, rats ate less and ran more than when the feeding period was in the active phase (Aravich, Rieg, & Doerries, 1992). This has implications for hyperactive calorically restricted women who eat only at night. Chronic anabolic steroid administration before and during the syndrome also increased rate of weight loss, without affecting food intake or running (Aravich, Choi, et al., 1993). This has implications for competitive female athletes who have a markedly greater incidence of eating disorders. Conversely, chronic nicotine exposure before and during the syndrome failed to affect rate of weight loss, running behavior, or food intake but exacerbated immune organ atrophy (Chiou, Amos, Funk, Rieg, & Aravich, 1994). This raises the possibility that nicotine may worsen the immunological consequences of exercise stress in malnourished people. We also showed that exposure to the syndrome after lactation markedly increased rate of weight loss (Downing et al., 1992). This has implications for normal weight women initiating dieting and exercise programs after weaning. And the stress of isolation housing prior to the syndrome (as opposed to group housing) also increased weight loss in the syndrome (Ness et al., 1995). This is relevant to the social isolation that accompanies AN and starvation.

CHANGES SPECIFIC TO THE SYNDROME

In addition to the opioid and serotonin changes reported above, we have evidence for other syndrome-specific abnormalities in the acute variant of the model. For example, animals subjected to the syndrome have an increase in diet-induced thermogenesis (relative to estimated lean body mass) compared to weight-reduced or exercised controls when tested under resting conditions (Platt, Downing, Atkinson, & Aravich, 1992). This raises the possibility that other forms of energy expenditure are also altered. Region-specific vasopressin and oxytocin changes also occur that are not observed in weight-reduced and exercised controls; perturbations in both of these peptides have been reported for AN (Aravich, Rieg, et al., 1993). Finally, other investigators found neurochemical changes specific to the chronic variant of the model, including serotonergic (Broocks et al., 1991), dopaminergic and noradrenergic (Broocks, Liu, & Pirke, 1990) abnormalities.

CHANGES ATTRIBUTED TO THE SECONDARY CONSEQUENCES OF WEIGHT LOSS OR EXERCISE

Several changes occur to a comparable extent in animals subjected to the acute variant of the syndrome and weight-reduced controls. These changes are, therefore, attributed to the secondary effects of weight loss rather than to a specific effect of the syndrome. They include hypoglycemia and hypoinsulinemia (Aravich et al., 1995); a paradoxical suppression of feeding following the glucose antimetabolite 2-deoxy-D-glucose (Aravich et al., 1995); increased plasma osmolality (Aravich, Rieg, Ahmed, et al., 1993); increased plasma vasopressin (Aravich, Rieg, Ahmed, et al., 1993); reduced cell-mediated immunity (Aravich et al., 1990); and decreased resting total energy expenditure (Platt et al., 1992). It is worth noting that many of these changes also occur in AN, which further validates the clinical relevancy of the model. Other changes attributed to the secondary effects of weight loss include relative adrenal hypertrophy, immune organ atrophy and leukopenia (Aravich et al., 1990); increased plasma insulinlike growth factor II, which is homologous to the metabolically important hormones, insulin and insulinlike growth factor I (Lauterio, Rieg, Ahmed, & Aravich, 1993); and so-called activity-stress ulcers, which present themselves following a 30% weight loss (chapter 6, this volume) and are associated with increased gastric mucosal vasopressin content (Aravich, Downing, Stanley, Rieg, & Doerries, 1993). Neuropeptide Y (NPY), which is one of the most potent feeding stimulatory agents, is also not specifically altered in the chronic variant of the syndrome, because comparable changes occur in weight-reduced controls (Lewis et al., 1993). While this does not negate a potential therapeutic benefit for NPY, it reduces interest in the peptide as a specific mediator of the syndrome and, by extension, of AN. Finally, changes attributed to the general effects of exercise (because they also occurred in freely fed exercised animals) include an increase in immunoreactive pulmonary vasopressin, which has been linked to surfactant secretion and may contribute to the general effects of exercise on lung expansion (Almenoff, Rieg, Lauterio, & Aravich, 1993).

OTHER VARIABLES MANIPULATED
IN THE SYNDROME

We manipulated a variety of other variables in the acute variant of the syndrome. For example, the α2-adrenergic agonist, clonidine, stimulates food intake in normal subjects following either paraventricular hypothalamic nucleus injection or systemic injection. Noradrenergic abnormalities occur in AN (see Rieg & Aravich, 1992) and in both the chronic (previously discussed) and acute (Tsuda & Tanaka, 1990) variants of the syndrome. Finally, systemic clonidine injections suppress wheel-running in the chronic variant of the syndrome (Wilckens, Schweiger, & Pirke, 1992b).

These data suggest that clonidine should protect against the acute variant of the syndrome. Instead, we found that chronic clonidine infused into the paraventricular hypothalamus (via osmotic minipumps) suppressed food intake and increased vulnerability to the syndrome (Rieg & Aravich, 1992). This was attributed to a down regulation of α2-adrenergic receptors due continuous infusion of the drug. Neither did chronic systemic infusion of clonidine protect against weight loss in the syndrome (Rieg & Aravich, 1994). In fact, while there was small increase in food intake at the lower dose (i.e., 30 mg/kg/day, which was not sufficient to alter the rate of weight loss), there was a dramatic increase in running with the higher dose (i.e., 300 mg/kg/day). We proposed that the high dose decreased sympathetically mediated energy expenditure and lipolysis, which counteracted the increased energy expenditure produced by the elevated wheel-running. The lower dose, on the other hand, which marginally increased food intake, was argued to be insufficient to reduce overall energy expenditure (Rieg & Aravich, 1994). Finally, we concluded that the exacerbation of hyperactivity by the high dose of clonidine raises concerns regarding its use in clinical syndromes associated with hyperactivity and caloric restriction such as AN (Rieg & Aravich, 1994).

In addition to these data, we found that water deprivation produced an exercise-stress syndrome similar to that observed with food deprivation (Rieg, Doerries, O'Shea, & Aravich, 1993). This suggests that other factors that energize behavior may produce similar exercise-stress syndromes. Finally, we have data indicating that two treatments that exacerbate the relative adrenal hypertrophy of the syndrome, namely fetal alcohol exposure and chronic nicotine exposure, failed to affect rate of weight loss in the acute variant of the syndrome (Chiou et al., 1994; Goduti, Gravette, Rieg, Chawla, & Aravich, 1993). These findings suggest that the glucocorticoids are not causally related to the weight loss effect.

CONCLUSIONS

We conclude that the experimental syndrome is clinically relevant to anorexia nervosa and other disorders related to the adverse effects of exercise stress and malnutrition; that the self-starvation–anorexia nomenclature is debatable and detracts from the syndrome's overall clinical relevancy; that one of the strengths of the syndrome is the ability to expressly control for the general effects of weight loss while one of its weaknesses is the inability to control for the general effects of exercise; that a number of paradigmatic considerations affect induction and interpretation of the syndrome; that the endogenous opioids are not causally related to it, in marked contrast to serotonin, which may protect against the weight-loss effect; that there are a number of risk factors that have significant clinical relevancy; that there are physiological changes specific to the syndrome; that $\alpha2$-adrenergic receptors do not protect against it; and that changes in insulin-like growth factor II, NPY and the glucocorticoids may not be causally related to the weight loss.

The public has been inundated with information on the adverse effects of a sedentary life style and obesity. This is often misinterpreted as suggesting that the more we exercise and the less we eat, the healthier we will be. However, it is a fundamental tenant in neurobiology, nutrition and immunology that there are optimal levels of activation, and that excesses should be avoided as well as deficiencies. Despite this, much more attention has focused on exercise deficiency and nutritional excess. It has been known for nearly 35 years that freely induced exercise stress can be fatal in normal rats that are calorically restricted (Spear & Hill, 1962). More research is clearly needed to document the adverse effects of excessive exercise in malnourished subjects. The data generated from this laboratory and elsewhere demonstrate that the exercise-stress syndrome is in a unique position to model the interactive effects of these two variables on health and disease. This makes it especially relevant to normal weight women, who frequently engage in strenuous exercise and dieting to lose weight; to AN, which is highly correlated with hyperactivity; and to the development of exercise prescriptions for the prevention and treatment of disease.

ACKNOWLEDGMENTS

This author was primarily supported by a U.S. Department of Veterans Affairs Merit Award. The participation of Dr. Thomas S. Rieg (NRSA Postdoctoral Fellowship MH 09805) and Dr. Lee E. Doerries, Christopher Newport University, in various portions of this research is gratefully acknowledged. The contribution of various other colleagues and a large number of students from Christopher Newport University, Hampton University, the College of William and Mary and the Virginia Governor's School for Science and Technology, Hampton, Virginia, is also gratefully acknowledged.

REFERENCES

Almenoff, P. L., Rieg, T. S., Lauterio, T. J., & Aravich, P. F. (1993). Lung immunoreactive vasopressin is increased by exercise and decreased by obesity in the rat. *Annals of the New York Academy of Sciences, 689,* 458–460.

Aravich, P. F., Choi, J. J., & Rieg, T. S. (1993). Anabolic steroid administration increases vulnerability to an animal model of anorexia nervosa [Abstract]. *Society for Neuroscience Abstracts, 19,* 460.

Aravich, P. F., Doerries, L. E., Farrar, L. E., Downing, S., Elhady, A. H., Metcalf, A , & Johnson, A. M. (1990). Immunodeficiency and activity-based anorexia [Abstract]. *Society for Neuroscience Abstracts, 16,* 1199.

Aravich, P. F., Doerries, L. E., & Rieg, T. S. (1994). Exercise induced weight loss in the rat and anorexia nervosa. *Appetite, 23,* 196.

Aravich, P. F., Doerries, L. E., Stanley, E., Metcalf, A., & Lauterio, T. J. (1989). Glucoprivic feeding and activity-based anorexia in the rat. *Annals of the New York Academy of Sciences, 575,* 490–492.

Aravich, P. F., Downing, S. N., Stanley, E. Z., Rieg, T. S., & Doerries, L. E. (1993). Activity-stress ulcers are associated with increased gastric mucosa vasopressin content. *Annals of the New York Academy of Sciences, 689,* 461–464.

Aravich, P. F., Goduti, M., & Rieg, T. S. (1992). Rostral hypothalamic fetal transplants reduce activity-based anorexia in rats with lesions aimed at the suprachiasmatic nucleus. *Journal of Neural Transplantation and Plasticity, 3,* 299–300.

Aravich, P. F., Howell, R. A., Downing, S. N., Rieg, T. S., & Doerries, L. E. (1992). Persistent supraoptic (SON) & suprachiasmatic (SCN) dynorphin-A abnormalities in adult activity-based anorexic (ABA) rats exposed to neonatal morphine [Abstract]. *Society for Neuroscience Abstracts, 18,* 824.

Aravich, P. F., Kaminski, L. A., & Rieg, T. S. (1994). Dietary tryptophan: beneficial effects on an animal model of anorexia nervosa [Abstract]. *Society for Neuroscience Abstracts, 20,* 588.

Aravich, P. F., Rieg, T. S., Ahmed, I., & Lauterio, T. J. (1993). Fluoxetine induces vasopressin and oxytocin abnormalities in food restricted rats given voluntary exercise: Relationship to anorexia nervosa. *Brain Research, 612,* 180–189.

Aravich, P. F., Rieg, T. S., & Doerries, L. E. (1991). [Naloxone fails to protect against the weight-loss effect of exercise stress in food-restricted rats]. Unpublished raw data.

Aravich, P. F., Rieg, T. S., & Doerries, L. E. (1992). [Time of feeding affects the weight loss effect of exercise stress in food-restricted rats]. Unpublished raw data.

Aravich, P. F., Rieg, T. S., Lauterio, T. J., & Doerries, L. E. (1993). Beta-endorphin and dynorphin abnormalities in rats subjected to exercise and restricted feeding: relationship to anorexia nervosa. *Brain Research, 622,* 1–8.

Aravich, P. F., Stanley, E. Z., & Doerries, L. E. (1995). Exercise in food restricted rats produces 2DG feeding and metabolic abnormalities similar to anorexia nervosa. *Physiology and Behavior, 57,* 147–153.

Boer, D. E., Epling, W. F., Pierce, W. D., & Russell, J. C. (1990). Suppression of food deprivation-induced high-rate wheel-running in rats. *Physiology and Behavior, 48*, 339–342.

Broocks, A., Liu, J., & Pirke, K. M. (1990). Semistarvation-induced hyperactivity compensates for decreased norepinephrine and dopamine turnover in the mediobasal hypothalamus of the rat. *Journal of Neural Transmission, 79*, 113–124.

Broocks, A., Schweiger, U., & Pirke, K. M. (1991). The influence of semistarvation-induced hyperactivity on hypothalamic serotonin metabolism. *Physiology and Behavior, 50*, 385–388.

Chiou, A., Amos, D. M., Funk, H. A., Rieg, T. S., & Aravich, P. F. (1994). Adverse effects of chronic nicotine on immune organ atrophy in an animal model of anorexia nervosa [Abstract]. *Society for Neuroscience Abstracts, 20*, 947.

Devlin, M. J., & Walsh, B. T. (1992). Anorexia nervosa and bulimia nervosa. In P. Bjorntorp & B. N. Brodoff (Eds.), *Obesity* (pp. 436–444). New York: Lippincott.

Dey, S., Singh, R. H., & Dey, P. K. (1992). Exercise training: Significance of regional alterations in serotonin metabolism of rat brain in relation to antidepressant effect of exercise. *Physiology and Behavior, 52*, 1095–1099.

Doerries, L. E., Stanley, E. Z., & Aravich, P. F. (1991). Activity-based anorexia: relationship to gender and activity-stress ulcers. *Physiology and Behavior, 50*, 945–949.

Downing, S.N., Rieg, T. S., Doerries, L. E., Glenn, K.S., Bloxom, S., & Aravich, P. F. (1992). Lactation increases susceptibility to activity-based anorexia in the rat [Abstract]. *Society for the Study of Ingestive Behavior Abstracts, 87.*

Drewnowski, A., Kurth, C. L., & Krahn, D. D. (1994). Weight-loss strategies of young adults: Exercise versus dieting. *Obesity Research, 2*, 557–562.

Epling, W. F., & Pierce, W. D. (1984). Activity-based anorexia in rats as a function of opportunity to run on an activity wheel. *Nutrition and Behavior, 2*, 37–49.

Epling, W. F., & Pierce, W. D. (1988). Activity-based anorexia: A biobehavioral perspective. *International Journal of Eating Disorders, 7*, 475–485.

Epling, W. F., Pierce, W. D., & Stefan, L. (1983). A theory of activity-based anorexia. *International Journal of Eating Disorders, 3*, 27–46.

Garattini, S., Bizzi, A., Codegoni, A. M., Caccia, S., & Mennini, T. (1992). Progress report on the anorexia induced by drugs believed to mimic some of the effects of serotonin on the central nervous system. *American Journal of Clinical Nutrition, 55*, 160S–166S.

Goduti, M. E., Gravette, A. E., Rieg, T. S., Chawla, J. S., & Aravich, P. F. (1993). The effect of prenatal ETOH exposure on the weight-loss syndrome produced by exercise in food-restricted rats [Abstract]. *International Society for Developmental Psychobiology Abstracts, 29.*

Hara, C., Manabe, K., & Ogawa, N. (1981). Influence of activity-stress on thymus, spleen and adrenal weights of rats: Possibility for an immunodeficiency model. *Physiology and Behavior, 27*, 243–248.

Hellhammer, D. H., Hingtgen, J. N., Wade, S. E., Shea, P. A., & Aprison, M. H. (1983). Serotonergic changes in specific areas of rat brain associated with activity-stress gastric lesions. *Psychological Medicine, 45*, 115–122.

Hsu, L. K. G., Kaye, W., & Weltzin, T. (1993). Are eating disorders related to obsessive compulsive disorder? *International Journal of Eating Disorders, 14*, 305–318.

Jakubczak, L. F. (1967). Age differences in the effects of terminal food deprivation (starvation) on activity, weight loss, and survival of rats. *Journal of Gerontology, 22*, 421–426.

Kanarek, R. B., & Collier, G. H. (1983). Self-starvation: A problem of overriding the satiety signal? *Physiology and Behavior, 30*, 307–311.

Lauterio, T. J., Rieg, T. S., Ahmed, I., & Aravich, P. F. (1993). Fluoxetine induced insulin-like growth factor II (IGF-II) changes in hypothalami of normal, exercised and food restricted rats. *Regulatory Peptides, 48*, 21–28.

Lewis, D. E., Shellard, L., Koeslag, D. G., Boer, D. E., McCarthy, H. D., McKibbin, P. E., Russell, J. C., & Williams, G. (1993). Intense exercise and food restriction cause similar hypothalamic neuropeptide Y increases in rats. *American Journal of Physiology, 264*, E279–E284.

Marrazzi, M. A., & Luby, E. D. (1986). An auto-addiction opioid model of chronic anorexia nervosa. *International Journal of Eating Disorders, 5*, 191–208.

McKinney, W. T. (1988). *Models of mental disorders. A new comparative psychiatry.* New York: Plenum.

Ness, J. W., Marshall, T. R., & Aravich, P. F. (1995). Effects of rearing condition on activity-induced weight loss. *Developmental Psychobiology, 28*, 165–173.

Pare, W. P., & Houser, V. P. (1973). Activity and food-restriction effects on gastric glandular lesions in the rat: The activity-stress ulcer. *Bulletin of the Psychonomic Society, 2,* 213–214.

Pierce, W. D., & Epling, W. F. (1991). Activity anorexia: An animal model and theory of human self-starvation. In A. Boulton, G. Baker, & M. Martin-Iverson (Eds.), *Neuromethods, Vol. 19: Animal Models in Psychiatry I* (pp. 267–311). Toronto, ON: Humana Press.

Platt, K. H., Downing, S., Atkinson, R. L., & Aravich, P. F. (1992). Diet-induced thermogenesis & nocturnal energy expenditure abnormalities in activity-based anorexia [Abstract]. *Society for the Study of Ingestive Behavior Abstracts,* 75.

Rieg, T. S. & Aravich, P. F. (1992). Paraventricular hypothalamic clonidine increases rather than decreases susceptibility to activity-based anorexia in the rat. *Behavioral Neuroscience, 106,* 1015–1022.

Rieg, T. S., & Aravich, P. F. (1994). Systemic clonidine increases feeding and wheel-running but does not affect rate of weight loss in rats subjected to activity-based anorexia. *Pharmacology, Biochemistry and Behavior, 47,* 215–218.

Rieg, T. S., Burt, J. L., Contakes, L. M., Chiou, A., & Aravich, P. F. (1994). Central serotonergic depletion exacerbates activity-based anorexia [Abstract]. *Eastern Psychological Association Abstracts, 65,* 58.

Rieg, T. S., Doerries, L. E., O'Shea, J. G., & Aravich, P. F. (1993). Water deprivation produces an exercise-induced weight loss phenomenon in the rat. *Physiology and Behavior, 53,* 607–610.

Rieg, T. S., Jenkins, K., & Aravich, P. F. (1994). Serotonin 5HT1c/5HT2 receptor antagonism & the weight-loss syndrome produced by exercise in food-restricted rats [Abstract]. *Society for the Study of Ingestive Behavior Abstracts,* A-14.

Rieg, T. S., Maestrello, A. M., & Aravich, P. F. (1994). Weight cycling alters the effects of D-fenfluramine on susceptibility to activity-based anorexia. *American Journal of Clinical Nutrition, 60,* 494–500.

Rieg, T. S., Woynicz, B. A., Fulton, K. F., Downing, S. N., & Aravich, P. F. (1993). Neonatal monosodium glutamate (MSG) decreases vulnerability to the weight-loss syndrome produced in adult rats by voluntary exercise and food restriction [Abstract]. *Society for Neuroscience Abstracts, 19,* 1731.

Routtenberg, A. (1968). "Self-starvation" of rats living in activity wheels. Adaptation effects. *Journal of Comparative and Physiological Psychology, 66,* 234–238.

Routtenberg, A., & Kuznesof, A. W. (1967). Self-starvation of rats living in activity wheels on a restricted feeding schedule. *Journal of Comparative and Physiological Psychology, 64,* 414–421.

Sclafani, A., & Rendel, A. (1978). Food deprivation-induced activity in normal and hypothalamic obese rats. *Behavioral Biology, 22,* 244–255.

Spatz, C., & Jones, S..D. (1971). Starvation anorexia as an explanation of "self-starvation" of rats living in activity wheels. *Journal of Comparative and Physiological Psychology, 77,* 313–317.

Spear, N. E., & Hill, W. F. (1962). Methodological note: Excessive weight loss in rats living in activity wheels. *Psychological Reports, 11,* 437–438.

Stanley, E. Z., Doerries, L. E., Rieg, T. S., & Aravich, P. F. (1992). Suprachiasmatic nucleus (SCN) lesions increase susceptibility to activity-based anorexia [Abstract]. *Society for Neuroscience Abstracts, 18,* 1222.

Thibault, L., & Roberge, A. G. (1989). Comparative effects of carbohydrate restriction vs. starvation on biochemical parameters related to neurotransmitters in rat. *Journal of the American College of Nutrition, 8,* 35–46.

Tsuda, A., & Tanaka, M. (1990). Neurochemical characteristics of rats exposed to activity stress. *Annals of the New York Academy of Sciences, 597,* 146–158.

Vincent, G. P., & Pare, W. P. (1976a). The activity-stress ulcer in the hamster. *Physiological Psychology, 4,* 521–522.

Vincent, G. P., & Pare, W. P. (1976b). Activity-stress ulcer in the rat, hamster, gerbil and guinea pig. *Physiology and Behavior, 16,* 557–560.

Vincent, G. P., Pare, W. P., Isom, K. E., & Reeves, J. M. (1977). Activity-stress gastric lesions in the chipmunk (*Tamias striatus*). *Physiological Psychology, 5,* 449–452.

Watanabe, K., Hara, C., & Ogawa, N. (1992). Feeding conditions and estrous cycle of female rats under the activity-stress procedure from aspects of anorexia nervosa. *Physiology and Behavior, 51,* 827–832.

Wilckens, T., Schweiger, U., & Pirke, K. M. (1992a). Activation of 5-HT1C-receptors suppresses excessive wheel-running induced by semi-starvation in the rat. *Psychopharmacology, 109,* 77–84.

Wilckens, T., Schweiger, U., & Pirke, K. M. (1992b). Activation of α2-adrenoceptors suppresses excessive wheel-running in the semistarvation-induced hyperactive rat. *Pharmacology Biochemistry and Behavior, 43,* 733–738.

Woods, D. J., & Routtenberg, A. (1971). "Self-starvation" in activity wheels: Developmental and chlorpromazine interactions. *Journal of Comparative and Physiological Psychology, 76,* 84–93.

8

The Role of Neurotransmitters in Activity Anorexia in the Rat

K. M. Pirke
University of Trier

The syndrome of anorexia nervosa (AN) is often accompanied by severe hyperactivity (Epling & Pierce, 1988; Falk, Halmi, & Tyron, 1985). In some cases the symptom of hyperactivity is so prominent that the diagnosis of AN is missed (chapter 15, this volume). The interpretation of hyperactivity in anorexia is controversial. Although it is considered by many authors as a simple measure of anorectic patients to reduce their weight or keep it low, others have claimed that a biological mechanism is responsible for the development of hyperactivity in AN. From a theoretical point of view, there are two alternative explanations: (a) impaired eating behavior (starving and dieting) and hyperactivity are both caused by a single central nervous mechanism as yet unknown; or (b) hyperactivity is induced by reducing caloric intake.

The second alternative has been discussed by many authors because in rodents hyperactivity can be induced by food restriction (Richter, 1922; Routtenberg & Kuznesof, 1967; chapter 9, this volume). In order to understand the starvation-induced hyperactivity in rodents and especially in rats, I first review the neuroendocrine and neurotransmitter changes in the starved rat and then summarize the effects of starvation and semistarvation on hyperactivity related endocrine and neurotransmitter alterations.

ANIMAL MODELS

As in humans, in rats starvation causes a rapid decrease of luteinizing hormone (LH) in the plasma (Pirke & Spyra, 1981). As a consequence, gonadal hormone secretion is reduced. Stimulation of the gonads by human chorionic gonadotropine (HCG) results in a rapid increase of gonadal hormones. The increase of gonadotropic hormones after gonadotropin releasing hormone (GnRH) is reduced but not abolished indicates that starvation impairs the function of the hypothalamic–pituitary–gonadal (HPG) axis at the hypothalamic level.

The content of GnRH in the eminentia mediana of the starved rat is normal. In vitro superfusion experiments show that GnRH can be secreted from the median eminence by depolarizing stimuli (Warnhoff, Dorsch, & Pirke, 1983). We therefore conclude that GnRH is available in sufficient concentration and is in a releasable form. When studying gonadal–pituitary feedback in starved rats by implanting gonadal hormone capsules of different sizes into gonadectomized rats, we observed that castration induced LH increase is suppressed by much smaller testosterone plasma concentrations in starved than in control rats. This increased feedback sensitivity probably contributes to the reduced activity of the HPG axis as is the case in prepuberty.

As with humans, rats increase activity of the adrenal gland during starvation (Pirke & Spyra, 1982). This hormonal alteration, which is centrally mediated, stimulates gluconeogenesis and thus is of major importance for survival during food deprivation. In order to evaluate the neurotransmitter changes responsible for the neuroendocrine changes mentioned previously we have adopted two strategies:

1. Measurement of neurotransmitter turnover in the hypothalamus (norepinephrine, dopamine, serotonin).
2. Application of centrally active agonists and antagonists of neurotransmitters and neuromodulators.

Norepinephrine turnover was measured in the preoptic region, the medial basal hypothalamus, and the median eminence by two different techniques. In the alpha-methyl-paratyrosine technique, norepinephrine biosynthesis is blocked and the reduction of norepinephrine over two hours is measured (Pirke & Spyra, 1982). The other technique involves measurement of the norepinephrine metabolite 3-methoxy-5-hydroxyphenylethylenglycol (MOPEG; Schweiger, Warnhoff, & Pirke, 1985a, 1985b). Both methods revealed a starvation induced reduction of central norepinephrine activity. These data indicate that norepinephrine turnover in starvation is reduced not only in peripheral tissue (Landsberg & Young, 1978), but also in the brain.

We observed two mechanisms responsible for the impaired central sympathetic activity. Schweiger et al. (1985a) found a close correlation between the influx of the norepinephrine precursor tyrosine into the brain and norepinephrine turnover. Philipp and Pirke (1987) described a reduction of the activity of the rate-limiting enzyme of norepinephrine biosynthesis, tyrosine hydroxylase. As judged from the measurement of dopamine and serotonin metabolites in the brain, starvation reduces dopaminergic activity and increases serotonin turnover (Broocks, Liu, & Pirke, 1989). The mechanisms underlying these changes are unclear.

The second strategy involves neuropharmacological interventions to correct starvation-induced suppression of LH and the stimulation of corticosterone secretion. Norepinephrine neurons exert a stimulatory influence on the HPG axis and an inhibitory action on the hypothalamo–hypophyseal–adrenal (HPA) axis in the rat. Therefore, the observed reduction of norepinephrine in the medial basal hypothalamus, and especially in the median eminence, might explain the neuroendocrine findings. In order to test this hypothesis we injected centrally active noradrenergic agonists and precursors into starved and control animals (Pirke & Spyra, 1982).

L-Dopa abolished the starvation-induced corticosterone increase but did not stimulate the suppressed LH secretion. The data support the assumption that starvation-induced activity of the HPA axis may be caused by the reduced central norepinephrine turnover. It has been speculated that increased endorphinergic activity might suppress LH secretion in AN and starvation. However, application of the endorphin antagonist naloxone was not able to reverse LH suppression in anorexia nervosa and in the starved rat (Küderling, Dorsch, Warnhoff, & Pirke, 1984).

In summarizing the experiments described, we assume that starvation-induced reduction of noradrenergic activity stimulates the HPA axis. The mechanisms by which malnutrition suppresses the HPG axis remain unclear. An increased sensitivity of gonadal–pituitary feedback reduces gonadotropin and gonadal hormone secretion. Changes in neurotransmitter activity were not related to LH suppression. The possibility cannot be excluded that the GnRH neurons sense metabolic signs of malnutrition and reduce activity as a consequence.

STARVATION-INDUCED HYPERACTIVITY

When rats are given access to a running wheel under ad libitum feeding conditions, they gradually increase their running activity, which reaches its maximum around the time of feeding (Richter, 1922). Major differences exist between male and female rats. Female rats develop running activity faster, and their activity is modulated by the menstrual cycle, reaching a maximum at proestrus. When access to food is not restricted, food intake becomes smaller and weight gain is reduced in comparison with sedentary controls. Within 5 to 10 days (Levitsky, 1974) this effect vanishes and rats increase their body weight again.

It is well known that food restriction induces hyperactivity in rats and other rodents (Cornish & Mrosovsky, 1965; Dourish, Hutson, & Curzon, 1985; Finger, 1951; Hall & Hanford, 1954). Routtenberg and Kuznesof (1967) restricted the availability of food to one hour per day and observed a much more rapid increase of running activity and much higher peak values. This paradigm was studied in great detail by Kanarek and Collier (1983) and by Epling and Pierce (chapter 1, this volume).

We modified the Routtenberg and Kuznesof (1967) experiment by giving the rats a reduced amount of food so that their body weight decreased to 70% of its initial value (Broocks, Schweiger, & Pirke, 1990) and was then kept constant. Figure 8.1 shows an individual example of body weight development and running activity. Our studies indicate that hyperactivity is more rapidly developed as weight loss increases. It is remarkable that hyperactivity was maintained for up to 65 days when weight was kept constant at 70% of initial weight.

ENDOCRINE CONSEQUENCES OF STARVATION-INDUCED HYPERACTIVITY ADRENAL INVOLVEMENT

Broocks, Schweiger, and Pirke (1990) measured the circadian pattern of plasma corticosterone in male rats after hyperactivity had been induced by reduced feeding for 10 days (Fig. 8.2). Plasma corticosterone paralleled the circadian pattern of running activity. The average 24-hour concentrations were significantly greater in this group than in sedentary ad libitum fed rats and in freely fed rats having access to a running wheel. Starvation alone caused an increase in plasma corticosterone (Pirke & Spyra, 1982). When semistarved running rats and semistarved sedentary rats were compared, a synergistic effect of starvation and hyperactivity on corticosterone was observed (Broocks, Schweiger & Pirke, 1990).

Trijodothyronine (T3) was also reduced by semistarvation and hyperactivity in a synergistic way. Increased activity of the adrenal gland and reduced production of T3 can be considered adaptations to the reduced calorie supply and the increased energy demand. The main role of corticosterone is the stimulation of gluconeogenesis, whereas low T3 probably has a protein-sparing and more general energy-conserving effect. The hypercortisolism is of potential importance because we now

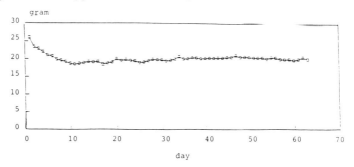

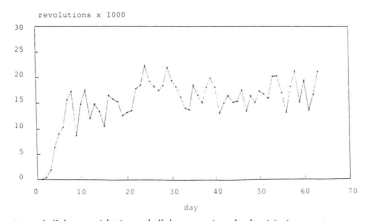

FIG. 8.1.   Upper half shows weight. Lower half shows running wheel activity in one rat.

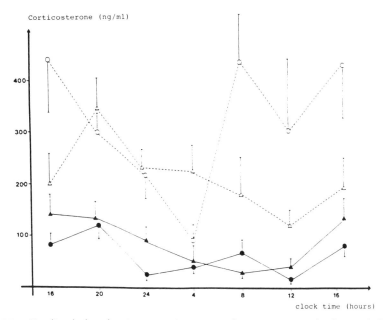

FIG. 8.2.   Circadian rhythm of cortiscosterone in semistarved running (O–O) and sedentary (Δ–Δ) rats and in ad lib-fed running (●–●) and sedentary controls (▲–▲) after 10 days of semistarvation. Feeding time in the starvation groups was 12 o'clock noon.

know that high glucocorticoid levels may modify glucocorticoid receptors at the amygdala and under certain circumstances may even cause cell damage in this area (Sapolsky, Krey, & McEwen, 1986). When semistarvation-induced running is continued at a constant body weight, the corticosterone values slowly normalize, as demonstrated by Pirke, Broocks, Wilckens, Marquard, and Schweiger (1993).

REPRODUCTIVE FUNCTION

Reproductive function is impaired by starvation induced hyperactivity in male and female rats. Broocks, Liu, and Pirke (1990) observed reduced LH and testosterone levels in male rats. Marquard (1991) monitored the menstrual cycle during weight loss in semistarved sedentary and semistarved running rats. Menstrual cycles disappear faster as a combined effect of semistarvation and hyperactivity: the faster the weight loss, the more rapidly the cycles disappeared. When weight loss was 3% of initial weight per day, the last proestrus occurred at a weight of 85 + 1.3%. With slower weight loss (2% per day) the last proestrus occurred at 74 + 2.3% of the initial weight. In the male rat, semistarvation alone and semistarvation-induced hyperactivity caused the same extent of suppression of LH and testosterone (Broocks, Liu, & Pirke, 1990). From these experiments it cannot be concluded that semistarvation-induced hyperactivity causes suppression of the HPG axis more rapidly than semistarvation alone.

NEUROTRANSMITTERS IN SEMISTARVATION-INDUCED HYPERACTIVITY

Central neurotransmitter changes in starvation-induced hyperactivity were studied by Broocks, Lui, and Pirke (1989, 1990) and Broocks, Schweiger, and Pirke (1990). Hyperactivity was again induced by reduced feeding after a 10-day period. Sedentary controls fed ad libitum, ad libitum fed rats with access to a running wheel, semistarved sedentary rats, and semistarved running rats were sacrificed at 4-hour intervals over a 24-hour period. The neurotransmitters norepinephrine, dopamine, serotonin, and their metabolites methoxyhydroxyphenyl-glycol (MHPG), dihydroxyphenylacetic acid (DOPAC), and hydroxy indolamine acetic acid (5-HIAA) were measured by high pressure liquid chromatography (HPLC) including eletrochemical detection in the medial basal hypothalamus and in the preoptic area. Although the limitations of the method should be kept in mind, we may consider the tissue concentrations of the metabolites as an indicator for transmitter turnover.

Freely fed rats run most during the dark hours, and semistarved rats show highest activity around the time of feeding, which was done at noon. Figure 8.3 shows the concentrations of MHPG in the medial basal hypothalamus (MBH). In the ad libitum fed and in the semistarved rats, MHPG concentrations parallel running

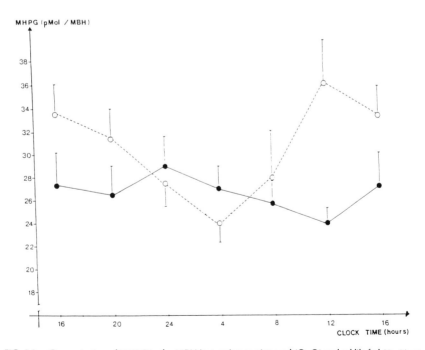

FIG. 8.3.   Concentration of MHPG in the MBH in running semistarved (O–O) and ad lib-fed (●–●) rats.

TABLE 8.1

Characteristics of the Groups of Restricted Diet,
Unrestricted Diet, Running, and Sedentary Rats

	A	B	C	D	Significance
	Semistarved Running	Semistarved Sedentary	Ad Libitum Running	Ad Libitum Sedentary	
[a]Body Weight (day 1)	262.4 ± 2.9	253.6 ± 4.6	250.0 ± 4.8	247.8 ± 2.1	ns
[a]Body Weight (day 10)	185.9 ± 1.7	183.9 ± 2.4	290.0 ± 5.6	306.0 ± 3.04	10
[b]MHPG (pMol/MBH)	29.0 ± 1.4	21.6 ± 0.8	26.5 ± 0.9	23.6 ± 0.4	2, 5, 7, 8, 10
[c]DOPAC (pMoL/MBH)	49.8 ± 1.9	41.8 ± 1.09	46.9 ± 2.4	44.8 ± 0.8	2, 4, 6, 8
[d]5-HIAA (pMol/MBH)	163.5 ± 7.9	134.3 ± 4.4	129.0 ± 5.6	113.4 ± 2.2	1, 3, 5, 9, 10

Note. [a]Body weight before and 10 days after semistarvation. [b]Concentrations of 3-methoxy-4-hydroxy-phenylgly-col (MHPG). [c]3, 4-dihydroxyphenylacetic acid (DOPAC). [d]5-hydroxy-indole-3-acetic acid (5-HIAA) in the medio-basal hypothalamus (MBH).

1 = A vs. B, $p < .05$; 2 = $p < .001$; 3 = $p < .001$; 4 = A vs. D, $p < .05$; 5 = $p < .001$; 6 = B vs. C, $p < .05$; 7 = $p < .001$; 8 = B vs. D, $p < .05$; 9 = $p < .001$; 10 = C vs. D, $p < .05$.

activity. Semistarvation alone reduces MHPG concentrations in the MBH as has been demonstrated in many earlier experiments (Pirke & Spyra, 1982; Schweiger et al., 1985a, 1985b). Hyperactivity reverses the effect of semistarvation on MHPG.

Table 8.1 gives a synopsis of the neurotransmitter findings in the medial basal hypothalamus. Serotonin turnover is stimulated by semistarvation. The assumption that an increased opioid activity in the brain is responsible for runner's high has been discussed at great length (for review see Epling & Pierce, 1988). Naloxon reduces running activity in the rat (Epling & Pierce, 1988). Data on central endorphin turnover and more detailed studies of endorphin agonist and antagonists are needed to clarify the role of opioids in this animal model.

The question arises whether the neurotransmitter changes observed can explain the endocrine findings. Semistarvation suppresses the activity of the HPG axis. Many experiments in the rat have clearly demonstrated the stimulatory effect of no-repinephrine (NE) on the HPG axis. We could therefore assume that reduced NE activity in semistarvation impairs LH secretion. Activity reverses the effect of starvation on NE; it does not, however, reverse the effect on LH and testosterone (T). If we assume that the effect of NE is inhibitory on the HPA axis, we could explain high corticosterone values in semistarvation, but not even higher values in semistarvation nduced hyper-activity.

There are probably many reasons why we have failed to explain neuroendocrine observations by changes in the neurotransmitter systems in the experimental paradigm discussed here. The comparison of findings in the preoptic area (POA) and in the MBH already shows that there may be major local differences in the effects of semistarvation and hyperactivity on neurotransmitters. Many more than the classic three neurotrans-mitters studied here are involved in the regulation of the HPG and the HPA axes. The same considerations discussed here for neuroendocrine regulation also are relevant for the suppressing effect of hyperactivity on food intake in this animal model. More detailed studies on more neurotransmitter and neuromodulator systems are necessary to understand this animal model.

NEUROPHARMACOLOGICAL STUDY

The first study of this kind was conducted by Routtenburg and Kuznesof (1967), who observed that the development of hyperactivity and anorexia could be prevented by giving neuroleptic drugs. Because these drugs influence different neurotransmitter systems, it is not possible to determine how these drugs act on hyperactivity and anorexia. Later studies focused on more specific interference with these neurotransmitter sy+stems, the function of which is altered in semistarvation-induced hyperactivity (Broocks, Liu, & Pirke, 1990; Broocks, Schweiger, & Pirke, 1991).

Wilckens, Schweiger, and Pirke (1992a) studied the serotonergic system. In these experiments, stable running was achieved for up to 6 weeks after an initial weight loss of 20% to 30%. Serotonin agonists and antagonists were injected intraperitoneal in different doses either alone or in different combinations. Running activity was observed for two hours after injection. Different serotonin agonists were used in the study. None of these substances is totally specific for any one of the serotonin receptors (1A, 1B, 1C, 1D, 2, and 3). Among these substances only m-trifluoro-methylphenylpiperazine HCl (TFMPP), 1-(metachlorophenyl)-piperazine di HCl (mCPP), (+-)-1-(2,5-dimethoxy-4-iodophenyl)- 2-amino-propane HCl (DOI), and quipazine, which share a relatively high affinity for the serotonin 1c receptor, suppress running activity in a dose-dependent manner. Agonists that act only on peripheral 5-HT receptors did not suppress running activity.

Among the antagonists tested, only those substances that shared a high affinity for the serotonin 1c receptors blocked the effects of the agonists mentioned above on running activity (Van de Kar et al., 1989). These data indicate that semistarvation induced hyperactivity can be blocked by serotonin 1c agonists. The involvement of other 5-HT-receptors seems unlikely, because 8-OHDPAT (8-hydroxy-2-[di-n-propylamino] tetralin), which is selective for 5-HT1A receptors, increased locomotion at a low, presynaptic dose and decreased activity only at doses at which symptoms of the serotonin syndrome occurred. Behavioral stereotypes arise in food-restricted rats at lower doses than in rats on a free feeding schedule (Bendotti & Samanin, 1987). 8-OHDPAT (1 mg/kg) was also given 2 hours before the experiment (at T = 2 h) because of its known biphasic effect (Duda & Bolles, 1963), but no effect was observed when running wheel activity (RWA) was recorded at T = 4, 5, and 6 (data not shown). We therefore suggest that the suppression of (RWA) by 8-OHDPAT is a consequence of a behavioral impairment resulting from the serotonin syndrome and not a suppression of the stimulus to run.

The 5-HT18/D receptor ligand RU 24969 (possibly also an agonist at 5-HT2 receptor, Van de Kar et al., 1989) showed no effect on RWA. During the second hour after injection, the 5-HT1B/D receptor agonist CGS 12066B slightly increased RWA at the higher dose. This could reflect activation of presynaptic 5-HT1B receptors that results in a decreased 5-HT release.

Because mCPP is thought to be a 5-HT2 receptor antagonist (Conn & Sanders-Busch, 1987; Simansky & Schechter, 1988), whereas DOI acts as an agonist at this receptor (Wing, Tapson, & Geyer, 1990), we concluded from the present results that 5-HT1A/B and 5-HT2 receptors are not directly involved in the suppression of semistarvation-induced hyperactivity. Although the presence of 5-HT1B receptors in rat brain is established, there is presently no evidence for 5-HT1D receptors in rats (Hoyer & Middlemiss, 1989). Central 5-HT3 receptors might be involved in the observed behavior because they interact with the dopaminergic neurotransmitter system, and we also found an increased dopamine turnover under these experimental conditions (Broocks et al., 1989). However, until now no selective 5-HT3 receptor agonist with good penetration of the blood-brain barrier by systemic administration is available.

The effect of mCPP would not appear to be mediated via 5-HT3 because ICS 205930, a highly selective 5-HT3 antagonist, did not restore excessive RWA, which had been suppressed by mCPP. 2-ME-5-HT, a 5-HT3 agonist with only peripheral action when administered systematically, was without effect.

NORADRENERGIC SYSTEM

Studies of the noradrenergic system were inspired because the noradrenergic system is impaired by semistarvation (Schweiger et al., 1985a, 1985b) but stimulated by semistarvation-induced hyperactivity (Broocks et al., 1989). Alpha2-(clonidine), but not alpha1- and beta-agonists, suppressed running activity. This specific effect of the alpha2-agonists was prevented by alpha2-antagonists. Alpha- and beta-antagonists alone had no effect on semistarvation-induced running (Wilckens, Schweiger, & Pirke, 1992b). The assumption that clonidine suppresses running simply by lowering blood pressure must be rejected because neither prazozine nor phentolamine, which also reduce blood pressure, inhibited running activity.

Semistarvation-induced RWA has been shown to be accompanied by an increased NE-turnover (Broocks, Liu, & Pirke, 1990). Therefore, one likely explanation for clonidine suppression of hyperlocomotion is that it reduces central NE-turnover, thus reducing the stimulation of postsynaptic alpha-receptors. This would reduce the drive for feeding mediated via postsynaptic alpha2 receptors (Leibowitz, 1984). Such an interpretation would be in line with reports that demonstrate clonidine-induced sedation to be a result of stimulation of somatodentric autoreceptors at ascending noradrenergic neurons (Heal, Prow, & Buckett, 1989; Scheinin & MacDonald, 1989).

In summarizing the results of the pharmacological studies two questions should be answered:

1. Do these studies tell us why semistarved rats start running?
2. Do these studies suggest pharmacological treatment of hyperactivity in anorectic patients?

Although the pharmacological studies reported here used more specific drugs than the neuroleptic drugs given by Routtenberg and Kuznesof (1967), they also used drugs of limited specificity simply because agonists and antagonists that have a high specificity for any one of the serotonin receptor subtypes are not yet available. Thus any explanation must remain highly speculative. We could, for instance, assume that semistarved rats learn to run faster and faster because the increased serotonergic activity thus achieved makes them feel less hungry. Similarly, the semistarved rat may learn to overcome starvation-induced reduction of norepinephrine turnover and thus "feel better." Although the first assumption is supported by the fact that wheel running reduces food intake (Epling & Pierce, 1984) it remains extremely speculative and must be proven by further experiments that study the effect of running on food intake on a neurotransmitter basis. The second assumption appears to be rather unlikely, because we should assume that increasing the noradrenergic activity by giving alpha1 and beta-agonists should be able to substitute running as a measure to raise norepinephrine turnover. However, this is not the case.

RELEVANCE OF THE ANIMAL MODEL FOR THE UNDERSTANDING OF HYPERACTIVITY IN AN

In attempts to interpret hyperactivity in patients with AN, different causes have been discussed. Some argue that anorectics increase their activity on purpose because it helps them to burn more energy and get thin even faster. Others investigators believe that the permanent physical activity and the fidgeting could be biological in origin. Indeed, hyperactivity in some anorectic patients impresses the physician by its similarity to addiction. Although we do not understand the nature of starvation-induced hyperactivity in the rat and other rodents, it is clear that all rats without exception develop hyperactivity when starved. There are two reasons to assume that this mechanism is not relevant in human beings.

First, not all patients with AN are hyperactive (Falk, Halmi, & Tyron, 1985). Second, the semistarved young men in the Minnesota experiment conducted by Keys, Brozek, Henschel, Mickelson, and Taylor (1950) did not develop signs of hyperactivity. It may be that only women develop hyperactivity during weight reduction, because in the female rat the effect is much more pronounced than in males. However, our own studies in young women who participated in weight reducing diets over a three- to six-week period and who kept event, eating, and activity diaries give no clear evidence for the development of hyperactivity (Pirke et al., 1986; Schweiger et al., 1987).

To summarize, we cannot expect an explanation for the hyperactivity of anorectic patients from the study of semistarved rodents living in running wheels.

However, the study of central neurotransmitter changes in the animal model can help us to generate hypotheses on neurotransmitter changes attributable to starvation and hyperactivity in the brain of the anorectic patient. As previously shown, we demonstrated that several drugs interfering with the noradrenergic and serotonergic systems can inhibit hyperactivity. Among these, serotonin 1-C-agonists appear to be the most promising. They could provide a pharmacological way of inhibiting hyperactivity without inhibiting eating. The suppression of hyperactivity in anorectic patients is clinically important because many patients expend a huge amount of calories while exercising (Pirke, Trimborn, Platte, & Fichter, 1991), which makes it difficult for the patient to gain weight.

REFERENCES

Bendotti, C., & Samanin, R. (1987). The role of putative 5-HT1A and 5-HT1B receptors in the control of feeding in rats. *Life Sciences, 41*, 635–642.

Broocks, A., Liu, J., & Pirke, K. M. (1989). Influence of hyperactivity on the metabolism of central monoaminergic neurotransmitters and reproductive function in the semistarved rat. In K. M. Pirke, W. Wuttke, & U. Schweiger (Eds.), *The menstrual cycle and its disorder* (pp. 88–96). Berlin: Springer-Verlag.

Broocks, A., Liu, J., & Pirke, K. M. (1990). Semistarvation-induced hyperactivity compensates for decreased norepinephrine and dopamine turnover in the mediobasal hypothalamus of the rat. *Journal of Neural Transmission, 79*, 113–124.

Broocks, A., Schweiger, U., & Pirke, K. M. (1990). Hyperactivity aggravates semistarvation-induced changes in corticosterone and triiodothyronine concentrations in plasma but not luteinizing hormone and testosterone levels. *Physiology and Behavior, 48*, 567–569.

Broocks, A., Schweiger, U., & Pirke, K. M. (1991). The influence of semistarvation induced hyperactivity on hypothalamic serotonin metabolism. *Physiology and Behavior, 50*, 385–388.

Conn, J. P., & Sanders-Busch, E. (1987). Relative efficiencies of piperazines at the phosphoinositide hydrolysis-linked serotonergic (5-HT1C and 5-HT2) receptors. *Journal of Pharmacology and Experimental Therapy, 242*, 552–557.

Cornish, E. R., & Mrosovsky, N. (1965). Activity during food deprivation and satiation of six species of rodent. *Animal Behavior, 13*, 242–248.

Dourish, C. T., Hutson, P. H., & Curzon, G. (1985). Characteristics of feeding induced by the serotonin agonist 8-hydroxy-2- (di-n-propylamino) tertralin (8-OHDPAT). *Brain Research Bulletin, 15*, 377–384.

Duda, J. J., & Bolles, R. C. (1963). Effects of prior deprivation, current deprivation and weight loss on the activity of the hungry rat. *Journal of Comparative Physiology and Psychology, 56*, 569–571.

Epling, W. F., & Pierce, W. D. (1984). Activity-based anorexia in rats as a function of opportunity to run on an activity wheel. *Nutrition and Behavior, 2*, 37–49.

Epling, W. F., & Pierce, W. D. (1988). Activity-based anorexia: A biobehavioral perspective. *International Journal of Eating Disorders, 7*, 475–485.

Falk, J. R., Halmi, K. A., & Tyron, W. T. (1985). Activity measures in anorexia nervosa. *Archives of General Psychiatry, 42*, 811–814.

Finger, F. W. (1951). The effect of food deprivation and subsequent satiation upon general activity in the rat. *Journal of Comparative Physiology and Psychology, 44*, 557–564.

Hall, J. F., & Hanford, P. V. (1954). Activity as a function of a restricted feeding schedule. *Journal of Comparative Physiology and Psychology, 47*, 362–363.

Heal, D. J., Prow, M. R., & Buckett, W. R. (1989). Clonidine-induced hypoactivity and midriasis in mice respectively are mediated via pre- and postsynaptic alpha-2-adrenoceptors in the brain. *European Journal of Pharmacology, 170*, 19 – 28.

Hoyer, D., & Middlemiss, D. N. (1989). Species differences in the Pharmacology of terminal 5-HT autoreceptors in mammalian brain. *TIPS, 10*, 130–132.

Kanarek, R. B., & Collier, G. H. (1983). Self-starvation: A problem of overriding the satiety signal? *Physiology and Behavior, 30*, 307–311.

Keys, A., Brozek, J., Henschel, A., Mickelson, O., & Taylor, H. L. (1950). *The biology of human starvation* (pp. 340–396). Minneapolis: University of Minnesota Press.

Küderling, I., Dorsch, G., Warnhoff, M., & Pirke, K. M. (1984). The actions of prostaglandin E2, naloxone and testosterone on starvation-induced suppression of luteinizing hormone-releasing hormone and luteinizing-hormone secretion. *Neuroendocrinology, 39*, 530–537.

Landsberg, L., & Young, J. B. (1978). Fasting, feeding and regulation of the sympathetic nervous system. *New England Journal of Medicine, 298*, 1295–1301.

Leibowitz, S. F. (1984). Noradrenergic function in the medial hypothalamus: Potential relation to anorexia nervosa and bulimia. In K. M. Pirke & D. Ploog (Eds.), *The psychobiology of anorexia nervosa* (pp. 35–45). Berlin: Springer-Verlag.

Levitsky, D. A. (1974). Feeding conditions and intermeal relationships. *Physiology and Behavior, 12*, 779–787.

Marquard, R. (1991). *Tiermodell zur Anorexia nervosa: Mangelernährungsbedingte Hyperaktivität bei der weiblichen und bei der männlichen Ratte* [Animal model of anorexia nervosa: Malnutrition-based hyperactivity in female and male rats]. Doctoral dissertation, Technical University, Munich.

Philipp, E., & Pirke, K. M. (1987). Effect of starvation on hypothalamic tyrosine hydroxylase activity in adult male rats. *Brain Research, 413*, 53–59.

Pirke, K. M., Broocks, A., Wilckens, T., Marquard, R., & Schweiger, U. (1993). Starvation-induced hyperactivity in the rat: The role of endocrine and neurotransmitter changes. *Neuroscience and Biobehavioral Reviews, 17*, 287–294.

Pirke, K. M., Schweiger, U., Laessle, R. G., Dickhaut, B., Schweiger, M., & Waechtler, M. (1986). Dieting influences the menstrual cycle: Vegetarian versus nonvegetarian diet. *Fertility and Sterility, 46*, 1083–1088.

Pirke, K. M., & Spyra, B. (1981). Influence of starvation on testosterone luteinizing hormone feedback in the rat. *Acta Endocrinologica, 96*, 413–321.

Pirke, K. M., & Spyra, B. (1982). Catecholamine turnover in the brain and the regulation of luteinizing hormone and corticosterone in starved male rats. *Acta Endocrinologica, 100*, 168–176.

Pirke, K. M., Trimborn, P., Platte, P., & Fichter, M. (1991). Average total energy expenditure in anorexia nervosa, bulimia nervosa, and healthy young women. *Biology and Psychiatry, 30*, 711–718.

Richter, C. P. A. (1922). A behavioristic study of the activity of the rat. *Comparative Psychology Monographs*, 1–55

Routtenberg, A., & Kuznesof, A. W. (1967). Self-starvation of rats living in activity wheels on a restricted feeding schedule. *Journal of Comparative Physiology and Psychology, 64*, 414–421.

Sapolsky, R. M., Krey, L. C., & McEwen, B. S. (1986). The neuroendocrinology of stress and aging: The glucocorticoid cascade hypothesis. *Endocrine Review, 7*, 284–301.

Scheinin, M., & MacDonald, E. (1989). An introduction to the pharmacology of a-2-adrenoceptors in the central nervous system. *Acta Veterinerica Scandinavica, 85*, 11–19.

Schweiger, U., Laessle, R. G., Pfister, H., Hoehl, C., Schwingenschloegel, M., Schweiger, M., & Pirke, K. M. (1987). Diet-induced menstrual irregularities: Effects of age and weight loss. *Fertility and Sterility, 48*, 746–751.

Schweiger, U., Warnhoff, M., & Pirke, K. M. (1985a). Central noradrenergic turnover and corticosterone secretion in semistarvation. *Acta Endocrinologica, 108*, 267.

Schweiger, U., Warnhoff, M., & Pirke, K. M. (1985b). Norepinephrine turnover in the hypothalamus of adult male rats: Alteration of circadian patterns by semistarvation. *Journal of Neurochemistry, 45*, 706–709.

Simansky, K. J., & Schechter, L. E. (1988). Properties of some 1-Arylpiperazines as antagonists of sterotyped behaviors mediated by central serotonergic receptors in rodents. *Journal of Pharmacology Experimental Therapy, 247*, 1073–1081.

Van de Kar, L. D., Carnes, M., Maslowski, J., Bonadonna, A. M., Rittenhouse, P. A., Kunimoto, K., Piechowski, R. A., & Bethea, C. L. (1989). Neuroendocrine evidence for denervation supersensitivity of serotonin receptors: Effects of the 5-HT agonist RU 24969 on corticotropin, corticosterone, prolactin and renin secretion. *Journal of Pharmacology Experimental Therapy, 251*, 428–434.

Warnhoff, M., Dorsch, G., & Pirke, K. M. (1983). Effect of starvation on gonadotrophin secretion and on in vitro release of LRH from the isolated median eminence of the male rat. *Acta Endocrinologica, 103*, 293–301.

Wilckens, T., Schweiger, U., & Pirke, K. M. (1992a). Activation of 5-HT1C-receptors suppresses excessive wheel running induced by semi-starvation in the rat. *Psychopharmacology, 109*, 77–84.

Wilckens, T., Schweiger, U., & Pirke, K. M. (1992b). Activation of alpha2-adrenoceptors suppresses excessive wheel-running in the semistarvation-induced hyperactive rat. *Pharmacology Biochemistry and Behavior, 43*, 733–738.

Wing, L. L., Tapson, G. S., & Geyer, M. A. (1990). 5-HT-2 mediation of acute behavioral effects of hallucinogens in rats. *Psychopharmacology, 100*, 417–425.

9

The Induction and Maintenance of Hyperactivity During Food Restriction in Rats

James C. Russell
Allen D. Morse
University of Alberta

The laboratory rat is a domesticated species that has been developed for almost 90 years as a model for biomedical research relevant to humans (Baker, Lindsay, & Weisbroth, 1979). The rat has also proven to be invaluable for behavioral studies and, as described in the preceding chapters, clearly can develop activity anorexia. Thus the rat provides us with a model that can allow for integrated study of the physiological basis of behavior, in particular that of activity anorexia.

Hyperactivity is a central component of activity anorexia that, from the early studies of Epling, Pierce, and Stefan (1983), is essential for the full development of the syndrome. These studies, based on time-limited access to food (a single 90-minute meal), showed that the distance run daily by rats given access to a running wheel increased exponentially with time. Figure 9.1 shows the typical distance run day by day by young rats under these conditions, with peak running of some 7,000 meters a day. With a decreasing food intake and an associated continuously falling body weight, the increased running leads rapidly to a fatal outcome if not interrupted. In contrast, rats without the opportunity to exercise manage to eat sufficient food to survive in good health. This phenomenon appears to have the characteristics of a physiological control

113

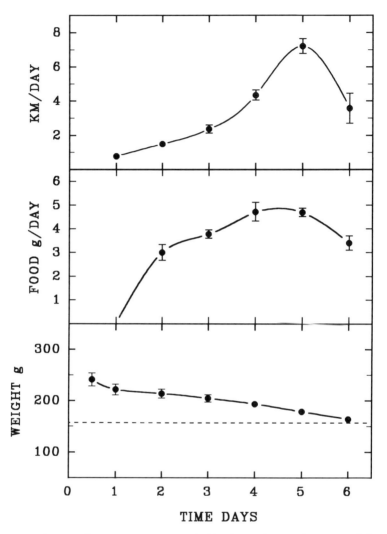

FIG. 9.1.   Development of activity anorexia in 6-week-old male rats. The animals were provided access to a running wheel, starved for 24 hours, and given 90-minute access to food once every 24 hours. The distance run increased exponentially to day 5, followed by a collapse in running and a reduction in food intake. Body weight showed a continuous decline from the initial value to 65% of entry weight, as indicated by the dashed line. These data represent mean ±*SEM* for 4 rats.

mechanism that has been driven into a range in which responses are grossly decompensated. Clarification of the nature of this system may prove essential to a real understanding of activity anorexia. Some key questions arise from this concept:

- Are the hyperactivity and anorexia mutually maintained by a regular dysfunction?

- If so, what are the physiological and behavioral reward mechanisms?

If the fatal anorexia of the rat restricted to the 90-minute meal is due to a decompensated control mechanism, it should be possible to restore control through exogenous feedback. Russell, Epling, Pierce, Amy, and Boer (1987) provided such feedback through control by the experimenter of the absolute amount of food provided each day. The experimental protocol provided young rats with an initial allocation of 15 grams of food each day. The daily distance run increased essentially linearly with time (Fig. 9.2) more slowly than in the case of the rats with the single

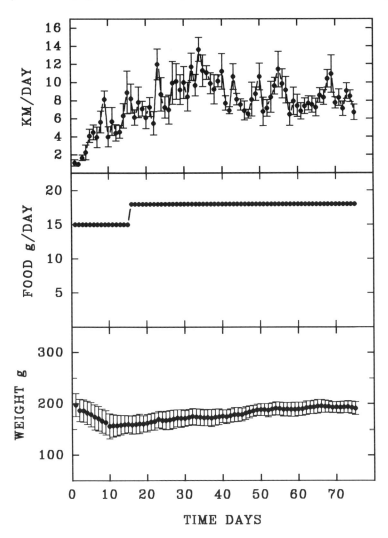

FIG. 9.2.   Development of prolonged steady-state running in 6-week-old male rats. The rats were initially given 15 grams of food daily, as shown, and this increased to 18 grams at day 15. The mean daily distance run was approximately 8,000 meters from day 20 to 75. Mean body weight remained below 200 grams, in contrast to sedentary control animals with mean weight of 261 ± 19.9 grams at day 75. The results are mean ±SEM, with six rats in the group.

90-minute daily meal. If left on this regimen, in time the rats reach very high daily running (15,000 to 25,000 m/day) and decompensate, with the development of anorexia. In contrast, if the animals, on reaching a more moderate level of running (e.g., 8,000 to 10,000 m/day, at day 15), are given 18 grams of food a day, the running stabilizes. Figure 9.2 illustrates that such rats will run 8,000 to 10,000 meters a day over long periods. The animals in this study remained at about 75% of the body weight of freely eating sedentary rats. The daily distance run is strongly dependent on daily food allocation. Boer (1989) showed that changes of plus or minus 1 gram in the amount of food provided significantly altered the distance run, with greater amounts of food decreasing and lesser amounts increasing the running. The interaction between food supplied and running appears to depend on the degree of food restriction relative to metabolic requirements. As the running increases, so do energy output and metabolic need. Thus careful control of the amount of food supplied can lead to a gradual increase in running with concomitantly increased food allocation. The end-stage result is a rat's running 25,000 meters a day while maintaining a diet of 25 grams of food per day. For comparison, a control sedentary rat would spontaneously consume 21 grams a day.

The rat is a nocturnal species that sleeps during the light phase of a diurnal cycle and is active during the dark phase. As shown in Fig. 9.3 (panel B), rats established in a state of long-term running under the mild food restriction described above essentially run only during the dark period (Morse et al., 1995). The stable pattern of activity shows a consistent biphasic pattern, with a trough of activity about two thirds of the way through the dark period. Animals that are not food-deprived show a similar pattern of running activity at a much lower level (Fig. 9.3, panel A). Thus the rats in the steady hyperactivity and food-restricted state, although running substantial and abnormal distances, retain their normal circadian rhythm. These animals may be regarded as analogous to the quite common group of humans who are highly athletic (particularly runners), exhibit a lean phenotype, but are not frankly anorectic (Katz, 1986).

In contrast to the fixed-food paradigm, the 90-minute meal protocol induces a rapid and complete breakdown of the diurnal pattern of activity in rats. Figure 9.4 shows a continuous record of activity over a 4-day experiment. The regular pattern of behavior was disrupted on the first day of this experiment, and by day 4 the rats were running continuously throughout the dark and light periods. They paused only briefly when provided access to food. This continuous activity must reflect a significant alteration of central nervous system functioning. It is also incompatible with survival and makes clear why this form of activity anorexia is fatal. Rats left in the fixed-food allocation protocol for long periods and allowed to run over 20,000 meters a day also show a breakdown of the diurnal pattern of activity. These rats become unstable and can degenerate into exhibiting the full-blown anorectic syndrome and die (Morse & Russell, 1995).

The ability to control the distance run precisely through variation in food allocation confirms that food intake is a critical controlling factor in activity anorexia. Our results also indicate that it is the relative food intake compared with the metabolic requirements of the animal that is relevant, not the absolute amount. All this is consistent with the hypothesis of the existence of a regulated physiological and metabolic control of activity that is determined by relative food intake. The stable hyperactivity of the rats restricted to a fixed amount of food each day reflects

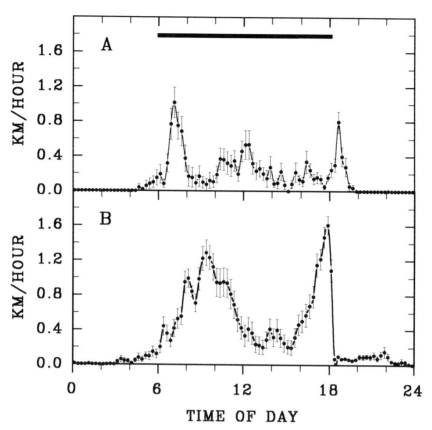

FIG. 9.3.   Diurnal variation of spontaneous running activity in male rats. Panel A, ad libitum fed rats, 20 days in a running wheel; panel B, rats in the food-restricted steady state protocol at 25 days in the wheel. This group were fed 18 grams per day at 1800 hours. The heavy horizontal line indicates the dark period of the light cycle. Data are rate of running measured every 15 minutes; mean ±SEM. There were 10 rats in each group.

a highly perturbed state of this system, a state barely maintained in the functional range by the intervention of the experimenter. The rats with full-blown activity anorexia (induced by timed access to food) are in a state where the physiological mechanism has exceeded its functional range and the system has decompensated.

The existence of a physiological mechanism inducing and maintaining hyper-activity implies the presence of an effector mechanism in either the central nervous system or the reward system for the behavior. The endogenous opioid system is well documented as playing a significant role in the regulation of spontaneous food intake (Brands, Thornhill, Hirst, & Gowdey, 1979; Reid, 1985). Activation of this system also provides an intrinsic reward that is powerful in both humans and other animals such as rats (Stolerman, 1985). This leads us to consider the possibility that effector mechanisms for hyperactivity involve an endogenous opioid reward. An initial study conducted by Boer, Epling, Pierce, and Russell (1990) showed that the

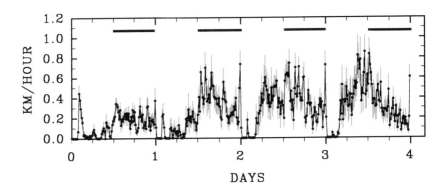

FIG. 9.4.   Running activity of rats developing activity anorexia on a daily 90-minute meal. The data cover the entire experiment and represent the rate of running over each 15-minute period, mean $\pm SEM$. The rats were provided with free access to food for 90 minutes each day at the end of the dark period. The heavy horizontal bars indicate the dark periods. The study was stopped at the end of day 4, as the rats' body weights were in the range of 70% of initial weight and physical condition was declining rapidly.

opiate antagonist naloxone caused a modest, but significant, reduction in daily total running. Naloxone has a short half-life, and only some 6% of the peak plasma concentration may be expected to remain 2 hours following an intraperitoneal injection. Recent, more detailed study has been made of the effects of naloxone on steady-state running. Naloxone, as shown in Fig. 9.5, inhibits running markedly in the 4-hour period following intraperitoneal injection, $p < .001$; (Morse, Epling, Pierce, & Russell, 1994). However, the effect of naloxone treatment is not immediate and is not evident on the first day of treatment. By the third and fourth day of treatment, the effect in the 4-hour period following the naloxone injection is marked. Similarly, on removal of the opiate antagonist, the recovery of the diurnal pattern of behavior is delayed, with some four days required to reach the pattern preceding naloxone administration.

The response to naloxone administration is relatively short, with the inhibition of hyperactivity confined to the four-hour period following injection of the drug. The dose of naloxone used (50 mg/kg) is sufficient to antagonize all three known opioid receptors (mu, delta, and kappa) for at least 2 hours (Michel, Bolger, & Weissman, 1985). Identification of the receptor type responsible for the inhibition of hyperactivity will require the use of receptor-specific antagonists such as peptides. The delayed onset and recovery from inhibition by naloxone suggests that the effect of the drug is not directly on the neural mechanisms controlling activity. Rather, the effects suggest the inhibition of a reward mechanism. As the endogenous reward provided by activity-induced opioid release is reduced, the animals respond by not running at those times of the day. In effect, the naloxone induces a negative conditioning. On cessation of the opioid antagonism, a relatively slow reconditioning occurs over a number of diurnal cycles.

Food intake in the presence of an excess is regulated and influenced by various factors, including exogenous opiates (Brands et al., 1979). The hypothalamic peptide neuropeptide Y (NPY) is the most potent known stimulant of eating behavior (Stanley, Kyrkouli, Lambert, & Leibowitz, 1986). Lewis et al. (1993) have shown that food-restricted rats in a state of stable hyperactive running (8 km/day) have significantly elevated levels of NPY in the arcuate nucleus, the medial preoptic area, and the dorsomedial hypothalamus. Similar but smaller increases in NPY were found in the same areas in the brains of rats food-restricted so as to maintain weight pairing with the running rats. Thus, although NPY levels are increased in the presence of reduced body weight, hyperactivity is associated with an even greater rise in NPY. Such an effect is consistent with a reduced sensitivity to NPY in the hyperactive animal, perhaps through modulation of the reward system for eating behavior. The mechanisms underlying the relationships between food intake and hyperactivity are complex and may involve insulin, corticotrophin and its releasing factor, and NPY (Lewis et al., 1993). An understanding of these mechanisms would open the possibility of specific, effective pharmacologic treatment of activity anorexia.

The available data on activity anorexia and hyperactivity behavior allow for a speculative physiological model that may be subjected to experimental testing. In healthy animals and humans, body weight is precisely regulated through both a modulation of food intake and internal metabolism. This system responds effectively to large changes in metabolic demand due to environmental factors and to changes in food supply and composition; however, if the food available is decreased (for whatever reason—famine or, in humans, self-induced dieting) beyond a certain

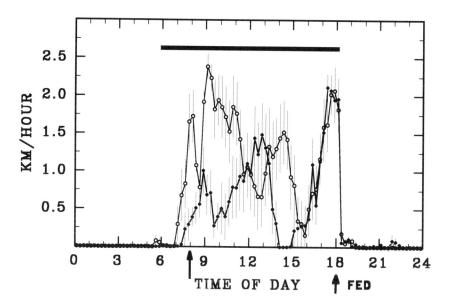

FIG. 9.5.   The effect of naloxone on the diurnal pattern of running of male rats in the steady state protocol. Open circles represent control rats (injected with saline), and filled circles rats injected with naloxone. Naloxone (50 mg/kg) was injected as indicated by the arrow at 0800 hours and the animals were fed 18 grams per day at 1800 hours. Data represent the rate of running measured every 15 minutes, mean ±SD; there were 10 rats in the group.

point, the individual becomes more active. Hyperactivity causes the release of endogenous opioids providing a strong intrinsic reward. In the food-restricted protocols, the system changes with the running increasing day by day, with a concomitant increase in metabolic demand. With a fixed food supply, the relative degree of food restriction increases, leading to further increased running and consequent increased endogenous opioid-mediated reward. The opioid reward may not only reinforce the running behavior, but may also antagonize the effects of the NPY-mediated drive to eat. This sequence is inherently unstable, involving positive feedback for the running. Without intervention, a state is reached where the physiological system decompensates and a rapid runaway occurs. The sequence is greatly accelerated in the protocol with a 90-minute timed access to food. In the fixed-food allocation protocol, the animal may be stabilized at a new state of equilibrium over a wide range of hyperactivity through external regulation of the food supply. In such a state the physiological regulatory system is functioning more or less normally, but at or near the extreme end of its range of operation.

The inhibitory effect of naloxone confirms the role of an endogenous opioid reward in hyperactivity. However, it is evident that the opioid receptor mechanism is not the initiator–controller of the running, but rather probably acts as a conditioning reward mechanism. Thus it acts to maintain, rather than start, the hyperactivity. The identification of the hormones, neurotransmitter(s), and brain areas responsible for initiating the hyperactivity remains an experimental challenge.

Nonetheless, some conclusions may be drawn from the animal experiments that have implications for clinical practice and research. It is obvious that highly active individuals who tend to restrict their food intake, such as long distance runners and ballet dancers, are at serious risk of decompensation. This is not a new observation, but the steady state hyperactivity model with the rats is highly analogous to and provides a physiological explanation for the propensity of such individuals to full-blown activity anorexia. From a clinical perspective, behavior patterns that emphasize strict dieting and high levels of activity in both artistic and sporting contexts should be regarded as risky and to be avoided. The slow response to naloxone in the rat suggests that opiate antagonists would have limited and probably even slower effects in humans exhibiting activity anorexia. This has been borne out by clinical trials showing limited effects (de Zwaan & Mitchell, 1992). Effective treatment through such an approach will require much longer-acting opioid antagonists and a relatively long period of treatment. Opiate antagonists would appear also to offer only a temporary inhibition of hyperactivity.

The downregulation of food intake in activity anorexia and its upregulation in states of obesity probably represent misregulation of the same physiological mechanism. The responsible physiological system appears to involve NPY or related neurotransmitters and/or hormones. Elucidation of this mechanism would permit broad treatment of eating disorders through the inhibition and/or stimulation of specific pathways. Combined with the inhibition of the positive feedback through the opioid reward system, this should ultimately provide an effective clinical approach to treating activity anorexia.

ACKNOWLEDGMENTS

We are indebted to D. P. Boer, who performed some of the experiments, and especially to D. G. Koeslag and S. E. Graham for their expert assistance with the rats. This work was supported in part by a grant from Alberta Mental Health.

REFERENCES

Baker, H. J., Lindsay, J. R., & Weisbroth, S. H. (1979). *The laboratory rat*. Orlando, FL: Academic Press.

Boer, D. P. (1989). *Determinants of excessive running in activity anorexia*. Unpublished doctoral dissertation, University of Alberta, Edmonton, Alberta.

Boer, D. P., Epling, W. F., Pierce, W. D., & Russell, J. C. (1990). Suppression of food deprivation-induced high-rate wheel running in rats. *Physiology and Behavior, 48*, 339–342.

Brands, B., Thornhill, J. A., Hirst, M., & Gowdey, G. W. (1979). Suppression of food intake and body weight gain by naloxone in rats. *Life Sciences, 24*, 1773–1778.

de Zwaan, M., & Mitchell, J. E. (1992). Opiate antagonists and eating behavior in humans: A review. *Journal of Clinical Pharmacology, 32*, 1060–1072.

Epling, W. F., Pierce, W. D., & Stefan, L. (1983). A theory of activity-based anorexia. *International Journal of Eating Disorders, 3*, 27–46.

Katz, J. L. (1986). Long distance running, anorexia nervosa and bulimia: A report of two cases. *Comprehensive Psychiatry, 27*, 74–78.

Lewis, D. E., Shellard, L., Koeslag, D. G., Boer, D. P., McCarthy, H. D., McKibbin, P. E., Russell, J. C., & Williams, G. (1993). Intense exercise and food restriction cause similar hypothalamic neuropeptide Y increases in rats. *American Journal of Physiology, 264*, E279–E284.

Michel, M. E., Bolger, G., & Weissman, B. A. (1985). Binding of a new opiate antagonist, nalmefene, to rat brain membranes. *Methods and Findings in Experimental and Clinical Pharmacology, 7*, 175–177.

Morse, A. D., Epling, W. F., Pierce, W. D., & Russell, J. C. (1994). Inhibitory effects of naloxone on hyperactivity in activity-anorexia demonstrated in JCR:LA-cp/+ rats [Abstract]. *Canadian Journal of Physiology and Pharmacology, 72*, Axxix.

Morse, A. D., & Russell, J. C. (1995). [Studies of extreme running in activity anorexia]. Unpublished raw data.

Morse, A. D., Russell, J. C., Hunt, T. W. M., Wood, G. O., Epling, W. F., & Pierce, W. D. (1995). Diurnal variation of intensive running in food deprived rats. *Canadian Journal of Physiology and Pharmacology, 73*, 1519–1523.

Reid, L. D. (1985). Endogenous opioid peptides and regulation of drinking and feeding. *Journal of Clinical Nutrition, 43*, 1099–1132.

Russell, J. C., Epling, W. F., Pierce, W D., Amy, R. M., & Boer, D. P. (1987). Induction of prolonged running by rats. *Journal of Applied Physiology, 63*, 2549–2553.

Stanley, B. G., Kyrkouli, S. E., Lambert, S., & Leibowitz, S. F., (1986). Neuropeptide Y chronically injected into the hypothalamus: A powerful neurochemical inducer of hyperphagia and obesity. *Peptides, 7*, 1189–1192.

Stolerman, J. P. (1985). Motivational effects of opioids: Evidence on the role of endorphins in mediating reward or aversion. *Pharmacology, Biochemistry and Behavior, 23*, 877–881.

IV

Extending Activity Anorexia
to Humans

10

Nutrition, Physical Activity, Menstrual Cycle, and Anorexia

Eliza B. Geer
Michelle P. Warren
*St Luke's-Roosevelt Hospital
and Columbia College of Physicians and Surgeons*

Menstrual abnormalities have a widely documented correlation to eating disorders. In a study conducted by Stewart, Robinson, Goldbloom, and Wright (1990), it was found that 58% of women with altered cyclicity had eating disorders, whereas only 7% of normally cycling women did. Investigating more severe forms of disorder, a study of ballet dancers showed that 50% of those with amenorrhea also had anorexia, but only 13% of those with normal cycles did (Brooks-Gunn, Warren, & Hamilton, 1986). In women particularly, both nutritional intake and body weight have been associated with normal development and reproductive maturity. This is reflected by the fact that girls develop twice as much fat as boys during puberty. Similarly, reports have shown the female reproductive system to be sensitive to its environment, and that it can alter during situations of crowding, starvation, travel, communal living, weight change, exercise, and stress (Fries, Nillius, & Petterson, 1974; Warren, 1982).

The incidence of eating disorders is widespread. In a survey of women between the ages of 16 and 35 attending a family practice, King (1986) found an incidence of eating disorders and partial eating disorders of 4%. The complications of eating disorders are numerous and broadly based, spanning psychological and medical domains. Specific physical dysfunctions include electrolyte disturbances, gastro-intestinal problems, and reproductive complications.

ANOREXIA AND REPRODUCTIVE FUNCTION

Incidence and Relation to Physical Activity

Theander (1976) and Kendell, Hall, Hailey, and Babigan (1973) found that anorexia occurs in .24 to 1.6 per 100,000 people, but incidence varies greatly according to population type. Kalucy, Crisp, Lacey, and Harding (1977) found that one in every 100 middle class White girls develops a serious form of anorexia, indicating this population to be at high risk. Values vary according to study method and definition (Stangler & Printz, 1980), and another study has identified a lifetime prevalence of anorexia of .3% among high school girls (Whitaker, 1992). In a study of over 2,500 girls between the ages of 13 and 18, secondary amenorrhea was associated with binge eating behavior and weight control and was found to have a one-year prevalence of 8.5% (Johnson & Whitaker, 1992). Populations involved in high activity levels are similarly at great risk for developing anorexia. Studies have indicated that 38% to 75% of all cases of anorexia may occur in highly active women (Theander, 1976).

Professional ballet dancers are a targeted population, because of their high level of exercise and the imposed standards of thinness in their profession. It has been found that 1 in 20 to 1 in 5 ballet dancers develop anorexia, depending on the level of competition in the company (Hamilton, Brooks-Gunn, & Warren, 1985). The level of competition probably relates to the level of training and physical activity, but stress may also play a role. Undoubtedly linked to the prevalence of eating disorders is the high incidence of menstrual dysfunction in this population. One source indicates that 30% of ballet dancers had delayed menarche and secondary amenorrhea (Warren, 1991). Anorexia is rare in men, occurring at a 1:9 ratio with women, but it has been found in men involved in competitive training and weight reduction (Smith, 1980).

Diagnosis

Anorexia is characterized by weight loss of 20% or more below normal, severe food restriction, and amenorrhea (Warren, 1985b). Diagnosis of anorexia includes associated behavioral changes such as hyperactivity, obsession with food and weight, distorted body image, and gorging alternating with periods of semistarvation. Patients with anorexia show an interest in low calorie and artificially sweetened food, an increased intake of raw vegetables, and an avoidance of foods with a high fat content (Warren, 1985a).

Endocrinology

The hormonal alterations present in anorexia, probably involving both psychological and neurochemical changes, are useful in elucidating the neuroendocrine mechanisms involved in reproductive cyclicity. The endocrine changes in anorexia probably involve an extreme example of the physiological changes seen in weight-loss-induced amenorrhea. Endocrine profiles indicate hypothalamic dysfunction, and anorexia can be seen as the basic model for the hypothalamic amenorrhea seen with eating disorders and nutritional restriction.

Specifically, the hormonal changes that occur during anorexia include low gonadotropin, especially luteinizing hormone (LH), and reversion from the normal episodic pattern to the prepubertal pattern of a low baseline 24-hour LH secretion (Fig. 10.1). Some patients with anorexia also produce nocturnal LH spurting, a pattern common in early puberty (Boyar et al., 1974). These changes in gonadotropin secretion are accompanied by uniformly low estradiol levels.

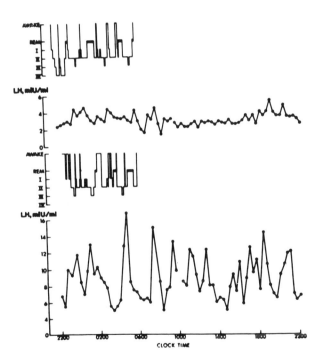

FIG. 10.1. Plasma LH concentration every 20 minutes for 24 hours during acute exacerbation of anorexia nervosa (upper panel) and after clinical remission with a return of body weight to normal (lower panel). The latter represents a normal adult pattern. Reprinted from "Anorexia Nervosa: Immaturity of the 24-Hour Luteinizing Hormone Secretory Pattern," by R. M. Boyar, 1974, *New England Journal of Medicine, 291*, p. 865. Copyright 1974 Massachusetts Medical Society. Reprinted by permission of *The New England Journal of Medicine.*

The basic hypothalamic dysfunction stems from altered pulsatile secretion of gonadotropin releasing hormone (GnRH). Both pulse frequency and amplitude are reduced from the normal bursts that occur every 60 to 90 minutes. This leads to inefficient stimulation of pituitary gonadotropins that are essential for folliculo-genesis, estrogen secretion, and consequent normal menstruation. The neurons that contain (GnRH) are situated in the arcuate nucleus in the brain. ß-endorphin, an opiate, may be involved in GnRH modulation. Dopamine and norepinephrine, other neurotransmitters, may also be modulators; excessive amounts of these transmitters have been found to alter behavior and appetite (Warren, 1985a). Similarly, ß-endorphin, cortisol, epinephrine, norepinephrine, and prolactin are involved in stress reactions and may also affect the GnRH pulse generator.

Anorectic patients exhibit immature patterns of hormone secretion: there is a prepubertal response to GnRH challenge with a greater follicle stimulating hormone (FSH) than LH response. With a subcutaneous or intravenous pulsatile administration of GnRH every 2 hours, patients produce adultlike secretion of gonadotropin after 4 days (Fig. 10.2). Eventual ovulation and menstruation is induced in this manner and occurs when the LH response supersedes that of the FSH. Normal recovery and weight gain also cause reversion to the adultlike pattern of hormone secretion (Warren, 1985a).

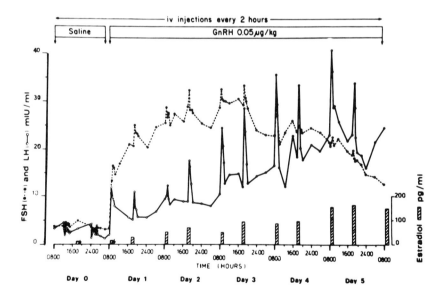

FIG. 10.2.   Plasma FSH, LH, and estradiol responds to GnRH (0.05 ug/kg) every two hours. The arrow indicates values below the sensitivity of the estradiol assay. Reprinted from "Low Dose Pulsatile Gonadotropin-Releasing Hormone in Anorexia Nervosa: A Model of Human Pubertal Development," by J. C. Marshall and R. P. Kelch, 1979, *Journal of Clinical Endocrinology and Metabolism, 49*, 712–718, p. 714. © The Endocrine Society. Reprinted with permission.

Other mechanisms may also influence estrogen secretion in anorexia. Hypercarotenemia (elevated levels of carotene in the blood) develops in some cases. This results from metabolic alterations in addition to a possible increased consumption of raw vegetables. Studies have indicated that dieting may cause a metabolic deficit that inhibits the normal metabolism of carotene, a precursor of vitamin A (Frumar, Meldrum, & Judd, 1979). This yellow substance accumulates in the subcutaneous layer of the skin and gives a yellow tone to the palms and soles, leaving sclera clear. One study postulates that lowering carotene levels by reducing intake of foods high in carotenoids restores eumenorrhea (Kemmann, Pasquale, & Skaf, 1983).

Patients with anorexia show signs of hypothyroidism other than hypercarotenemia. These symptoms include constipation, cold intolerance, hypotension, dry skin, and low basal metabolic rates (Warren, 1988). A metabolic adaption to a state of starvation appears to occur in cases of anorexia and is reflected by lowered serum levels of Thyroxine (T_4) and Triiodothyronine (T_3), especially T_3. Low T_3 levels are most likely caused by the conversion of T_4 predominantly into the inactive form reverse T_3, instead of the active form, T_3. Although the secretion of thyroid-stimulating hormone (TSH) appears normal in anorectic patients, thyroid-releasing factor (TRF) stimulation produces a delayed TSH response from 30 to 120 minutes (Warren, 1985a). This may suggest an alteration in the set point for endogenous TRF regulation.

Reduced metabolic clearance may cause the elevated plasma cortisol levels found in anorectic patients, reflecting yet another consequence of metabolic dysfunction. An increase in cortisol, which stimulates gluconeogenesis and reduces peripheral glucose utilization, reflects the body's compensation to an energy deficit. Thus the multiple physiological changes seen in anorexia suggest an adaptation to the semistarved state.

WEIGHT-LOSS RELATED AMENORRHEA

Simple weight loss is defined as dieting to achieve a weight of 10% to 15% below normal (Warren, 1985b). This condition occurs in the absence of the extreme behavioral and physiological symptoms associated with anorexia, such as hyperactivity. However, excessive dieting causes hormonal abnormalities and menstrual dysfunction similar to those seen in anorexia (Fig. 10.3), and women with eating disorders not otherwise specified frequently have menstrual dysfunction. In fact it has been observed that reduced ovarian function is one of the first adaptations to occur in the setting of caloric reduction (Schweiger et al., 1987). Amenorrhea may occur preceding, during, or following weight loss and was correlated to the time of food restriction whether or not significant weight loss has occurred (Warren, 1985a). Studies have shown that normal-weight young women, after dieting for 6 weeks (800 to 1,000 kcal/day), develop a range of alterations in endocrine function. Moreover, the menstrual cycles in 20% of these normal-weight young women were disrupted for 3 to 6 months after dieting (Pirke, Dogs, Fichter, & Tuschil, 1988).

Specifically, weight loss interferes with the normal release of gonadotropins from the anterior pituitary. The hormonal changes that result from excessive dieting

ITEM TESTED	PATIENTS WITH SIMPLE WEIGHT LOSS	PATIENTS WITH ANOREXIA NERVOSA
GROWTH HORMONE	↑	↑
PROLACTIN	N l	N l
TSH	N l	N l
LH	N l	↓
FSH	↓	↓
CORTISOL	N l	N l
FREE THYROXINE	N l	N l
3,5,3'−TRI−IODOTHYRONINE	↓	↓
N l = NORMAL		
LH RESPONSE TO GnRH	LATE PEAK	LATER PEAK
FSH RESPONSE TO GnRH	N l	LATE PEAK
TSH RESPONSE TO TRH	LATE PEAK	LATER PEAK
PROLACTIN RESPONSE TO TRH	N l	LATE PEAK
RATE OF CHANGE IN CORE TEMPERATURE	↓	↓

FIG. 10.3. Pituitary end-organ function in patients with simple weight loss and anorexia nervosa. Adapted with permission from "Hypothalamic Dysfunction in Secondary Amenorrhea Associated with Simple Weight Loss," by R. A. Vigersky, A. E. Anderson, R. H. Thompson, and D. I. Loriaux, 1977, *New England Journal of Medicine, 297*, p. 1143. Copyright 1974 Massachusetts Medical Society. Reprinted by permission of *The New England Journal of Medicine*.

are similar to those seen in anorexia, namely, reversion to nocturnal pubertal spiking of gonadotropins. Weight reducing diets have been shown to affect follicular development and progesterone secretion during the leutal phase (Schweiger et al., 1992). The less severe weight loss that occurs in simple dieting, as opposed to anorexia, facilitates reversal of symptoms. Treatment includes weight gain and consequent restoration of eumenorrhea.

One study compared a group of restrained eaters with a group of controls matched for age, age of menarche, absolute height and weight, and body-mass index (expressed as the weight in kilograms divided by the square of the height in meters) and found significant differences in menstrual cyclicity (Schweiger et al., 1992). The restrained eaters showed a high level of concern about physical appearance, reduced caloric intake (23% lower than the controls), avoidance of fat, increased intake of artificial sweeteners and diet products, and increased variability of food intake (suggesting alternating episodes of overeating with semistarvation). Despite this control of food intake, it was found that the maximum adult weight was higher in the restrained eaters than in the controls. The restrained eaters did not manifest any of the psychopathological features associated with eating disorders such as low self-confidence, depression, or fear of intimacy.

In this study, 11 of the 13 women in the control group had normal cycles, whereas only 2 of the 9 women in the restrained group had normal cycles. The luteal phase of the restrained eaters had a reduced or shortened progesterone production. Because luteal phase length has been associated with elevated energy expenditure, the reduction in progesterone secretion may be an energy conservation mechanism.

EXERCISE-INDUCED AMENORRHEA

Altered reproductive function has also been found in women who exercise strenuously, specifically in sports such as running, swimming, and ballet dance. The incidence seems to be linked particularly to the sports that require thinness for athletic success, and hormonal studies have shown that it is the combination of both exercise and dieting to achieve a weight below the ideal level that commonly leads to reversible reproductive dysfunction in women. Bullen et al. (1985) conducted a study on 28 women that investigated the effects of exercise on cyclicity in two groups of women, one that maintained their weight level, and one that lost weight in conjunction with exercising. This study found that the weight-loss group experienced delayed menses and loss of LH surge more frequently than in the weight-maintenance group. Another study found that amenorrheic runners exhibit greater oral control (neglecting to eat even when hungry) and a higher level of aberrant dietary patterns when compared with eumenorrheic runners and particularly to sedentary controls (Myerson et al., 1991).

Exercise-induced reproductive abnormalities generally include delayed menarche, secondary amenorrhea, and irregular cyclicity with prolonged cycles or shortened cycles as a result of diminished luteal phases. Body fatness as a causal mechanism continues to receive wide publicity in the popular press, although numerous cross-sectional studies have established that this factor is probably not causal (Sanborn, Albrecht, & Wagner, 1987). Twenty-two percent body fat is thought to be necessary for maintenance of regular cycles, but regular cycles are seen in athletes with less than 17% body fat. Amenorrheic and eumenorrheic runners have been found to have similar percentages of body fat. Reproductive dysfunction is uncommonly seen in athletes who have a high percentage of body fat, so the weight or body fat probably reflects other metabolic parameters (Cameron, Nobisch, Helmreich, & Parfitt, 1990; Highet, 1989; Sanborn et al., 1987).

Several studies support the observation that athletic women have dietary intakes that are lower than expected for their activity level (Loucks, Mortola, Girton, & Yen, 1989; Marcus et al., 1985; Myerson et al., 1991). Lowered metabolic rates and low T_3 levels, a sign of energy deficiency, occur in this group. Endurance training may be associated with reproductive dysfunction when caloric intake decreases and energy output cannot be met. These experiments also suggest that a physiological paradox exists: A large energy output is not compensated for by increased caloric intake, yet weight loss does not occur. Thus training appears to be associated with increased caloric efficiency and may represent an adaptive syndrome. Initial studies examining energy balance are conflicting. A number of studies found resting metabolic rate (RMR) increases during exercise training program (with an increase in dietary intake), and others have shown no effect of training on RMR; still others have speculated that dietary and intense exercise deplete energy stores, stimulating the body to increase food efficiency (Wilmore et al., 1992). How these adaptive changes tie in with reproductive dysfunction is unclear. The well-documented reductions in GnRH pulses suggest that the GnRH pulse generator may be affected by metabolic fuels. In fact, recent physiologic experiments on normal women suggest that reproductive hormones (measured by LH pulsatility) are not affected in exercising women until nutrition is restricted (Loucks, Brown, King, Thuma, & Verdun, 1995; Loucks & Heath, 1994).

Another pathway that has stimulated studies in the animal model is the possible effect of activation of the hypothalamic pituitary adrenal axis on the GnRH pulse generator. Corticotropin releasing factor (CRF) decreases LH pulses in animals (Petraglia, Vale, & Rivier, 1986; Sapolsky & Krey, 1988; Xiao, Luckhaus, Niemann, & Ferin, 1989). Adrenocorticotrophic hormone (ACTH) and cortisol levels are elevated during exercise, with disturbances of rhythms of both ACTH and cortisol in amenorrheic runners (Fig. 10.4; Loucks & Horvath, 1984; Loucks et al., 1989). These may be

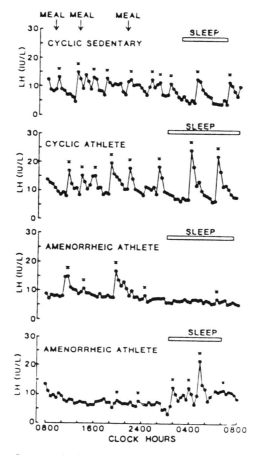

FIG. 10.4.   Exercise influences pulsatile LH activity in women athletes, the severity of the inhibition depending on the strenuousness of the exercise and the particular sensitivity of each individual. With ongoing function of the GnRH pulse generator, the athlete continues to have normal ovulatory menstrual cycles. Menstrual cycle disturbances will parallel the severity of the decrease in pulse frequency. The asterisks (*) indicate pulses as identified by the cluster pulse analysis program using a 2x1 cluster size and balanced T criteria of 2.1. Reprinted from "Alterations in the Hypothalamic-Pituitary-Ovarian and the Hypothalamic-Pituitary-Adrenal Axes in Athletic Women," by A. B. Loucks, J. F. Mortola, L. Girton, and S. S. C. Yen, 1989, *Journal of Clinical Endocrinology and Metabolism, 68*(2), p. 407. © The Endocrine Society. Reprinted with permission.

a side effect of the activation of CRF, which may be the factor that directly suppresses GnRH. The stress of chronic exercise or competition may be the initiating factor that induces reproductive dysfunction. Alternatively, this type of amenorrhea may be different from that seen with an "energy drain" or may be superimposed on it.

Recent literature has also begun to examine the frequency with which eating disorders occur in the athletic population. Eating disorders have recently been recognized as a contributing cause of so-called athletic amenorrhea, and have been recognized as part of a clinical symptom complex called the *female athlete triad*, which consists of amenorrhea, eating disorders, and osteoporosis. Eating disorders may occur initially as chronic dieting to try to lower weight or may progress to full-blown anorexia or bulimia. Lower resting metabolic rates, possibly reflecting an energy conservation mechanism, have also been found in amenorrheic runners when compared with eumenorrheic runners and sedentary controls (Myerson et al., 1991). Interestingly, in this study, the amenorrheic runners had similar percentage of body fat to the eumenorrheic runners, a finding that is supported elsewhere (Loucks, Horvath, & Freedson, 1984) and that suggests that a critical amount of body fat is not necessary for regular menses.

The hormonal changes in exercise-induced amenorrhea are similar to those of anorexia, including reduced LH pulse frequency and mild hypercortisolism (Loucks et al., 1989), but these alterations are probably less severe, and the problem appears to be reversible with exercise reduction, weight gain, or both (Warren, 1991).

IDIOPATHIC HYPOTHALAMIC AMENORRHEA

Most women with idiopathic hypothalamic amenorrhea have major nutritional aberrations and eating disorders, although this may not be obvious without in-depth testing. A study investigating the correlation between abnormal nutrition and idiopathic hypothalamic amenorrhea found that the amenorrheic subjects showed more eating disorders when compared with controls (55% versus 26%; Warren et al., 1994). Similarly, these women had higher scores on a scale of eating behavior, indicating higher occurrence of dieting, bulimia, food preoccupation, and oral control.

The hormonal profile includes normal levels of prolactin (PRL), testosterone, and dehydroepiandrosterone (DHEAS), and low to normal levels of FSH and LH. One study showed that 61% of women with hypothalamic amenorrhea had elevated cortisol levels when compared with controls, which is similar to the profile in patients with eating disorders (Warren et al., 1994).

MEDICAL COMPLICATIONS
OF MENSTRUAL DYSFUNCTION

Long-term medical complications associated with menstrual dysfunction include osteopenia, particularly of trabecular bone. This problem is common in amenorrheic athletes, who during the first years of menstrual dysfunction exhibit a rate of vertebral bone loss similar to that seen in menopause, 5% per year. Scoliosis has been reported in adolescent ballet dancers, but has not been reported in other athletic fields (Warren, 1991). Evidence suggests that anorectic women and ballet dancers have an increased risk of fracture.

In a study in which 27 women with anorexia were followed for 25 months, no significant difference in the change in bone density was found between women who attained 80% of their ideal weight and those who did not, or between groups who did or did not reverse amenorrhea, take calcium or estrogen, or exercise strenuously (Rigotti, Neer, Skates, Herzog, & Nussbaum, 1991). This suggests that recovery from anorexia does not rapidly reverse the loss in cortical bone density.

TREATMENT

Patients with eating disorders should be treated on both psychiatric and nutritional levels. Treatment for amenorrhea includes reducing carotene levels, encouraging weight gain, and reducing exercise. If the patient is reluctant to gain weight or reduce exercise, artificial administration of GnRH, which mimics normal pulsatile secretion, induces puberty, folliculogenesis, ovulation, and menses. Estrogen and progestin therapy has been beneficial in reversing postmenopausal hypoestrogenism, although there is insufficient evidence that this treatment is successful with premenopausal women.

Infertility occasionally results from inadequate luteal phases or amenorrhea and can be treated with ovulation induction with human menopausal gonadotropins. Nutritional and psychiatric treatment should precede treatment for infertility, because women with eating disorders have been shown to gain less weight during pregnancy, experience more complications associated with the pregnancy and with postpartum adjustment, have smaller babies, and have more problems with breastfeeding (Stewart, Raskin, Garfinkel, MacDonald, & Robinson, 1987).

Menstrual irregularities have been found to be reversible when weight is gained. In one study, 73% of normal infertile patients below ideal body weight because of caloric restriction conceived spontaneously on weight gain (Bates, Bates, & Whitworth, 1982). Delayed menarche and weight-loss-related amenorrhea may be the body's reversible and natural form of fertility control in response to an energy deficit, whether from increased energy expenditure, reduced food intake, or both. The !Kung of the Kalahari Desert in South Africa have a birthpeak exactly 9 months after a time when their weight is at a maximum (Vander Walt, Wilmsen, & Jenkins, 1978). This and hormonal studies indicate a naturally occurring and readily reversible suppression of ovulation during the seasons when the women weigh less and are more active. Nutritional insult, whether self-induced or environmentally induced, appears to lead to suppression of the hypothalamic–pituitary–ovarian axis. The exact mechanisms by which undernutrition and energy drain cause menstrual irregularities remain unclear and require further investigation.

REFERENCES

Bates, G. W., Bates, S. R., & Whitworth, N. S. (1982). Reproductive failure in women who practice weight control. *Fertility and Sterility, 37*, 373-378.

Boyar, R. M., Katz, J., Finkelstein, J. W., Kapen, S., Weiner, H., Weitzman E., & Hellman, L. D. (1974). Anorexia nervosa: Immaturity of the 24-hour luteinizing hormone secretory pattern. *New England Journal of Medicine, 291*, 861–865.

Brooks-Gunn, J., Warren, M. P., & Hamilton, L. H. (1986). The relation of eating problems and amenorrhea in ballet dancers. *Medicine and Science in Sports and Exercise, 19*, 41–44.

Bullen, B. A., Skrinar, G. S., Beitins, I. Z., von Mering, G., Turnbull, B. A., & McArthur, J. W. (1985). Induction of menstrual disorders by strenuous exercise in untrained women. *New England Journal of Medicine, 312*, 1349–53.

Cameron, J. L., Nosbisch, C., Helmreich, D. L., & Parfitt, D. B. (1990). Reversal of exercise-induced amenorrhea in female cynomolgus monkeys (Macaca Fascicularis) by increasing food intake [Abstract]. *Endocrine Society Annual Meeting, 72*, 285.

Fries, H., Nillius, S. J., & Pettersson F. (1974). Epidemiology of secondary amenorrhea: A retrospective evaluation of etiology with special regard to psychogenic factors and weight loss. *American Journal of Obstetrics and Gynecology, 118*, 473–479.

Frumar, A. M., Meldrum, D. R., & Judd, H. L. (1979). Hypercarotenemia in hypothalamic amenorrhea. *Fertility and Sterility, 32*, 261–264.

Hamilton, L. H., Brooks-Gunn, J., & Warren, M. P. (1985). Sociocultural influences on eating disorders in professional female ballet dancers. *International Journal of Eating Disorders, 4*, 465–477.

Highet, R. (1989). Athletic amenorrhea: An update on aetiology, complications and management. *Sports Medicine, 7*, 82–108.

Johnson, J., & Whitaker, A. H. (1992). Adolescent smoking, weight changes, and binge-purge behavior: Associations with secondary amenorrhea. *American Journal of Public Health, 82*, 47–54.

Kalucy, R. C., Crisp, A. H., Lacey, J. H., & Harding, B. (1977). Prevalence and prognosis in anorexia nervosa. *Australia and New Zealand Journal of Psychiatry, 11*, 251–257.

Kemmann, E., Pasquale, S. A., & Skaf, R. (1983). Amenorrhea associated with carotenemia. *Journal of American Medical Association, 249*, 926–929.

Kendell, R. E., Hall, D. J., Hailey, A., & Babigan, H. M. (1973). The epidemiology and anorexia nervosa. *Psychological Medicine, 3*, 200–203.

King, M. B. (1986). Eating disorders in general practice. *British Medical Journal, 293*, 1412–1414.

Loucks, A. B., Brown, R., King, K., Thuma, J. R., & Verdun, M. (1995). A combined regimen of moderate dietary restriction and exercise training alters luteinizing hormone pulsatility in regularly menstruating young women [Abstract]. *Endocrine Society Annual Meeting, 77*, 558.

Loucks, A. B., & Heath, E. M. (1994). Induction of low-T3 syndrome in exercising women occurs at a threshold of energy availability. *American Journal of Physiology, 266*, R817–R283.

Loucks, A. B., & Horvath, S. M. (1984). Exercise-induced stress responss of amenorrheic and eumenorrheic runners. *Journal of Clinical Endocrinology and Metabolism, 59*, 1109–1120.

Loucks, A. B., Horvath, S. M., & Freedson, P. S. (1984). Menstrual status and validation of body fat prediction in athletes. *Human Biology, 56*, 383–392.

Loucks, A. B., Mortola, J. F., Girton, L., & Yen, S. S. C. (1989) Alterations in the hypothalamic-pituitary-adrenal axes in athletic women. *Journal of Clinical Endocrinology and Metabolism, 68*, 402–411.

Marcus, R., Cann, C. E., Madvig, P., Minkoff, J., Goddard, M., Bayer, M., Martin, M. C., Gaudiani, L., Haskell, W., & Genant, H. K. (1985). Menstrual function and bone mass in elite women distance runners. *Annals of Internal Medicine, 102*, 158–163.

Marshall, J. C., & Kelch, R. P. (1979). Low dose pulsatile gonadotropin-releasing hormone in anorexia nervosa: A model of human pubertal development. *Journal of Clinical Endocrinology and Metabolism, 49*, 712–718.

Myerson, M., Gutin, B., Warren, M. P., May, M. T., Contento, I., Lee, M., Pi-Sunyer, F. X., Pierson, R. N., & Brooks-Gunn, J. (1991). Resting metabolic rate and energy balance in amenorrheic and eumenorrheic runners. *Medicine and Science in Sports and Exercise, 23*, 15–22.

Petraglia, F., Vale, W., & Rivier, C. (1986). Opioids act centrally to modulate stress-induced decrease in luteinizing hormone in the rat. *Endocrinology, 119*, 2445–2450.

Pirke, K. M., Dogs, M., Fichter, M. M., & Tuschil, R. J. (1988). Gonadotropins, oestradiol, and progesterone during the menstrual cycle in bulimia nervosa. *Clinical Endocrinology, 29*, 265–270.

Rigotti, N. A., Neer, R. M., Skates, S. J., Herzog, D. B., & Nussbaum, S. R. (1991). The clinical course of osteoporosis in anorexia nervosa. *Journal of American Medical Association, 265*, 1133–1138.

Sanborn, C. F., Albrecht, B. H., & Wagner, W. W., Jr. (1987). Athletic amenorrhea: Lack of association with body fat. *Medicine and Science in Sports and Exercise, 19*, 207–212.

Sapolsky, R. M., & Krey, L. C. (1988). Stress-induced suppression of luteinizing hormone concentrations in wild baboons: Role of opiates. *Journal of Clinical Endocrinology and Metabolism, 66*, 722–726.

Schweiger, U., Laessle, R., Pfister, H., Hoehl, C., Schwingenschoegel, M., Schweiger, M., Pirke, K. M. (1987). Diet-induced menstrual irregularities: Effects of age and weight loss. *Fertility and Sterility, 48*, 36–41.

Schweiger, U., Tuschl, R. J., Platte, P., Broocks, A., Laessle, R. G., & Pirke, K. M. (1992). Everyday eating behavior and menstrual function in young women. *Fertility and Sterility, 57*, 771–775.

Smith, N. J. (1980). Excessive weight loss and food aversion in athletes stimulating anorexia nervosa. *Pediatrics, 66*, 139–142.

Stangler, R. S., & Printz, A. M. (1980). DSM-III: Psychiatric diagnosis in a university population. *American Journal of Psychiatry, 137*, 937–940.

Stewart, D. E., Raskin, J., Garfinkel, P. E., MacDonald, O. L., & Robinson, G. E. (1987). Anorexia nervosa, bulimia, and pregnancy. *American Journal of Obstetrics and Gynecology, 157*, 1194–1198.

Stewart, D. E., Robinson, G. E., Goldbloom, D. S., & Wright, C. (1990). Infertility and eating disorders. *American Journal of Obstetrics and Gynecology, 163*, 1196–1199.

Theander, S. (1976). Anorexia nervosa. *Acta Psychiatrica Scandinavica, 214*, 1.

Vander Walt, L. A., Wilmsen, E. N., & Jenkins, T. (1978). Unusual sex hormone patterns among desert dwelling hunter gatherers. *Journal of Clinical Endocrinology and Metabolism, 46*, 658– 663.

Vigersky, R. A., Anderson, A. E., Thompson, R. H., & Loriaux, D. L. (1977). Hypothalamic dysfunction in secondary amennorrhea associated with simple weight loss. *New England Journal of Medicine, 297*, 1141-1145.

Warren, M. P. (1982). The effects of altered nutrition states, stress, and systemic illness on reproduction in women. In J. L. Vaitukaitis (Ed.), *Clinical reproductive neuroendocrinology* (pp. 177–206). New York: Elsevier Biomedicals.

Warren, M. P. (1985a). Anorexia nervosa and related eating disorders. *Clinical Obstetrics and Gynecology, 28*, 588–597.

Warren, M. P. (1985b). When weight loss accompanies amenorrhea. *Contemporary Obstetrics/Gynecology, 25*, 183–190.

Warren, M. P. (1988). Anorexia nervosa. In J. W. Sciarra (Ed.), *Gynecology and obstetrics* (pp. 1–14). Philadelphia, PA: Harper & Row.

Warren, M. P. (1991) Anorexia nervosa and exercise induced amenorrhea. In *Precis IV: An update in obstetrics and gynecology* (pp. 331–333). Washington, DC: American College of Obstetricians and Gynecologists.

Warren, M. P., Holderness C. C., Lesobre, V., Tzen R., Vossoughian, F., & Brooks-Gunn, J. (1994). Hypothalamic amenorrhea and hidden nutritional insults. *Journal of Society for Gynecologic Investigation, 1*, 84–88.

Whitaker, A. H. (1992). An epidemiological study of anorectic and bulimic symtoms in adolescent girls: Implications for pediatricians. *Pediatric Annals, 21*, 752–759.

Wilmore, J. H., Wambsgans, K. C., Brenner, M., Broeder, C. E., Paijmans, I., Volpe, J. A., & Wilmore, K. M. (1992). Is there energy conservation in amenorrheic compared with eumenorrheic distance runners? *Journal of Applied Physiology, 72*, 15–22.

Xiao, E., Luckhaus, J., Niemann, W., & Ferin, M. (1989). Acute inhibition of gonadotropin secretion by CRH in the primate: Are the adrenal glands involved? *Endocrinology, 124*, 1632–1637.

11

The Female Athlete Triad and the Critical Body Fat Hypothesis

David C. Cumming
University of Alberta

Disordered eating, oligomenorrhea, and osteoporosis have been linked together as the female athlete triad. The frequency and nature of disordered eating in relation to exercise are dealt with extensively in this book. In this chapter, we examine the relationship of disordered eating and poor nutritional status to reproductive dysfunction, long considered one of the hallmarks of anorexia nervosa (AN) and only recently associated with disordered eating and endurance training.

The rhythmic patterns of hormonal changes that together form the menstrual cycle are relatively robust despite their apparent complexity. The events and timing of menarche in a normal population are well described. More than 99% of young women have started breast development by age 14; by age 16 more than 99% have begun to menstruate (Zachiarias, Rand, & Wurtman, 1976). In the mature population the prevalence of amenorrhea and oligomenorrhea approximate 2% and 5%, respectively (Drew, 1961; Petterson & Fries, 1973; Sher, 1942). The apparent delay in onset of menstruation and suggestions of high frequency of oligomenorrhea in women athletes caused concern and led to an extensive literature on the topic (for a review see Cumming, 1995).

The endocrine system at rest is characterized by endogenous rhythmic fluctuations in hormone levels. Superimposed on the internal rhythms is the capacity to respond to acute and longer-term changes in the external environment. Thus stress, feeding, food abstinence, trauma, exercise, training, and other stimuli are followed by adjustments in hormonal control that can include overt and concealed alterations in reproductive function. From a teleological perspective, it is reasonable to suggest that reproductive development and reproduction itself will not occur when environmental and physical factors are such that a successful pregnancy outcome is unlikely. It is not surprising, therefore, that physical activity, nutrition, and reproduction have been linked.

Two conflicting theories have developed to explain the mechanism through which disordered eating and/or excessive exercise could cause reproductive dysfunction. The critical body fat hypothesis has been for many years a prime explanation for the reproductive dysfunction that is associated with AN, dietary amenorrhea, and exercise-associated amenorrhea. An alternative concept is that the diminished energy flux and/or specific macronutrient deficits from disordered eating and poor nutrition are directly responsible for oligomenorrhea. Similar discussions over the relative importance of energy stores (in the form of body fat) versus energy flow (in the form of dietary intake, work output, and metabolic rate/thermal responses to diet) are found in literature examining work in women in developing countries and breastfeeding (Lunn, 1994; Panter-Brick & Ellison, 1994).

The role of nutrition and body composition in determining the onset and maintenance of normal reproductive function has been explored extensively in animals (Kirkwood, Cumming, & Aherne, 1987), but ethical constraints on experiments on humans result in studies that are generally indirect and observational. Human studies, however, are consistent in implicating a nutritional component in determining menstrual function. Epidemiological evidence showed that the mean age at menarche declined from the mid-1800s, when consistent records began, until the 1960s or 1970s as more young women entered puberty at an early age (Brown, 1966; Damon, 1974; Tanner, 1962, 1981). The change in age at menarche was accompanied by increased stature clearly apparent in school-age children (Tanner, 1962). Physical size correlates better with age at menarche than chronological age (Frisch, 1972). In circumstances in which poorer nutrition has not engendered accelerated physical growth, average age at menarche has been stable over the past generation (Bojilen & Bentzoin, 1968). When famine and starvation from warfare produced short-term involuntary nutritional stresses, reproductive consequences (amenorrhea or infertility) were seen first in women whose previous nutrition was marginally adequate (Stein & Susser, 1975). That nutrition and/or body composition may affect menarche has been confirmed in different populations (Baanders-Van Halewin & de Ward, 1968; Dreizen, Spirakis, & Stone, 1967; Kantero & Widholm, 1971; Van Noord & Kaaks, 1991; Weir, Dunn, & Jones, 1971; Wolanski, 1968). Low body weight, dieting, weight loss, and reduced body fat are associated with amenorrhea (Fries, Nillius, & Petterson, 1974; Warren, 1973). In this chapter we examine the question of how amenorrhea develops in circumstances of poor nutrition and voluntary self-starvation.

THE CRITICAL BOY FAT HYPOTHESIS

Based on the observations linking poor nutrition with delayed menarcheal age, it was suggested that, even in circumstances in which adequate nutrition is not in question, the age at which menarche occurs is more closely related to body weight than to chronological age (Frisch & Revelle, 1971). However, maturation involves a relative reduction in body water throughout puberty (Fries-Hansen, 1956), suggesting a relative gain in body fat. Total body water and lean and fat body mass were calculated at three pubertal milestones (growth spurt, peak height velocity, and menarche) using a formula based on height and weight (Frisch, Revelle, & Cook, 1973; Mellits & Cheek, 1970). There was a relative increase in body fat compared with lean mass between the initiation of the adolescent growth spurt and menarche (Frisch et al., 1973). The increase in body fat roughly corresponded to the energy requirement of pregnancy and 3 months of breastfeeding, a finding that was considered to have teleological significance (Frisch, 1984). It was also found that late maturers gain fat more slowly than early maturers, again focusing attention on percentage of body fat as a determinant for menarche. Some data supporting the hypothesis have been published. Gonadotropins increase with increasing body fat (Penny, Goldstein, & Frasier, 1978).

Support for an association of low body fat with amenorrhea in women who exercise has been inconsistent. Amenorrheic athletes were lighter, leaner, and had lost more weight following the onset of running than their normally menstruating counterparts (Carlberg, Buckman, Peake, & Riedesel, 1983; Dale, Gerlach, & Wilhite, 1979; Schwartz et al., 1981; Speroff & Redwine, 1979). Others failed to find reduced percentage of body fat (Dale & Goldberg, 1982; Sanborn, Albrecht, & Wagner, 1987; Toriola, 1988; Wakat, Sweeney, & Rogol, 1978). There are method-specific differences in body fat estimates, and differing conclusions can be drawn from the same population depending on the means of calculation (Cumming & Rebar, 1984). It is clear that low body fat is not invariably associated with menstrual irregularity, nor is menstrual irregularity invariably associated with reduced body fat. However, menstrual irregularities are much more common in those sports and activities where low body fat is beneficial (Brooks-Gunn, Burrow, & Warren, 1988; Sanborn, Martin, & Wagner, 1982) even if there is no clear difference within the individual sports activity. It is also apparent that disordered eating is more frequent in the same groups of subjects attempting to initiate and maintain the low body fat.

Four mechanisms through which fat may modify the functioning of the hypothalamic–pituitary–gonadal axis have been postulated (Frisch, 1985). First, fat tissue may influence the conversion of androgens to estrogens, particularly forming estrone from androstenedione (Siiteri & MacDonald, 1973). Estrone levels begin to increase 3 to 6 years before menarche, and the rise is progressive and linear throughout puberty, suggesting that precursor availability may be a more significant drive than the late increase in body fat (Bidlingmaier, Wagner-Barnack, Butenandt, & Knorr, 1973; Gupta, 1975; Saez & Morera, 1973). The second factor suggested was that increasing fat can modify the direction of estrogen metabolism to more or less potent forms (Fishman, Boyar, & Hellman, 1975). These were at nonphysiological extremes of obesity and AN. Third, obese women have diminished sex hormone binding globulin (SHBG) levels (Plymate, Fariss, Bassett, & Majej, 1981). Again, this is a nonphysiological extreme. SHBG levels are lower in pubertal children and adults than in prepubertal children (Forest & Bertrand, 1972; Moll & Rosenfeld, 1979). The transition is gradual, beginning at about 9 to 10 years of age, and the reduction in SHBG is inversely related to the increasing testosterone levels, suggesting that this factor, and not body fat, is responsible for the reduced SHBG levels (Bartsch, Horst, & Derwahl, 1980). Finally, it was felt that the storage of steroids in fat may influence reproduction, but it unclear how this might influence reproductive maturity.

Detailed criticisms of the minimal body fat hypothesis have been published. The basic assumption of a changing age of menarche over time has been questioned (Bullough, 1981). The variability of subjects in Frisch's (1984) own study can be seen from her scattergrams. Others have disputed the repeatability of the data (Billewicz, Fellowes, & Hytten, 1976: Johnston, Roche, Schell, & Wettenhall, 1975), the methodology (Cumming & Rebar, 1984; Reeves, 1979; Trussel, 1978), and the statistical validity of the conclusions (Johnston et al., 1975; Trussel, 1978). The use of the Mellits and Cheek (1970) nomogram for low body weight women, including athletes, is clearly inaccurate (Johnston, 1985). The simplicity of the critical body fat hypothesis is appealing, but its very simplicity in a complex metabolic organism makes it unlikely to be true (Bronson & Manning, 1991). Correlation can only imply causality if there are good supporting evidence and good mechanistic explanations. Girls who go through an early puberty are taller and heavier than their counterparts by six years of age (Garn & Haskell, 1960; Reynolds, 1946). This implies that growth, development, and sexual maturation are determined by a genetic plan that long precedes changes around menarche.

Puberty begins long before the onset of menses, and Warren (1980) showed that not only menarche is delayed with activity, but also early gonadotropin releasing hormone (GnRH)–pituitary axis maturation. The start of puberty is not dependent on the attainment of a specific body composition, although it may be inhibited by voluntary or involuntary malnutrition, or perhaps a relative excess of energy output over intake. Menarche occurs when there is sufficient variability in estrogen levels to permit endometrial build-up and breakdown. The physiological developments required for initiation of puberty precede peak height velocity, fat deposition, and menarche: The increments in circulating sex steroids remain linear during late puberty when peripheral fat deposition occurs. Exogenous sex steroids may cause physical changes, for example, the growth spurt, and deposition of fat in breasts, over the abdomen, and in the buttocks (Lucky et al., 1979). It is tempting to suggest that any change in body fat is a consequence of pubertal endocrine changes rather than a determinant factor.

NUTRITIONAL DEFICIT AS AN ETIOLOGY FOR AMENORRHEA

Abnormal eating patterns have been reported in a high proportion of female athletes (Brooks-Gunn, Warren, & Hamilton, 1987; Rosen, McKeag, Hough, & Curley, 1976; Walberg & Johnston, 1991; Zucker et al., 1985), although there is no unanimity (Borgen & Corbin, 1987; Snead et al., 1992). The accuracy of the standard tools for detecting abnormalities of dietary function and attitudes in this population has been questioned (Snead et al., 1992), and the accuracy of the methodology for tracking dietary intake in free-field conditions is also open to question.

There is evidence that disordered eating may induce reproductive problems through either low caloric intake and/or through macronutrient deficits. Short-term (6-week) vegetarian diets associated with low caloric intake produced a shortening of the menstrual cycle by a mean of 5 days and induced anovulation in the majority of the women (Pirke et al., 1986). Others reported a similar experience (Hill, Garbaczewski, Daynes, & Gaire, 1984). A high frequency of vegetarianism has been reported in female athletes (Brooks, Sanborn, Albrecht, & Wagner, 1984; Slavin, Lutter, & Cushman, 1984). Brooks et al. (1984) reported 83% of amenorrheic athletes had vegetarian diets compared with 13% of eumenorrheic athletic women, whereas Slavin et al. (1984) found only 4 of 36 amenorrheic cyclists had a mixed diet, the remainder being modified vegetarians, excluding red meat from their diet.

The young are particularly susceptible to nutritional insults (Tanner, 1962). Malnutrition reduces gonadotropin levels before puberty and in adults (Beumont, George, Pimstone, & Vinik, 1976; Chakravarty, Sreedhar, Ghosh, & Bulusu, 1982; Kulin, Bwibo, Mutie, & Santner, 1984; Vigersky, Andersen, Thompson, & Loriaux, 1977). Attempts to define specific nutrient deficiency associated with reduced gonadotropin levels have been inconclusive (Steiner, 1987).

Injuries preventing exercise in amenorrheic young ballet dancers precipitated menarche or were followed by resumption of menses without weight change (Warren, 1980), who postulated that an energy drain of exercise may delay menarche or result in amenorrhea without alteration of body composition. A relatively small change in weight of 1 to 2 kilograms around the critical level can regulate menstruation in some athletes (Frisch et al., 1981; Schwartz et al., 1981). It is unclear how such a small alteration in body fat could influence menstrual function. An early study of dietary intake found no difference in caloric intake, but reported a relative but not absolute reduction in protein (Schwartz et al., 1981). Subsequent cross-sectional studies of diet have provided conflicting evidence of macronutrient and caloric deficiencies in amenorrheic and eumenorrheic athletes and sedentary controls. Schweiger et al. (1988), Nelson et al., (1986) and Kaiserauer, Snyder, Sleeper, and Zierath (1989) found caloric deficits in amenorrheic athletes. Deuster et al. (1986) and Kaiserauer, Snyder, Sleeper, and Zierath (1989) reported fat deficiency in athletes; Loucks, Mortola, Girton, and Yen (1989) found dietary fat to be lower in athletes in general, but similar in amenorrheic and eumenorrheic women. Other reported deficits include red meat (Brooks et al., 1984), zinc (Deuster et al., 1986), excess fiber (Lloyd et al., 1987), and meat deficiency (Kaiserauer et al., 1989)

It has been difficult to demonstrate caloric deficits in either eumenorrheic or oligomenorrheic runners. However, dietary intake even in normally menstruating runners does not seem to match the increase in energy output that their activity requires (Broocks et al., 1990; Dahlstrom, Jansson, Nordevand, & Kaijser, 1990; Drinkwater et al., 1984; Loucks et al., 1989; Mulligan & Butterfield, 1990; Myerson et al., 1991; Wilmore et al., 1992). The long-held belief that if dietary intake is constant and energy output is increased, weight will be progressively lost must be open to some question. It may be that, as the requirements for the body to remain efficient become more stringent, reproductive function may be initially compromised and later sacrificed to minimize energy loss.

Caloric intake in the luteal phase of the cycle is increased by 500 calories (Dalvit, 1981), and energy expenditure is increased by 8% to 16% in the luteal phase of the cycle in normally menstruating women, representing somewhat less than the increased intake (Dalvit, 1981; Solomon, Jurzer, & Howes, 1982; Webb, 1986). Suppression of luteal progesterone levels might well be the first of a series of energy saving measures that culminate in total reproductive shutdown. The resting metabolic rate is reduced in states of calorie deprivation (Luke & Schoeller, 1992; Shetty, 1984). Significantly lower resting metabolic rates were observed in amenorrheic runners compared with controls in one study (Myerson et al., 1991); but no difference was found in another (Wilmore et al., 1992). The mechanism of reduced metabolic rate could involve lowered serum tri-iodothyronine levels that have been reported (Myerson et al., 1991). Despite the consistency of the reports suggesting a caloric deficit, it remains to be confirmed that the mechanism of conservation involves changes in the metabolic rate.

CONCLUSION

The relative importance of specific dietary deficiencies, energy balance, and physical activity in the genesis of reproductive change and dysfunction remains to be clarified. Dietary evaluation is an imprecise art, and investigators must balance the difficulty of accuracy versus freedom and lack of interference in energy balance measurements. The conceptual barrier erected by the body fat theory has to be dealt with before progress can finally resolve the complex interrelationships. Clearly nutrition is important in modulating reproductive function, but it is unclear whether the prime messenger is energy reserve or whether disordered eating associated with exercise exerts an effect through changes in energy balance or macronutrient intake, or indeed through changes in micronutrients. How would a nutritional inadequacy involved in the genesis of exercise-associated amenorrhea pass the message to the hypothalamus? Possible metabolic signals could include neurotransmitter precursor deficiencies, alteration in thyroid function, activation of hormones related to stress, alterations in glucoregulatory and other metabolic hormones, changes in steroid metabolism in fat tissue, changes in hepatic metabolism of binding proteins, or an exaggerated peripheral response to exercise in a nutritionally stressed subject. Other sources of materials influencing reproductive function include increased dietary fiber, which is common in athletes (Snow, Schneider, & Barbieri, 1990) and phytoestrogens (plant estrogens), which are common in vegetarian diets (Adlercreutz et al., 1987). The range of possibilities makes this area important for further studies.

REFERENCES

Adlercreutz, H., Hockerstedt, K., Bannwart, C., Hamalainen, E., Fotsis, T., & Ollus, A. (1987). Effect of dietary components, including lignans and phytoestrogens, on enterohepatic circulation and liver metabolism of estrogens and on sex hormone binding globulin (SHBG). *Journal of Steroid Biochemistry, 27,* 1135–1144.

Baanders-Van Halewin, E. A., & de Ward, F. (1968). Menstrual cycles shortly after menarche in European and Bantu girls. *Human Biology, 40*, 314–322.

Bartsch, W., Horst, H-J., & Derwahl, K. M. (1980). Interrelationships between sex-hormone binding globulin and 17-b estradiol, testosterone, 5-a dihydrotestosterone, thyroxine and tri-iodothyronine in prepubertal and pubertal girls. *Journal of Clinical Endocrinology and Metabolism, 50*, 1053–1056.

Beumont, P. J. V., George, G. C. W., Pimstone, B. L., & Vinik, A. I. (1976). Body weight and the pituitary response to hypothalamic releasing hormones. *Journal of Clinical Endocrinology and Metabolism, 43*, 487–496.

Bidlingmaier, F., Wagner-Barnack, M., Butenandt, O., & Knorr, D. (1973). Plasma estrogens in childhood and puberty under physiologic and pathologic conditions. *Pediatric Research, 7*, 901–907.

Billewicz, W. S., Fellowes, H. M., & Hytten, C. A. (1976). Comments on the critical metabolic mass and the age of menarche. *Annals of Human Biology, 3*, 51–59.

Bojilen, K., & Bentzoin, M. (1968). Influence of climate and nutrition on age at menarche: A historical review and a modern hypothesis. *Human Biology, 40*, 69–85.

Borgen, J. S., & Corbin, C. B. P. (1987). Eating disorders among female athletes. *Physican and Sportsmedicine, 15*(2), 89–95.

Bronson, F. H., & Manning, J. L. (1991). The energetic regulation of ovulation: A realistic role for body fat. *Biology of Reproduction, 44*, 945–950.

Broocks, A., Pirke, K. M., Schweiger, U., Tuschl, R. J., Laessle, R. G., Strowitzki, T., Horl, E., Horl, T., Haas, W., & Jeschke, D. (1990). Cyclic ovarian function in recreational athletes. *Journal of Applied Physiology, 68*, 2083–2086.

Brooks, S. M., Sanborn, C. F., Albrecht, B. H., Wagner, W. W., Jr. (1984). Diet in athletic amenorrhea. *Lancet, 1*, 559–560.

Brooks-Gunn, J., Burrow, C., & Warren, M.P. (1988). Attitudes toward eating and body weight in different groups of female adolescent athletes. *International Journal of Eating Disorders, 7*, 749–757.

Brooks-Gunn, J., Warren, M. P., & Hamilton, L. H. (1987). The relation of eating problems and amenorrhea in ballet dancers. *Medicine and Science in Sports and Exercise, 19*, 41–44.

Brown, P. E. (1966). The age at menarche. *British Journal Social and Preventive Medicine, 20*, 9–14.

Bullough, V. L. (1981). Age at menarche: A misunderstanding. *Science, 213*, 365–366.

Carlberg, K. A., Buckman, M. T., Peake, G. T., & Riedesel, M. L. (1983). Body composition of oligo/amenorrheic athletes. *Medicine and Science in Sports and Exercise, 15*, 215–217.

Chakravarty, I., Sreedhar, R., Ghosh, K. K., & Bulusu, S. (1982). Circulating gonadotropin profile in severe cases of protein calorie malnutrition. *Fertility and Sterility, 37*, 650–654

Cumming, D. C. (1995). Hormones and athletic performance. In P. Felig, J. D. Baxter, & L. A. Frohman (Eds.), *Endocrinology and metabolism* (3rd ed., pp. 1837–1885). New York: McGraw-Hill.

Cumming, D. C., & Rebar, R. W. (1984). Lack of consistency in the indirect methods of estimating body fat. *Fertility and Sterility, 41*, 739–742.

Dahlstrom, M., Jansson, E., Nordevand, E., & Kaijser, L. (1990). Discrepancy between estimated energy intake and requirement in female dancers. *Clinical Physiology, 10*, 11–25.

Dale, E., Gerlach, D. H., & Wilhite, A. L. (1979). Menstrual dysfunction in distance runners. *Obstetrics and Gynecolology, 54*, 47–53.

Dale, E., & Goldberg, D. L. (1982). Implications of nutrition in athletes' menstrual cycle irregularity. *Canadian Journal of Applied Sport Science, 7*(2), 74–78, .

Dalvit, S. P. (1981). The effect of the menstrual cycle on patterns of food intake. *American Journal of Clinical Nutrition, 34*, 1811–1815.

Damon, A. (1974). Larger body size and earlier menarche: The end may be in sight. *Social Biology, 21*, 8–11.

Deuster, P. A., Kyle, S. B., Moser, P. B., Vigersky, R. A., Singh, A., & Schoomaker, E. B. (1986). Nutritional intakes and status of highly trained amenorrheic and eumenorrheic women runners. *Fertility and Sterility, 46*, 636–643.

Dreizen, S., Spirakis, C. N., & Stone, R. E. (1967). A comparison of skeletal growth and maturation in undernourished and well nourished girls before and after menarche. *Journal of Pediatrics, 70*, 256–263.

Drew, F. L. (1961). The epidemiology of secondary amenorrhea. *Journal of Chronic Diseases, 14*, 396–401.

Drinkwater, B. L., Nilson, K, Chesnut, C. H., III, Bremner, W. J., Shainholtz, S., Southworth, M. B. (1984). Bone mineral content of amenorrheic and eumenorrheic athletes. *New England Journal of Medicine, 31*, 277–281.

Fishman, J., Boyar, R. M., & Hellman, L. (1975). Influence of body weight on estradiol metabolism in young women. *Journal of Clinical Endocrinology and Metabolism, 41*, 489–491.

Forest, M. G., & Bertrand, J. (1972). Studies of the binding of dihydrotestosterone (17-b-hydroxy-5a androstane-3-one) in human plasma in different physiological conditions and the effect of medroxyprogesterone (17-hydroxy 6-amethyl-4-pregnene-3,20 dione, 17-acetate). *Steroids, 19*, 197–214.

Fries, H., Nillius, S. J., & Petterson, F. (1974). Epidemiology of secondary amenorrhea. *American Journal of Obstetrics and Gynecology, 118*, 473–479.

Fries-Hansen, B. J. (1956). Changes in body water compartments during growth. *Acta Paediatrica, 101*(supplement), 1–67.

Frisch, R. E. (1972). Weight at menarche: Similarity for well nourished and under-nourished girls at differing ages, and evidence for historical constancy. *Pediatrics, 50*, 445–450.

Frisch, R. E. (1984). Body fat, puberty and fertility. *Biological Review, 59*, 161–188.

Frisch, R. E. (1985). Body fat, menarche and reproductive ability. *Seminars in Reproductive Endocrinology, 3*, 45–54.

Frisch, R. E., Gotz-Welbergen, A. V., McArthur, J. W., Albright, T. E., Witschi, J., Bullen, B., Birnholtz, J., Reed, R. B., & Herman, H. (1981). Delayed menarche and amenorrhea of college athletes in relation to age of onset of training. *Journal of the American Medical Association, 246*, 1559–1563.

Frisch, R. E., & Revelle, R. (1971). Height and weight at menarche and hypothesis of critical body weights and adolescent events. *Science, 169*, 397–399

Frisch, R. E., Revelle, R., & Cook, S. (1973). Components of weight at menarche and the initiation of the adolescent growth spurt in girls: Estimated total body water, lean body weight and fat. *Human Biology, 45*, 469–483.

Garn, S. M., & Haskell, J. A. (1960). Fat thickness and developmental status in childhood and adolescence. *American Journal of Diseases of Children, 99*, 746–751.

Gupta, D. (1975). Changes in gonadal and adrenal steroid patterns during puberty. *Clinics in Endocrinology and Metabolism, 4*, 27–56,

Hill, P., Garbaczewski, L., Daynes, G., & Gaire, K. S. (1984). Diet and follicular development. *American Journal of Clinical Nutrition, 39*, 771–777

Johnston, F. E. (1985). Systematic errors in the use of the Mellits–Cheek equation to predict body fat in lean females. *New England Journal of Medicine, 312*, 588–589.

Johnston, F. E., Roche, A. F., Schell, L. M., & Wettenhall, N. B. (1975). Critical weight at menarche: Critique of a hypothesis. *American Journal of Diseases of Children, 129*, 19–23.

Kaiserauer, S., Snyder, A. C., Sleeper, M., & Zierath, J. (1989). Nutritional, physiological and menstrual status of distance runners. *Medicine and Science in Sports and Exercise, 21*, 120–125.

Kantero, R-L., & Widholm, O. (1971). The age of menarche in Finnish girls in 1969. *Acta Obstetrica et Gynaecologica Scandanavica, Supplement 14*, 7–18.

Kirkwood, R. F., Cumming, D. C., & Aherne, F. X. (1987). Nutrition and puberty in the female. *Proceedings of the Society of Nutrition, 46*, 177–192.

Kulin, H. E., Bwibo, N., Mutie, D., & Santner, J. S. (1984). Gonadotropin excretion during puberty in malnourished children. *Journal of Pediatrics, 105*, 325–328.

Lloyd, T., Buchanan, J. R., Bitzer, S., Waldman, C. J., Myers, C., & Ford, B. G. (1987). Interrelationships of diet, athletic activity, menstrual status and bone density among collegiate women. *American Journal of Clinical Nutrition, 46*, 681–684

Loucks, A. B., Mortola, J. F., Girton, L., & Yen, S. S. (1989). Alterations in the hypothalamic-pituitary-ovarian and the hypothalamic-pituitary-adrenal axes in athletic women. *Journal of Clinical Endocrinology and Metabolism, 68*, 402–411.

Lucky, A. W., Marynick, S. P., Rebar, R. W., Cultcr, G. B., Glen, M., Johnsonbaugh, R. E., & Loriaux, D. L. (1989). Replacement ethinyl oestradiol therapy for gonadal dysgenesis. *Acta Endocrinologica, 91*, 519–528.

Luke, A., & Schoeller, D. A. (1992). Basal metabolic rate, fat free mass and body cell mass during energy restriction. *Metabolism, 41*, 450–456.

Lunn, P. G. (1994). Lactation and other metabolic loads affecting lactation. *Annals of the New York Academy of Science, 709*, 77–85.

Mellits, E. D., & Cheek, D. B. (1970). The assessment of body water and fatness from infancy to adulthood. In J. Brozek (Ed.), Physical growth and body composition. *Monographs of the Society for Research in Child Development, 35*(7), 12–26.

Moll, G. W. Jr., & Rosenfeld, R. L. (1979). Testosterone binding and free plasma androgens under physiological conditions: Characterization by flow dialysis technique. *Journal of Clinical Endocrinology and Metabolism, 49*, 730–736.

Mulligan, K., & Butterfield, G. E. (1990). Discrepancies between estimated energy intake and expenditure in physically active women. *British Journal of Nutrition, 64*, 23–36.

Myerson, M., Gutin, B., Warren, M. P., May, M. T., Contento, I., Lee, M., Pi-Sunyer, F. X., Pierson, R. N., & Brooks-Gunn, J. (1991). Resting metabolic weight and energy balance in amenorrheic and eumenorrheic runners. *Medicine and Science in Sports and Exercise, 23*, 15–22.

Nelson, M. E., Fisher, E. C., Catsos, P. D., Meredith, C. N., Turksoy, R. N., & Evans, W. J. (1986). Diet and bone status in amenorrhic runners. *American Journal of Clinical Nutrition, 43*, 910–916.

Panter-Brick, C., & Ellison, P. T. (1994). Seasonality of workloads and ovarian function in Nepali women. *Annals of the New York Academy of Science, 709*, 234–235.

Penny, R., Goldstein, I. P., & Frasier, R. D. (1978). Gonadotropin excretion and body composition. *Pediatrics, 61*, 294–300.

Petterson, F., & Fries, H. (1973). Epidemiology of secondary amenorrhea. *American Journal of Obstetrics and Gynecolology, 117*, 80–86.

Pirke, K. M., Schweiger, U., Laessle, R., Dickhaut, B., Schweiger, M., & Waechtler, M. (1986). Dieting influence on the menstrual cycle, vegetarian versus nonvegetarian diet. *Fertility and Sterility, 46*, 1083–1088.

Plymate, S. R., Fariss, B. L., Bassett, M. L., & Majej, L. (1981). Obesity and its role in polycystic ovarian syndrome. *Journal of Clinical Endocrinology and Metabolism, 52*, 1246–1248.

Reeves, J. (1979). Estimating fatness. *Science, 204*, 881.

Reynolds, E. L. (1946). Sexual maturation and the growth of fat, muscle and bone in girls. *Childhood Development 17*, 121–127.

Rosen, L. W., McKeag, D. B., Hough, D. O., & Curley, V. (1986). Pathogenic weight control behavior in female athletes. *Physician Sportsmedicine, 14*(1), 79–86.

Saez, J. M., & Morera, A. M. (1973). Plasma oestrogens before puberty in humans. *Acta Paediatrica Scandanavica, 62*, 84.

Sanborn, C. F., Albrecht, B. H., & Wagner, W. W., Jr. (1987). Athletic amenorrhea: Lack of association with body fat. *Medicine and Science in Sports and Exercise, 19*, 207–212.

Sanborn, C. F., Martin, B. J., & Wagner, W. W. (1982). Is athletic amenorrhea specific to runners? *American Journal of Obstetrics and Gynecology, 143*, 859–861.

Schwartz, B., Cumming, D. C., Riordan, E., Selye, M., Yen, S. S. C., & Rebar, R. W. (1981). Exercise associated amenorrhea: A distinct entity? *American Journal of Obstetrics and Gynecology, 114*, 662–670.

Schweiger, U., Laessle, R., Schweiger, M., Herrman, F., Riedel, W., & Pirke, K. M. (1988). Caloric intake stress and menstrual function in athletes. *Fertility and Sterility, 49*, 447–450.

Sher, N. (1942). Causes of delayed menstruation and its treatment. *British Medical Journal, 1*, 347–349.

Shetty, P. S. (1984). Adaptive changes in basal metabolic rate and lean body mass in chronic undernutrition. *Human Nutrition and Clinical Nutrition, 38C*, 443–451.

Siiteri, P. K., & MacDonald, P. C. (1973). Role of extraglandular estrogen in human endocrinology, In S. R. Geiger, F. R. Astwood, & R. O. Greep (Eds.), *Handbook of physiology* (pp. 615–629). Washington, DC: American Physiological Society.

Slavin, J., Lutter J., & Cushman, S. (1984). Amenorrhea in vegetarian athletes. *Lancet, 2*, 1474–1475.

Snead, D. B., Stubbs, C. C., Weltman, J. Y., Evans, W. S., Veldhuis, J. D., Rogol, A. D., Teates, C. D., & Weltman, A. (1992). Dietary patterns, eating behaviors, and bone mineral density in women runners. *American Journal of Clinical Nutrition, 56*, 705–711.

Snow, R. C., Schneider, J. L., & Barbieri, R. I. (1990). High dietary fibre and low saturated fat intake in among oligomenorrheic undergraduates. *Fertility and Sterility, 54*, 632–637.

Solomon, S. J., Jurzer, M. S., & Howes, D. (1982). Menstrual cycle and basal metabolic rate in women. *American Journal of Clinical Nutrition, 36*, 611–616.

Speroff, L., & Redwine, D. B. (1979). Exercise and menstrual dysfunction. *Physician and Sportsmedicine, 8*(5), 42–52.

Stein, Z., & Susser, M. (1975). Fertility, fecundity, famine: Food rations in the Dutch famine 1944/5 have a causal relationship to fertility and probably to fecundity. *Human Biology, 47*, 131–154.

Steiner, R. A. (1987). Nutritional and metabolic factors in the regulation of reproductive hormone secretion in the primate. *Proceedings of the Nutrition Society, 46*, 159–175.

Tanner, J. M. (1962). *Growth at adolescence* (2nd ed.). Philadelphia, PA: Blackwell Scientific.

Tanner, J. M. (1981). Menarcheal age. *Science, 214*, 614.

Toriola, A. L. (1988). Survey of menstrual function in young Nigerian athletes. *International Journal of Sports Medicine, 9*, 29–34.

Trussel, J. (1978). Menarche and fatness: A re-examination of the critical body composition hypothesis. *Science, 200*, 1506–1509.

Van Noord, P. A. H., & Kaaks, R. (1991). The effect of wartime conditions and the 1944 "Dutch Famine" on recalled menarcheal age in participants of the DOM breast cancer screening program. *Annals of Human Biology, 18*, 57–70.

Vigersky, R. A., Andersen, A. E., Thompson, R. H., & Loriaux, D. L. (1977). Hypothalamic dysfunction in secondary amenorrhea associated with simple weight loss. *New England Journal of Medicine, 297*, 1141–1145.

Wakat, D. K., Sweeney, K. A., & Rogol, A. D. (1978). Reproductive system function in women cross country runners. *Medicine and Science in Sports and Exercise, 14*, 263–269.

Walberg, J. L., & Johnston, C. S. (1991). Menstrual function and eating behavior in female recreational weight lifters and competitive body builders. *Medicine and Science in Sports and Exercise, 23*, 30–36.

Warren, M. P. (1973). Clinical and metabolic features of anorexia nervosa. *American Journal of Obstetrics And Gynecology, 117*, 435–449.

Warren, M. P. (1980). The effects of exercise on pubertal progression and reproductive function in girls. *Journal of Clinical Endocrinology and Metabolism, 51*, 1150–1157.

Webb, P. (1986). 24 hour energy expenditure and the menstrual cycle. *American Journal of Clinical Nutrition, 44*, 614–619.

Weir, J., Dunn, J. E., Jr., & Jones, E. G. (1971). Race and age at menarche. *American Journal of Obstetrics and Gynecology, 111*, 594–596.

Wilmore, J. H., Wambsgans, K. C., Brenner, M., Broeder, C. E., Paijmans, I., Volpe, J. A., & Wilmore, K. M. (1992). Is there energy conservation in amenorrheic compared with eumenorrheic distance runners? *Journal of Applied Physiology, 72*, 15–22.

Wolanski, N. (1968). Environmental modification of human form and function. *Annals of the New York Academy of Science, 134*, 826–840.

Zacharias, L., Rand, W. M., & Wurtman, R. J. (1976). A prospective study of sexual development and growth in American girls: The statistics of menarche. *Obstetrical and Gynaecological Survey, 31*, 325-336.

Zucker, P., Avener, J., Bayder, S., Brotman, A., Moore, K., & Zimmerman, J. (1985). Eating disorders in young athletes. *Physician and Sportsmedicine, 13*(11), 89–106.

12

The Effects of Food Restriction and Training on Male Athletes

Diane G. Symbaluk
University of Alberta

This chapter addresses the implications of combining athletic training with food restriction for anorexia and associated endocrine problems in men. Epling and Pierce's (1991) theory of activity anorexia suggests that eating problems occur with a high frequency in people who combine dieting with intense exercise. Amateur wrestlers are a predominantly male athletic group that engage in food restriction while exercising, placing themselves at considerable risk for anorexia. The negative effects of training and dietary practices may be pronounced in wrestlers who compete in low-weight categories because they have less than ideal body masses to begin with. Wrestlers who have little or no experience with the sport may also be at increased risk if they are unable to adjust physiologically to weight cycling methods and strenuous exercise regimes.

ATHLETES AND ANOREXIA

Anorexia nervosa (AN) is a psychological term used to describe individuals who reduce their food intake to alarming levels in order to lose weight. Supplementing a reduction in food intake, use of laxatives, vomiting, and exercise may be employed to enhance weight reduction, even to the point of starvation. Epling and Pierce (1988) argue that AN as a diagnostic category incorporates a broad spectrum of individuals, some of whose conditions may be better understood from a more specific functional category.

Activity anorexia is one such classification that refers to a condition in which loss of appetite is induced through physical activity. Paradoxically, as individuals of normal to low body weight increase their level of exercise, their appetite declines. Lowered food intake leads to a reduction in body weight. As a person loses weight, the value of exercise and level of activity increases, initiating a reciprocal, exercised-based starvation cycle termed activity anorexia (Epling & Pierce, 1988).

An involvement in performing arts or sports that require thin physiques (e.g., gymnastics, ballet dancing) or use weight classification systems (e.g., boxing, wrestling) may foster motivational conditions that result in activity anorexia. Increasing physical activity and dieting are techniques used by athletes to shed unwanted pounds in an attempt to reach a desired weight or improve performance. Occasionally, food restriction may be combined with excessive exercise in a way that results in anorexia (Epling & Pierce, 1991).

Garner and Garfinkel (1980) examined risk for anorexia in a group of female ballet dancers, fashion models, and university students. Ballet dancers are required to maintain lean physiques while engaged in highly competitive, intense physical training. Models also compete with one another and must maintain low weights, but they are not required to exercise. Finally, university students may compete with one another, but they do not have to diet or exercise excessively. According to Epling and Pierce's (1991) theory, risk of anorexia should be greatest in ballet dancers, followed by models, then university students.

In accordance with these predictions, scores on the Eating Attitudes Test (EAT)[1] place ballet dancers at greatest risk for anorexia, followed by models and students. Almost 40% of the 69 ballet dancers in Garner and Garfinkel's (1980) study were classified as being at risk, and 12 of these were subsequently diagnosed as exhibiting anorectic symptoms. Only 4 (7%) of the fashion models and none of the university students were diagnosed with anorexia. These findings suggest that a requirement to stay thin and maintain a high level of exercise can promote anorexia in females.

Although anorexia is far more prevalent in females that in males, it is not exclusive to this group. The low prevalence rate of AN among males in general may reflect reluctance to obtain help for eating problems. Even when males seek help, AN often goes unrecognized by clinicians because of female-specific inclusion criteria such as presence of amenorrhea (Scott, 1986). Not surprisingly, research on risk of anorexia in male subgroups is lacking. Activity anorexia, however, is not gender-specific, and all who combine exercise and dieting are at risk for the disorder.

Racing jockeys, for example, constitute a predominantly male subgroup at risk for anorexia due to a low body weight requirement. Low weight is essential for employment and is often the most important criterion of success in this profession.

---

[1]The Eating Attitudes Test (EAT) is a 40-item self-report questionnaire developed by Garner and Garfinkel (1979) as an instrument for assessing risk for AN. The EAT contains a range of items characteristic of anorectics, including "Find myself preoccupied with food" or "Avoid eating when I am hungry." Scores for the EAT range from 0–120, with 30 or greater indicating a high risk for AN.

King and Mezey (1987) examined eating attitudes, body weights, and risk of anorexia in a group of male jockeys. Findings indicated that jockeys were 13% to 21% below ideal weight relative to matched standards. In addition, scores on Garner, Olmstead, and Garfinkel's (1982) EAT placed this group at high risk for AN.

Detailed interviews with a subsample of jockeys revealed a preoccupation with weight and weight-loss behaviors. Self-reported weight reduction methods correspond to those frequently used by diagnosed anorectics including excessive food restriction, strenuous exercise, abuse of laxatives and diuretics, and self-induced vomiting. Although activity levels and food intake were not directly measured, all but one jockey reported the use of strenuous exercise in conjunction with dietary restriction. Racing jockeys are subject to weight-related pressures analogous to those experienced by female fashion models. As a result, jockeys may be a male subgroup that shows a high incidence of activity anorexia, and future investigations are warranted in this regard.

Apart from an emphasis on low body weight, some sports necessarily entail high levels of physical activity that may induce activity anorexia in males. Katz (1986) reported two case studies involving male runners who developed anorexia following increases in level of exercise. Psychological traits associated with anorexia, including a preoccupation with food and a fear of becoming fat, followed rather than proceeded weight loss and strenuous exercise in these runners (Katz, 1986).

Yates, Leehey, and Shisslak (1983) compared interview responses from male long-distance runners whose training consisted of running at least 50 miles a week with those of adolescent women diagnosed with AN. Although it is unclear whether anorectic symptoms in runners existed prior to training or developed as a result of intense exercise, Yates et al. (1983) reported similarities in personality traits between the two groups including a preoccupation with food and body weight. Runners and anorectics also behaved in similar ways by adhering to strict diets and by increasing exercise levels following lapses in diet regimes. These studies suggest that extreme exercise, alone or in conjunction with weight loss, may trigger eating disorders among runners. Although excessive exercise has been noted in individuals with anorexia, it has not been given much significance in the etiology of eating disorders.

A STUDY OF AMATEUR WRESTLERS

Olympic-style wrestling is one the few male-dominated sports that requires rapid weight loss in conjunction with intense physical exercise. Weight loss is achieved primarily through food restriction prior to tournament weigh-ins, a period when wrestlers are also increasing their levels of physical activity. Wrestlers frequently compete in tournaments according to weight classes and are encouraged to engage in food and fluid restriction in order to "make weight."

Making weight (also called weight-cycling) includes attempts to lose body fat and water quickly to achieve a lower than average weight prior to a tournament weigh-in. The average wrestler fasts for 20 hours prior to a weigh-in and loses 3.2

kilograms (Oppliger, Landry, Foster, & Lambrecht, 1993). Although the benefits of this practice are questionable, most wrestlers and coaches believe that competing in a lower weight class gives an otherwise heavier wrestler a strength advantage over an opponent who may not have made weight prior to the match. In this case, the opponent would be competing at his regular or standard weight.

One risk of combining food restriction with excessive exercise involves generating eating disorders among wrestlers. Enns, Drewnowski, and Grinker (1987) examined the risk for sports-induced eating disorders by comparing male swimmers and Nordic skiers with a group of wrestlers on measures of body composition, caloric intake, and attitudes toward dieting at the beginning and end of the athletic season. Although all groups engaged in intense physical exercise on a regular basis, only wrestlers were required to lose weight throughout the season. All the athletes reduced food intake from fall to winter, but self-reported daily caloric intake and body weight was lowest for wrestlers from the start of the season. Moreover, wrestlers' total caloric intake at the end of the season ($M = 2125 \pm 203$ kcal) was well below population standards for young adult males, which range from 2,500 to 3,300 kcal.

In terms of attitudes toward dieting, wrestlers scored higher than skiers and swimmers on a questionnaire measuring restraint from eating; this difference was even more pronounced at the end of the season. Wrestlers also scored higher than swimmers and skiers on the EAT (administered at the end of the season only). Importantly, four of the wrestlers but none of the other athletes scored more than 30 on the EAT, showing a high risk for anorexia.

In addition to developing an eating disorder such as anorexia, wrestlers are at increased risk for hormonal disturbances as a result of combining food restriction with exercise. Female athletes often show hormonal disturbances associated with menstrual irregularities such as delays or interruptions in menses (Frisch et al., 1981; Frisch, Wyshank, & Vincent, 1980). Evidence is also accumulating that suggests male athletes undergo parallel hormonal changes as a result of training requirements. For example, testosterone levels in wrestlers may be lowered as a result of excessive weight loss and/or intense exercise (Strauss, Lanese, & Malarkey, 1985; Symbaluk, 1990; Wheeler, McFadyen, Symbaluk, Pierce, & Cumming, 1992).

Strauss et al. (1985) examined the effects of competitive training on several measures of endocrine function in a group of wrestlers. Testosterone levels were lower than average for individuals of comparable age during the competition season, but the levels recovered during the posttraining period. Intense physical activity negatively affected testosterone levels, and this effect may have been exacerbated by low body weight.

Wheeler et al. (1992) also investigated changes in serum testosterone and cortisol levels in amateur wrestlers during training and competition periods. Results indicated that in general testosterone levels were low, whereas serum cortisol levels were high relative to standards. Testosterone decreased even further during heavy training and competition periods, whereas cortisol increased with training but showed no specific change at time of competition. The results for testosterone accord with earlier findings reported by Strauss et al. (1985) and parallel findings for hormonal changes in female athletes.

This study[2] was designed to examine whether or not the adverse effects of combining food restriction with intense training are more pronounced in wrestlers who have little or no experience in the sport. Novices are relatively new to the sport and thus have little opportunity to adjust to imposed weight cycling and training schedules prior to competitions. In addition, the effects of diet and exercise are expected to be more noticeable in low-weight wrestlers. Finally, novice wrestlers in low-weight classes may constitute a subgroup of wrestlers that show the greatest risk for endocrine problems and/or anorexia.

Methods

The design was a 2 × 2 repeated-measures analysis of variance. There were two levels of wrestling experience (novice or senior) and two levels of weight class (high or low) with four phases of training (pretraining, training, precompetition, and postcompetition), the repeated factor.

Sixteen male wrestlers between the ages of 15 and 23 years were classified by wrestling experience into novice or senior categories. Senior wrestlers were nearly 3 years older ($M = 19.4 \pm 2.4$) than novices ($M = 16.6 \pm 1.2$), and were involved in the sport for twice as long ($M = 7.0 \pm .4$ vs. $M = 3.5 \pm$ years). Based on their coach's report, novice wrestlers were expected to make weight for twice as many matches as seniors ($M = 8.8 \pm 1.7$; $M = 4.4 \pm 2.7$).

Wrestlers were also classified as high or low in weight class. High-weight class wrestlers weighed between 67.0 and 94.0 kilograms, and low-weight class athletes weighed from 49.0 to 65.0 kilograms. There were 4 wrestlers in each of the wrestling experience categories (novice, senior) by weight class categories (high, low).

Throughout a season, wrestlers engage in various cycles of food restriction combined with intense training to prepare for competitions. This study examines the first four-stage weight cycle in a wrestling club. A baseline phase represented the postsummer start-up period, during which athletes have not engaged in food restriction or excessive exercise. Several dependent measures were taken. A measure of food intake could not be obtained for this phase because wrestlers were unable to complete diet diaries reliably without detailed instruction.

In the 4-week training phase that followed the baseline, wrestlers met for 2-hour workouts 5 days a week. Each workout involved warm-up exercises, practice in wrestling holds and techniques, games to develop agility and strength, running and sprinting, simulated wrestling matches, and warm-down exercises. Generally, physical activity was higher than baseline, but there was no requirement to restrict food intake. Most measures were taken once a week, and a 4-week average represented the effects of training on wrestlers. Food intake was measured every second week for a 3-day period (2 days during the week, 1 on the weekend).

The third stage was a 2-week precompetition phase (precomp) in which wrestlers continued training but were also encouraged to reach their preferred competition weight. Most wrestlers attempted to lose weight by fasting, dehydrating, and/or

[2]The information presented in this section includes highlights from research conducted for an honors thesis on activity anorexia and its implications for amateur wrestlers (Symbaluk, 1990).

sweating excessively by wearing many layers of clothing during practice. Efforts to prepare for competition also included intensified training during practice and increased involvement in physical activities outside of wrestling, such as cycling or swimming. Measures were based on a 2-week average except for food intake, which was based on 3 diet diaries filled out during the second week of this phase.

The final phase was a 2-week postcompetition period (postcomp) similar to the training stage, with regular workouts but no requirement to restrict food intake. Measures were based on a 2-week average with the exception of food intake, which was calculated from 3 diet diaries, starting 5 days after competition.

Dependent variables included body mass, ideal body mass, testosterone levels, food intake, and EAT-26 scores. Indices of body mass and ideal body mass were calculated for each wrestler during the pretraining phase. Body mass (BM) was calculated using the formula, $BM = w/h^2$, where w is the actual body weight and h is the height. Ideal body mass was calculated by comparing body mass with standardized body mass indexes given in the 1983 Metropolitan Height and Weight Tables.[3] Wrestlers' actual body mass was divided by the midpoint of the tabled value (based on body frame and height) and multiplied by 100. A person whose body mass matched the standard would have an ideal body mass of 100%, whereas deviations would be represented by scores that were above or below 100.

Testosterone levels were obtained from 10-ml blood samples taken biweekly during each of the four training phases. Blood samples were collected by venipuncture and centrifuged to separate serum. Samples were then stored at -20°C and analyzed using standard radioimmunoassay procedures.

In order to measure food intake, diet diary booklets were distributed to the wrestlers. Participants underwent a comprehensive training session wherein they were taught to complete the dietary information reliably. Each diary was divided into 6 eating periods consisting of morning meal, midmorning snack, midday meal, afternoon snack, evening meal, and evening snack. Adjacent columns on the diary forms allowed for detailed report of the amount eaten (entered in units such as ounce or number) or a description of the item (such as brand name, type of flavor, and method of cooking). Food intake was measured every 2 weeks. For each week three diaries were completed, two on weekdays and one on the weekend. Completed diaries were coded in terms of the caloric content in kilocalories using conversion tables (Reed, 1980). The mean number of kilocalories consumed was determined for each of the training phases previously described.

Attitudes toward dieting and food were also measured during pre- and postcompetition phases using Garner et al.'s (1982) 26-item EAT-26. Possible scores for the EAT-26 range from 0 to 78, with individuals at risk for AN scoring above 20.

Findings and Discussion

Findings show that wrestlers in the low-weight class had lower body masses ($M = 21.4 \pm 1.7$) than those in the high-weight class ($M = 24.0 \pm 2.7$), $F(1, 12) = 13.31$,

---

[3]It is appropriate to compare this sample with a male adult population (depicted in the Metropolitan Tables) because the mean age for wrestlers was 18 ± 2.3 years.

$p = .003$. In addition, novice wrestlers had lower ($M = 21.0 \pm 1.6$) body masses than seniors ($M = 24.4 \pm 2.3$), $F(1, 12) = 20.81$, $p = .0007$. There were no significant interactions.

Results for ideal body mass also indicated two main effects. Novice wrestlers-maintained less than ideal body masses ($M = 92.54 \pm 7.6$) relative to seniors who exceeded ideal body mass ($M = 105.0 \pm 10.0$), $F(1, 12) = 32.97$, $p = .0001$. Similarly, low-weight wrestlers had less than ideal body masses ($M = 91.4 \pm 6.8$), whereas those in the high-weight class were above ideal ($M = 106.0 \pm 9.0$), $F(1, 12) = 17.90$, $p = .0001$. The greatest deviations from ideal body mass were found in the high-weight senior group and the low-weight novice condition (see Fig. 12.1). Importantly, inexperienced (novice) wrestlers of low-weight were 14% below ideal body mass. This subgroup may be most adversely affected by the diet and training practices required in the sport.

Although analysis of variance indicated no main effect of weight class (high, low) on testosterone levels, actual body weight (averaged over training phases) was positively correlated with testosterone, $r = .53$, $p = .03$. Lower body weights are associated with lower levels of testosterone, which suggests that body weight is implicated in the regulation of testosterone. There was also a marginal main effect of wrestling experience on testosterone levels, $F(1, 12) = 4.29$, $p = .06$, which implies that negative effects of exercise on testosterone may be more pronounced in novices.

Further inspection of the means and standard deviations for testosterone levels indicated that the conditions lacked homogeneity of variance, and no appropriate linear transformation could be obtained. Nonparametric analyses revealed a significant interaction effect of training period and wrestling experience (but not body weight) on testosterone level, $\chi^2 = 7.74$, $df = 3$, $p = .05$. Senior wrestlers maintained testosterone levels over training phases, $Z = -1.70$, $p = .04$, whereas testosterone in

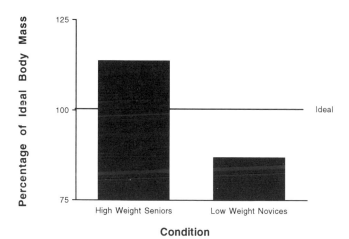

FIG. 12.1. Deviations from ideal body mass by wrestling subgroup. Ideal body mass is denoted as 100. Deviations are scores above or below ideal body mass.

novices declined during the precompetition phase, $Z = 1.72$, $p = .04$ (one-tailed). Figure 12.2 shows this interaction.

To determine if the decline in testosterone for novice wrestlers was due to training or lack of physical maturity, wrestlers were classified as younger (between the ages of 15 and 17) or older (18 to 23 years). Subsequent analyses showed that testosterone levels during precompetition did not differ between older and younger wrestlers, implicating training effects as a function of inexperience rather than physical maturity due to age. This contention is further supported by a positive correlation between testosterone levels and number of years in the sport, $r = .76$, $p = .0007$.

Like the findings for testosterone, results for food intake indicated differences by training phase, $F(2, 24) = 17.90$, $p = .0001$. Figure 12.3 shows the average caloric intake over training phases. Comparison of the means showed that the training and postcompetition phases did not differ; however, taken together these conditions differed from the precompetition phase, $F(1, 12) = 49.31$, $p = .0001$. Thus the extra effort of precompetition training lowered food intake for all wrestlers. All wrestlers restricted food intake prior to competition, but food intake recovered following competition to precompetition levels.

In accordance with the results for food intake, EAT scores did not differ by wrestling subgroups. EAT-26 scores were higher ($M = 9.13 \pm 8.2$) during the precompetition phase and lower ($M = 4.94 \pm 5.6$) during postcompetition when food intake recovered. Wrestlers' eating attitudes followed changes in food consumption, suggesting that these scores are more reflective of behaviors in relation to food than stable attitudes toward food. Although EAT scores were generally low in this sample, 2 of the wrestlers (or 12.5% of the sample) scored 30 and 25, thus falling in the range of those at risk for anorexia.

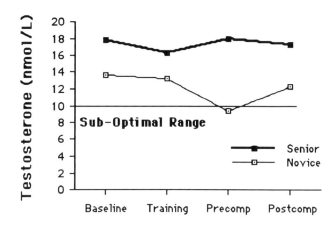

FIG. 12.2. Effects of wrestling experience and training phase on testosterone levels. Testosterone is measured in nmol/L. Testosterone for senior wrestlers is represented by the bold line and testosterone in novices is shown by the light line. Training phases (baseline, training, precompetition and postcompetition) are indicated by squares.

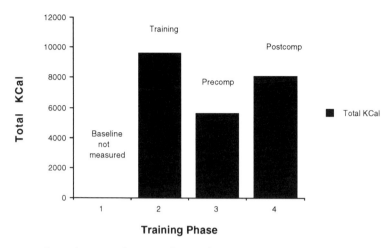

FIG. 12.3.   Effects of training phase on caloric intake in wrestlers. Caloric intake is measured in kilocalories. Training phases are as follows: 1 = *baseline*, 2 = *training*, 3 = *precompetition*, 4 = *postcompetition.*

CONCLUSION

All wrestlers restrict their food intake while exercising extensively. Food restriction occurs because athletes and their coaches believe that dieting is necessary in order to make competition weight. Within defined boundaries, some researchers claim that this practice does not have harmful implications (Morgan, 1970; Singer & Weiss, 1968; Smith, 1984; Steen & Brownell, 1990; Tcheng & Tipton, 1973; Woods, Wilson, & Masland, 1988).

The findings reported in this study, however, suggest the opposite. Testosterone levels were negatively affected by food restriction and exercise-based training in novices, a group that maintains less than ideal body mass. Findings for testosterone changes in novice wrestlers may be analogous to research on females that shows menstrual irregularities resulting from leanness, diet, and/or excessive exercise (Frisch, 1988; Frisch et al., 1980, 1981). Strenuous exercise, for example, reduced luteinizing hormone (LH) in female long-distance runners even when body weight was controlled (Cumming, Vickovic, Wall, Fluker, & Belcastro, 1985). A similar process may be evident in novice wrestlers whose testosterone levels dropped to subnormal ranges. Importantly, hormonal changes occurred during the precompetition stage of training where exercise was intense.

Evidence is accumulating that food restriction and excessive exercise combine to affect physiology adversely in male athletes (Strauss et al., 1985; Wheeler et al., 1992; Wheeler, Wall, Belcastro, Conger, & Cumming, 1986; Wheeler, Wall, Belcastro, & Cumming, 1984). The findings reported here support this research and provide an account of male subgroups at risk for anorexia, with particular emphasis on novice wrestlers. Future investigations of activity anorexia could focus on individuals who combine dieting with exercise, particularly those who are inexperienced with rigorous training and weight reduction schedules.

ACKNOWLEDGMENTS

I wish to express gratitude to individuals who have provided much needed support and advice. My honors thesis and this book chapter could not have been completed without the encouragement of these individuals. Very special thanks go to Dr. Garry Wheeler, whose friendship, knowledge, time, and support played an integral role in this study. I would like to extend my appreciation and gratitude to Dr. W. David Pierce, who supervised my thesis project. Finally, special thanks goes to Dr. W. Frank Epling for reading and rereading this manuscript, providing valuable comments and suggestions along the way.

REFERENCES

Cumming, D. C., Vickovic, M. M., Wall, S. R., Fluker, M. R., & Belcastro, A. N. (1985). The effect of acute exercise on pulsatile release of lutenizing hormone in women runners. *American Journal of Obstetrics and Gynecology, 141*, 482–485.

Enns, M. P., Drewnowski, A., & Grinker, J. A. (1987). Body composition, body size estimation, and attitudes towards eating in male college athletes. *Psychosomatic Medicine, 49*, 56–64.

Epling, W. F., & Pierce, W. D. (1988). Activity-based anorexia: A biobehavioral perspective. *International Journal of Eating Disorders, 7*, 27–46.

Epling, W. F., & Pierce, W. D. (1991). *Solving the anorexia puzzle: A scientific approach.* Toronto: Hogrefe & Huber.

Frisch, R. E. (1988). Fatness and fertility. *Scientific American, 258*, 88–95.

Frisch, R. E., Gotz-Welbergen, A. V., McArthur, J. W., Albright, T., Witschi, J., Bullen, B., Birnholtz, J., Reed, R. B., & Herman, H. (1981). Delayed menarche and amenorrhea of college athletes in relation to age of onset of training. *Journal of the American Medical Association, 246*, 1559–1563.

Frisch, R. E., Wyshank, G., & Vincent, L. (1980). Delayed menarche and amenorrhea in ballet dancers. *New England Journal of Medicine, 303*, 17–19.

Garner, D. M., & Garfinkel, P. E. (1979). The eating attitudes test: An index of the symptoms of anorexia nervosa. *Psychological Medicine, 9*, 1–7.

Garner, D. M., & Garfinkel, P. E. (1980). Socio-cultural factors in the development of anorexia nervosa. *Psychological Medicine, 10*, 647–656.

Garner, D. M., Olmstead, M. P., & Garfinkel, P. E. (1982). The eating attitudes test: Psychometric features and clinical correlates. *Psychological Medicine, 12*, 871–878.

Katz, J. L. (1986). Long-distance running, anorexia nervosa, and bulimia: Report of two cases. *Comprehensive Psychiatry, 27*, 74–78.

King, M. B., & Mezey, G. (1987). Eating behavior of male racing jockeys. *Psychological Medicine, 17*, 249–253.

Morgan, W. P (1970). Psychological effects of weight reduction in the college wrestler. *Medicine and Science in Sports, 2*, 24–27.

Oppliger, R., Landry, G., Foster, S., & Lambrecht, A. (1993). Bulimic behaviors among interscholastic wrestlers: A statewide survey. *Pediatrics, 91*, 826–831.

Reed, P. B. (1980). *Nutrition: An applied science.* St. Paul, MN: West Publishing.

Scott, D. (1986). Anorexia in the male: A review of clinical, epidemiological and biological findings. *International Journal of Eating Disorders, 5*, 799–821.

Singer, R. N., & Weiss, S. A. (1968). Effects of weight reduction on selected anthropometric, physical, and performance measures of wrestlers. *Research Quarterly, 39*, 361–368.

Smith, N. J. (1984). Weight control in the athlete. *Clinics in Sports Medicine, 3*, 693–704.

Steen, S. N., & Brownell, K. D. (1990). Patterns of weight loss and regain in wrestlers: Has the tradition changed? *Medicine and Science in Sports and Exercise, 22*, 762–768.

Strauss, R. H., Lanese, R. R., & Malarkey, W. B. (1985). Weight loss in amateur wrestlers and its effect on serum testosterone levels. *Journal of the American Medical Association, 254*, 3337–3338.

Symbaluk, D. G. (1990). *Activity anorexia and its implications for amateur wrestlers.* Unpublished master's thesis, University of Alberta, Edmonton.

Tcheng, T., & Tipton, C. M. (1973). Iowa wrestling study: Anthropometric measurements and the prediction of a "minimal" body weight for high school wrestlers. *Medicine and Science in Sports, 5*, 1–10.

Wheeler, G. D., McFadyen, S. G., Symbaluk, D., Pierce, W. D., & Cumming, D. C. (1992). The effects of training on serum testosterone levels in wrestlers. *Clinical Journal of Sport Medicine, 2*, 257–260.

Wheeler, G. D., Wall, S. R., Belcastro, A. N., Conger, P., & Cumming, D. C. (1986). Are anorexic tendencies prevalent in the habitual runner? *British Journal of Sports Medicine, 20*, 77–81.

Wheeler, G. D., Wall, S. R., Belcastro, A. N., & Cumming, D. C. (1984). Reduced serum testosterone and prolactin levels in male distance runners. *Journal of the American Medical Association, 252*, 514–516.

Woods, E. R., Wilson, C. D., & Masland, R. P. (1988). Weight control methods in high school wrestlers. *Journal of Adolescent Health Care, 9*, 394–397.

Yates, A., Leehey, K., & Shisslak, C. M. (1983). Running—An analogue to anorexia? *New England Journal of Medicine, 308*, 251–255.

13

Exercise, Sports, and Anorexia

Garry Wheeler
University of Alberta

Several researchers suggested that activity plays a central role in the development of eating disorders (Epling & Pierce, 1988; King, 1963; Kron, Katz, Gorzynski, & Weiner, 1978; Pierce & Epling, 1994). Cultural preoccupation with exercise and dieting, increased participation in competitive sports by younger individuals, and the demands of sport for certain body shapes have undoubtedly contributed to an increase in disordered eating and/or diagnosable eating disorders in athletes. Research consistently demonstrates higher than expected dietary problems in habitual exercisers and athletes, particularly in sports demanding slimness (Brownell & Rodin, 1992). The prevalence of eating disorder symptoms in athletes varies from fewer than 1% to as high as 33% of participants (Sundgot-Borgen, 1994a, 1994b). Whether individuals with eating disorders engage in sports or whether physical activity causes eating disorders remains a controversial and unanswered question.

Early comparisons of the athletic and the anorectic personality traits were based in part on observations of similarities between runners and those exhibiting frank anorectic behaviors and were summarized by Wheeler, Wall, Belcastro, and Cumming (1984; see Table 13.1).

Anecdotal reports of runners astoundingly resembling adolescents with anorexia nervosa (AN; Sours, 1980, 1981) have given way to a plethora of systematic investigations of disordered eating and eating disorders in a variety of athletic populations, using standardized assessment tools with and without control groups. Multifactor risk models (Sundgot-Borgen, 1994b) and animal-based theories

159

TABLE 13.1

Comparison of Habitual Runners and Patients with Anorexia Nervosa

Habitual/Obligatory Running	Anorexia Nervosa
Preoccupation of runners with body image and pursuit of ideal body	Distorted body image
Running as a means of weight control	A relentless pursuit of thinness and preoccupation with weight and food
Preoccupation with caloric value of food	Preoccupation with caloric value of food
Denial of addiction to running	Denial of illness
Running: a means of controlling life	Food avoidance/self-starvation: a means of achieving self-control
Ritual associated with running	Ritual associated with food and self-starvation
Excessive training up to three times per day	Hyperactivity in anorectics to burn off unwanted calories
Endocrine alterations in men and women runners including decreased total and free testosterone and amenorrhea	Endocrine changes in men and women associated with starvation including decreased total and free testosterone and amenorrhea

Note. From *Anorectic Tendencies in High Mileage Runners*, by G. Wheeler, 1984, Unpublished master's thesis, University of Alberta, Edmonton.

(Epling & Pierce, 1984) of the development of activity-associated eating disorders have also been developed.

The most compelling evidence of disordered eating or eating disorders in athletic populations is found in investigations of athletes in sports requiring leanness (Warren, Stanton, & Blessing, 1990). Indirect evidence of eating disorders in athletes has arisen from endocrine investigations in men (Wheeler et al., 1984, 1990) and women (Sundgot-Borgen, 1994a, 1994b, Warren, 1988) in which reproductive hormone changes, probably secondary to a negative energy balance, have been reported (Wheeler et al., 1989).

Comparisons of anorectic patients with athletic populations have also been described as simplistic (Leichner, 1986) and fraught with methodological problems (Sundgot-Borgen, 1994a, 1994b). Several researchers have failed to find similar psychological characteristics between male (Blumenthal, O'Toole, & Chang, 1984; Nudelman, Rosen, & Lietenberg, 1988), female (Borgen & Corbin, 1987; Evers, 1987; Hickson, Schrader, & Cunningham, 1986; Lindboe & Slettebo, 1984; Owens & Slade, 1987; Warren et al., 1990; Weight & Noakes, 1987) and mixed populations (Campbell, 1985) of habitual exercisers, athletes and anorectics. Other studies have been inconclusive in their findings (Wheeler et al., 1986). Failure to define patterns of disordered eating and/or eating disorders in athletic groups probably reflects a plethora of methodological approaches, use of instruments validated on patients with anorexia associated with lack of response integrity, choice of athletic populations, a search for classic AN, and subjective bias on the part of skeptical authors and reviewers.

Recently there have been increased reports of eating disorders in male athlete groups. Although the existence of AN in men has been refuted (Kidd & Wood, 1966; Selvini, 1965), it has been supported by others (Beumont, Beardwood, &

Russell, 1972; Hasan & Tibbetts, 1977; Swann, 1977), although the true incidence is probably masked by reluctance of the medical profession to diagnose the condition in men (Hogan, Huerta, & Lucas, 1974; Thompson & Sherman, 1993; Yates, Shisslak, Allender, & Crago, 1992). Men share the same concerns with body weight and food consumption as do women (Cash, Winstrad, & Janda, 1986; Stainsby, 1995), and several anecdotal and case reports describe similarities between male habitual exercisers, athletes, and anorectic individuals (Katz, 1986; Smith, 1980; Sours, 1980, 1981; Yates, Leehey, & Shisslak, 1983). Distorted body image was demonstrated in male runners (Wheeler et al., 1986); and elevated EAT scores were demonstrated in jockeys (King & Mezey, 1987), swimmers (Dummer, Rosen, & Heusner, 1987), and wrestlers (Enns, Drewnowski, & Grinker, 1987). Male athletes and men with eating disorders are alike in many ways; demonstrating tremendous psychological investment in their bodies; abuse of exercise; preoccupation with food; personality factors including commitment, perseverance, compulsivity, and alterations in endocrine profiles (Andersen, 1992) — although the motive for dieting may differ (Thomson & Sherman, 1993). For a comprehensive and historical overview of research in the area see Brownell & Rodin (1992).

A MODEL OF EATING DISORDERS IN ATHLETES AND HABITUAL EXERCISERS

An increase in eating disorders in the general population was associated with cultural influences (Garfinkel, Garner, & Olmstad, 1983),and in athletes with culture and sport-related emphasis on slimness (Hamilton, Brooks-Gunn, & Warren, 1985; Pierce & Epling, 1994; Rodin & Larson, 1992; Rodin & Plante, 1989; Smith, 1980; Yates et al., 1994). In addition to sociocultural models, risk factor models based on a complex interplay of social, cultural, psychological, and physiological factors were developed (Sundgot-Borgen, 1994b; Wilson & Eldredge, 1992). An animal model of activity anorexia was extended to humans (Pierce & Epling, 1994), representing the only systematic attempt to date to explain a viable process of the development of eating disorders associated with involvement in physical activity, although it has been criticized as failing to account for lack of universality of eating disorders in athletes, bulimia nervosa, and for placing exercise as the central point in the development of eating disorders (Thompson & Sherman, 1993).

Requirements of an Activity-Associated Model

A satisfactory model to explain a continuum of disordered eating in athletes must satisfy the following criteria:

1. Explain factors initiating the desire to lose weight, diet, and/or engage in an activity, weight reduction, or diet program.
2. Explain escalation from moderate dieting and activity toward severely curtailed caloric intake.
3. Account for a point of pathology: a shift from an exercise and diet habit to compulsive or addictive behavior; from rational to irrational thinking; from normal to aberrant behavior associated with food intake and exercise, and associated with changes in body image, personality, or psychological profile.
4. Explain the fundamental importance of alterations in endocrine and metabolic function in relation to exercise and food-related behaviors.
5. Describe factors that serve to maintain a cycle of self-starvation despite deleterious effects on health.

A Continuum of Normal Dietary Behavior to Eating Disorders

I suggest that the development of eating disorders in athletes represents progress along a continuum of normal eating behavior, to disordered eating, to diagnosable eating disorders, particularly in sports demanding leanness and/or thinness. Disordered eating in athletes and habitual exercisers represents a normal response to abnormal social, cultural, and sport demands and unrealistic sociocultural expectations pertaining to body shape and weight. Activity-associated eating disorders may be viewed as extensions of normative and culturally acceptable modes of behavior (Nylander, 1971) in certain sport and athletic environments. Normal eating behavior may progress to disordered eating, to activity-type anorexia, to full-blown AN.

The concept of a continuum in terms of personality and cognitive shifts has been suggested in relation to anorexia nervosa. Several authors suggest that cognition becomes pathologically altered on a continuum with chronicity of eating disorders (Katz, 1985; Manley, 1989). Kafman and Sadeh (1989) suggest that AN represents a monoideistic illness characterized by an underlying obsession with food and weight and a cognitive shift from normative concerns regarding body weight, size, and food to obsessional preoccupation. What begins as a normative social phenomenon becomes a condition beyond voluntary control, consistent with Garner and Garfinkel's (1980) concept of a "final common pathway" and Marrazzi and Luby's (1986) autoaddiction model.

Wilson and Eldredge (1992) suggested that eating disturbances in athletes lie on a continuum ranging from normative concerns about body weight and shape, to rigid dieting, to subclinical disordered eating patterns, to diagnosable eating disorders. Katz (1986) reported a shift from concerns regarding body weight to development of eating disorders in two men who developed AN. To date there is no satisfactory explanation of how movement occurs along a continuum of rational to irrational thought, from normal to disordered eating, to a full-blown eating disorder.

It is convenient to conceptualize the continuum as a linear process of initiation (entry into physical activity and/or dieting), escalation (increased activity with increased weight loss and social reinforcement), adaptation (psychological and physiological adaptations secondary to a negative energy balance or starvation), a point of pathology or psychopathology (altered cognitive schema, irrational thinking, and disturbed body image secondary to chronic starvation), and finally resolution (development of anorexia or bulimia or eating disorders not otherwise specified). Important in this process are multiple interacting factors that influence each stage of the model and determine the rate of progress along the continuum and the intensity with which individuals adopt caloric restriction practices and increase levels of activity, *oscillations* (movements backward and forward along it), and a final point of psychopathology characterized by psychological changes and *cognitive shifts* from which the athlete does not, or may not, recover. A *point of psychopathology* probably follows a critical energy threshold level and is characterized by potentially irreversible changes in personality factors and cognition, views regarding food and eating, and self or body perception. This inhibits the ability to perceive threats to health and body image accurately and is highly resistant to change. The entire process is conceptualized in Fig. 13.1.

The model does not deny, but rather subsumes, other models in that it recognizes multiple risk factors and synthesizes them with psychological and physiological adaptations to starvation. Activity anorexia (Pierce & Epling, 1994) might also be considered a subclinical variant on the continuum to a diagnosable eating disorder. I stress that the model proposed is at once based on theory and conjecture. It does not seek to refute the importance of predisposing genetic and psychological factors and/or family influences. Rather, it integrates these factors as part of the process. Finally, it is a heuristic designed to present evidence for activity or sport-related eating disorders that may develop into classic anorexia or bulimia nervosa.

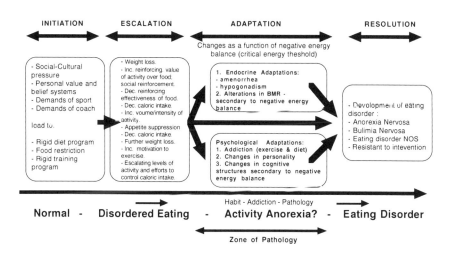

FIG. 13.1.   The development of activity-associated eating disorders: An integrated model.

PHASES AND PROCESSES IN ATHLETIC
AND ACTIVITY-ASSOCIATED EATING DISORDERS

Initiation Phase

Central to initiation to the continuum are an interaction of social and cultural pressures to be thin, social sanctioning of involvement in health-related physical activity and food deprivation, sport-related demands for a lean body shape, and cognitive factors. A prerequisite to the model is, of course, involvement in sports or intent to become involved in sport.

Culture has been considered a central factor in the development of eating disorders (Bruch 1978; DiNicola, 1990; Garfinkel et al., 1983; Nasser, 1988; Prince, 1985; Stevenson, 1990; Swartz, 1985), although cultural factors alone probably cannot explain the onset. A cultural factor in the initiation of disordered eating in athletes is consistent with observations of increased concerns with body shape described in men and women in the general population, superimposed on sport specific demands on body weight and shape (Cash et al., 1986; Drewnowski & Yee, 1987; Mellin, Sally, & Irwin, 1986; Yates, 1991; Yates et al., 1994).

Cultural demands for slimness combined with the demands of sport, exercise volume, intensity, and type are significant risk factors for the development of excessive concerns regarding body size and disordered eating patterns in male and female athletes, and often associated with sports in which thinness is emphasized (Davis & Cowles, 1989; Feldman, Hadgson, Corber, & Quinn, 1986; Friez, Olson, & Good, 1990; Hamilton, Brooks-Gunn, & Warren, 1985, 1986; Pierce & Epling, 1994; Richert & Hummers, 1986; Rodin & Larson, 1992; Rodin & Plante, 1989; Smith, 1980; Sundgot-Borgen, 1994b; Yaeger, Agostini, Nattive, & Drinkwater, 1993). In certain sports, athletes learn from coaches, other athletes, and observation that a lean body shape is required and that food deprivation and purging are effective, acceptable, or desirable means of weight control. Consistent with a social learning model (Bandura, 1977, 1986), the athlete models his or her behavior on that of other athletes with the expectation that he or she will achieve similar results. Athletes may learn from live (coaches), symbolic (media and culture), and verbal (literature) models expectations regarding body type and eating behavior. Such pressure and expectations lead to increased food awareness and to the adoption of disordered eating patterns. Athletes may observe behavior of models for some time and evaluate the potential for reinforcement before engaging in aberrant dietary behavior. Athletes learn through direct and vicarious reinforcement what weight control behaviors are acceptable and which behaviors will lead to success, a process termed self-regulation (Bandura, 1977, 1986).

Important in the initiation phase is the perception of normalcy. Potentially harmful excessive dieting and exercise behavior may be perceived by athletes, coaches, and others as perfectly acceptable in the context of a particular training and sport environment. Purging or total abstention from food, for example, may be viewed as a reasonable means of attenuating weight gain among athletes. Thus athletes in certain sports exist in a socially sanctioned environment in which to express food and weight obsessions (Henry, 1982). Normal cognition regarding food and activity may already be relatively abnormal to nonathletic populations.

A cumulative effect of cultural and social values and sport-related demands for thinness may initiate a process of dieting and weight reduction in athletes.

Escalation Phase

Several factors may contribute to an escalation in the amount of exercise and behaviors associated with limiting food intake. These include social reinforcement, appetite suppression, endogenous opiate-mediated motivation for (increased) activity, and time commitment. During this escalation phase, outcomes may appear to be positive in terms of increased performance and desirable weight loss.

Social Reinforcement.   Exercise combined with food restriction leads to weight loss and possibly improved performance. This not only reinforces exercise and diet behavior for the athlete, but also solicits reinforcement from significant others including peers, other athletes, coaches, teachers, and parents. This motivates the individual to maintain or increase activity, to adopt deliberate strategies such as exercising at mealtimes to replace food intake, or (continue) to restrict food. This results in further weight loss and serves to reinforce and maintain dieting and exercise behavior. Yates et al. (1994) describe this as a reciprocal feedback loop, and Pierce and Epling (1994) describe a similar process in their activity anorexia model.

Where attempts to maintain or lose weight fail, resulting in negative feedback from the coach and possible exclusion from the team, this also serves to motivate the athlete to adopt increased levels of activity or food deprivation strategies. In some sports, problems may occur around puberty when body type becomes less than ideal for a particular sport. Gymnastics is a classic example. The prepubertal athlete has positive self-efficacy with regard to weight control, and outcome expectations are achieved. However, at the onset of puberty a disparity occurs between perceived self-efficacy and outcome expectations in terms of weight control. This is consistent with self-efficacy theory (Bandura, 1986).

Exercise and Appetite Suppression.   Appetite suppression may occur with increased activity volume and intensity (Drinkwater ct al., 1984; Edholm, Fletcher, Widdowson, & McCance, 1955; Katch, Michael, & Jones, 1969; Marcus, Cann, & Madvig, 1985; Nelson et al., 1986; Short & Short, 1983) and has a physiological and psychological basis (Brouns, Saris, & Ten Hoor, 1986; Pierce & Epling, 1994; Sundgot-Borgen, 1994a, 1994b). Increased rate of change of activity has been shown to suppress food intake levels in animals (Tokuyama, Saito, & Okuda, 1982) and humans (Wheeler et al., 1989). Thus individuals who rapidly increase exercise intensity and volume may experience appetite reduction, which reinforces active decision-making regarding food restriction.

Endogenous Opiates and Appetite Suppression.   Evidence suggests that appetite is mediated by endogenous opiate peptides (Epling & Pierce, 1988; Marrazzi

& Luby, 1986; Pierce & Epling, 1994; Yates et al., 1994). Injections of opiates in the hypothalamus of animals stimulate feeding (Grandison & Guidotti, 1977; Liebowitz & Hor, 1982; McKay, Kenney, Edens, Williams, & Woods, 1981), which is attenuated by opiate antagonists including naloxone and naltrexone in animals (Fishman & Carr, 1983; Holtzman, 1975, 1979; Kirkham & Blundell, 1984; Maickel, Brauch, & Zabik, 1977; Margules, Moisset, Lewis, Shibuya, & Pert, 1978) and humans (Moore, Mills, & Forster, 1981). Conversely, food intake appears to be suppressed by a ß-endorphin-mediated effect in animals (Sanger & McCarthy, 1980) and humans at low body weight (Kaye, Pickar, Naber, & Ebert, 1982). Endogenous opiates seem to act to increase food intake at normal body weight and suppress appetite when food intake and body weight are low (Marrazzi & Luby, 1986; Epling & Pierce, 1988).

It is well established that acute bouts of physical activity are associated with increased peripheral circulating beta-endorphin levels for up to 2 hours after exercise in humans (Elias et al., 1986). As athletes lose weight and fall below a critical weight, ß-endorphins may mediate an appetite-suppressing effect while simultaneously enhancing mood. This may serve to motivate exercise even when caloric intake is restricted (Marrazzi & Luby, 1986; Pierce & Epling, 1994).

Time Commitment. Increased training volume and intensity, facilitated by increased fitness and weight loss, leaves less time for eating. Because training may take place at mealtimes, it may displace normal food intake. This may lead to accelerated weight loss, which concomitantly reinforces exercise and leads to further reduced food intake, as well as an elevation in food consciousness.

A combination of increased training commitment, social reinforcement, and ß-endorphin-mediated appetite suppression (at low body weight), accompanied by enhanced mood, may serve to motivate increases in exercise and reduce caloric intake.

Adaptation (to Energy Deficit) Phase

Initially, the body adapts positively to exercise and reduced caloric intake. However, at a critical energy threshold (CET), that is, a point where there is a critical energy deficit, potentially negative changes occur (see Fig. 13.2). The CET is specific to individuals and is based on a number of factors including activity level, dietary intake, and body size, for example. Achievement of a CET is probably followed by endocrine, physiological, and psychological changes.

Endocrine and Physiological Changes. High levels of physical training are associated with alterations in the hypothalamic–pituitary–gonadal (HPGA) axis in male and female athletic populations (Gadpaille, Feicht-Sanborn, & Wagner, 1987; Hamilton et al., 1985; Wheeler et al., 1984, 1986, 1989, 1990). Alterations of the HPGA and sex hormone production are probably due to a combination of factors including endogenous opiates, training volume, low caloric intake, and a negative

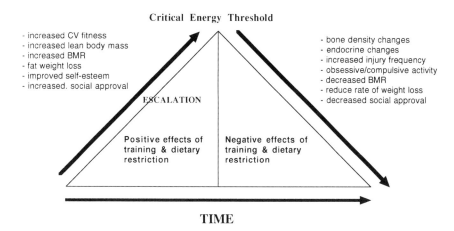

FIG. 13.2. The critical energy threshold: Transition from positive to negative effects of exercise and dieting.

energy balance (Cumming & Wheeler, 1987; Wheeler et al., 1989) and may represent a primary physiological adaption. Similar changes occur in women (Garner & Garfinkel, 1980) and men with eating disorders (Beumont, 1970; Beumont et al., 1972).

Alterations in Metabolic Rate. A second line of defense against a serious energy imbalance is an alteration in basal metabolic rate (BMR). Initially, exercise may result in an elevation in metabolic rate for up to 48 hours (Brehm & Gutin, 1986; Edwards, Thorndike, & Dill, 1935; Maehlum, Grandmontagne, Newsholme, & Sejersted, 1986), and weight loss is probably a function of chronically elevated BMR (Brehm, 1988). Anecdotal evidence from high mileage runners (Wheeler et al., 1984, 1986, 1989) suggests that, at certain levels of activity and food intake, maintaining body weight becomes problematic; that is, body weight appears to be gained easily with small fluctuations in caloric intake. This is consistent with reports of decreased BMR in overweight individuals under severe caloric restriction (Bray, 1969; Lammert & Hansen, 1982; Welle, Amatruda, Forbes, & Lockwood, 1984) and increased food efficiency in athletes (Marcus et al., 1985; Nelson et al., 1986). Warren (1988) has reported reduced BMR in amenorrheic high mileage female runners, and Phinney (1985) found a 10% reduction in BMR in women on diets, and a threefold reduction in BMR in women on a combined diet and exercise program. Myerson et al. (1991) reported reduced BMR in amenorrheic compared with eumenorrheic and sedentary women; Brownell, Steen, and Wilmore (1987) suggested that alterations in BMR in athletes reflect the defense of a set point of body weight; and Myerson et al. (1991) indicated that high mileage runners appear to maintain stable weight and energy balance through a reduction in BMR. As a consequence of decreased BMR, weight loss becomes difficult for the athlete (Yates et al., 1994). Alterations in BMR are possibly opiate-mediated (Marrazzi & Luby, 1986), and it has been suggested that beta-endorphins mediate homeostatic adaptations to starvation by conservation of energy and bodily resources by reduction of physiologic and metabolic functions to the minimum essential for a state of starvation (Margules et al., 1978). With declining BMR and stabilization of weight loss, the solution to maintaining or losing weight is to increase activity and/or reduce caloric intake (Yates et al., 1994). This has been described as dietary dyscontrol associated with anger, anxiety, and preoccupation with food (Herman & Polivy, 1985).

Addiction to Exercise and Food Restriction. Several authors suggested that runners become highly committed (Callen, 1983), addicted (Brownell & Rodin, 1992), negatively addicted (Morgan, 1979), obligatory or compulsive (Yates et al., 1983, 1994), unable to cease exercising in times of injury (Brownell & Rodin, 1992; Yates et al., 1994), and may develop neurotic symptoms as a function of having to cease exercise (Little, 1969, 1981). Others have suggested that individuals may become addicted to dieting and the process of caloric deprivation per se (Marrazzi & Luby, 1986). Overcommitment to exercise and to food restriction may be opiate-mediated (Yates et al., 1994; Marrazzi & Luby, 1986) and serve to motivate exercise and low caloric intake when body weight is low, increasing risk for activity-associated eating disorders (Pierce, Daleng, & McGowan, 1993; Pierce & Epling, 1994; Yates et al., 1994). Addiction to activity and dieting may be followed by changes in personality and cognitive schema or structures.

Alterations in Personality. Several authors suggested that participation in dieting and sport are associated with psychological changes including increased compulsivity and that efforts to control weight lead to general psychopathology (Davis, 1990; Davis, Fox, Cowles, Hastings, & Schwass, 1990; Katz, 1986; Keys, Brozek, Henschell, Mickelson, & Taylor, 1954; Wilson & Eldredge, 1992). This may also apply to food restriction (Marrazzi & Luby, 1986). It is unclear whether selection factors or socialization after entry into a highly competitive sport account for the development of personality characteristics consistent with those found in eating disordered patients (Andersen, 1992).

Alterations in Cognition. Alterations in cognitive structures and disruption of cognitive schema associated with eating, weight, and body size are central to cognitive–behavioral explanations of AN (Jordan, Canavan, & Steer, 1986; Kafman & Sadeh, 1989; Vitousek & Hollon, 1990).

Chronic preoccupation with diet, weight cycling, prolonged caloric deprivation, or chronic starvation in the athlete also may lead to a disruption in cognitive schema, as well as a shift from rational to irrational thought. Changes in body schema, for example, are associated with a distorted body image characteristic of eating disorders.

What is rational thinking in relation to diet in sports? Normal eating behavior in a gymnast, jockey, or ballet dancer would certainly not fit a definition of normal eating in a footballer or rugby football player. If an individual fails to lose or maintain weight in a thinness-related sport, self-starvation or purging may be a reasonable solution. In certain contexts this is acceptable thinking and serves to rationalize the behavior. Thus Yates et al. (1994) contended that compulsive athletes are generally rational persons who act in an irrational manner, suggesting that state-specific factors, that is, the situation in which the athlete finds him or herself, are partly responsible for compulsive exercise behavior.

Chronic starvation may eventually lead to organic changes and impaired cognitive processing. Yates et al. (1994) suggested that cognitive and emotional changes in overcommitted runners could be secondary to persistent caloric deficit.

The physiological and psychological changes suggested above may be conceptualized on the continuum as a zone of pathology: a transition from the beneficial effects of activity to potentially harmful physiological and psychological effects (see Fig. 13.1).

A Point of Psychopathology?   It is unclear at what point a shift occurs from rational to irrational thinking, from a normal to an impaired body image, or from the ability to inability to perceive the harmful impact of chronic starvation. It is hypothesized that this point is unique to an individual; probably follows physiological and metabolic changes including chronic elevation of endogenous opiates and downregulation of metabolic set point; and depends on the interaction of several mediating factors including the type, intensity, and rate of increase of activity, degree of reinforcement for weight loss, length of time engaged in weight loss behavior, and the age at which self-induced dietary deprivation begins. Premorbid personality factors complicate this picture and cannot be discounted.

Importantly, throughout the escalation and adaptation period, the athlete probably continues to receive positive reinforcement for his or her strict dietary regimen, high level of training, and body shape, that is, until a serious eating disorder is evident and a point of psychopathology has been reached.

Resolution Phase

The point of resolution represents the development of a diagnosable eating disorder, is highly individual, and undoubtedly reflects a unique interaction of predisposing psychological and environmental factors, the sport context, social reinforcement, degree of energy deficit, and severity of psychological changes and changes in cognitive schema. Not all athletes reach this point. At some point, aberrant eating behaviors and attitudes toward food and body image may become established, manifest as an eating disorder, and be highly resistant to change even in the absence of premorbid psychopathology (Hamilton et al., 1988; Katz, 1986). The critical energy threshold model may be expanded to incorporate these concepts in Fig. 13.3.

Progress and Maintenance.   Is progress along the continuum linear and inexorable, or does the athlete move backward and forward (oscillate) along the continuum? Many athletes (e.g., wrestlers) engage in repetitive weight cycling although it is unclear whether continuous cycling of this nature has a progressive effect of moving the athlete further along the continuum to developing an eating disorder. However, persistent weight cycling may result in increased energy efficiency and body weight preservation on low calorie diets and in increasingly dramatic efforts to maintain or lose weight. Progress along the continuum is a function of the following:

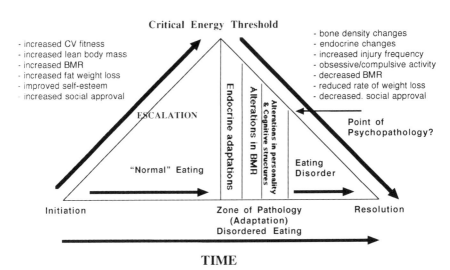

FIG. 13.3.   The critical energy threshold: Escalation, point of psychopathology, and resolution.

1. Type of physical activity or sport: the sport context;
2. Weight demands of the sport;
3. Body type required in a sport;
4. Volume, intensity and rate of increase of physical activity;
5. Degree of social reinforcement of exercise and dietary behavior from significant others;
6. Impact of culture and media as a contextual factor;
7. Premorbid personality or susceptibility factor (Thompson & Sherman, 1993);
8. Sex differences in physiology and anatomy;
9. Fundamental changes in gender role expectations.

Once established, what factors maintain behaviors associated with exercise and eating even when these behaviors become harmful? Pierce and Epling (1994) suggested that maintenance of disordered eating includes social, cultural, cognitive, behavioral, and physiological factors. Alterations in personality and cognition are probably critical factors. As well, potential financial rewards for excellence in certain sports probably serve as important maintenance factors of disordered eating and eventual eating disorders (Thompson & Sherman, 1993).

SUMMARY AND CONCLUSIONS

Increased participation in recreational activity combined with diet and weight reduction, increased and early participation in highly intensive training programs, and a cultural preoccupation with dieting, exercise, and body shape may interact with behavioral, physiological, and psychological processes to produce eating disorders in athletes. These behavioral processes constitute normal responses under abnormal training and body weight requirements and occur on a continuum along which an individual progresses as a function of multiple interacting factors, the most important of which appears to be the sport context (i.e., sports requiring leanness).

One question that has not been answered entirely is whether eating disordered individuals choose sports as a socially sanctioned environment in which to express pathological behaviors toward food and activity, whether dieting in sport leads to eating disorders in (psychologically or genetically) predisposed individuals, or whether involvement in activity results in the development of eating disorders.

REFERENCES

Andersen, A. E. (1992). Eating disorders in males: A special case? In K. Brownell, J. Rodin, & J. H. Wilmore (Eds.), *Eating, body weight and performance* (pp. 172–188). Philidelphia, PA: Lea & Febiger.

Bandura, A. (1977). *Social learning theory.* Englewood Cliffs, NJ: Prentice-Hall.

Bandura, A. (1986). *Social foundations of thought and action.* Englewood Cliffs, NJ: Prentice-Hall.

Beumont, P. J. V. (1970). Anorexia nervosa in male subjects. Recent research in psychosomatics. 8th European conference of psychosomatic research. *Psychotherapy and Psychosomatics, 18,* 365–371.

Beumont, P. J. V., Beardwood, C. J., & Russell, G. F. M. (1972). The occurrence of the syndrome of anorexia nervosa in male subjects. *Psychosomatic Medicine, 2,* 216–231.

Blumenthal, J. A., O'Toole, L. C., & Chang, J. L. (1984). Is running an analogue of anorexia nervosa? *Journal of the American Medical Association, 252,* 520–523.

Borgen, J. S., & Corbin, C. B. P. (1987). Eating disorders among female athletes. *Psychology Today, 15,* 89–95.

Bray G. A. (1969). Effect of caloric restriction on energy expenditure in obese patients. *Lancet, 2,* 397–398.

Brehm, B. A., & Gutin, B. (1986). Recovery energy expenditure for steady state exercise in runners and non-exercisers. *Medicine and Science in Sports and Exercise, 18,* 205–210.

Brehm, B. A. (1988). Elevation of metabolic rate following exercise. Implications for weight loss. *Sports Medicine, 6,* 72–78.

Brouns, F. J. P. H., Saris, W. H. M., & Ten Hoor, F. (1986). Dietary problems in the case of strenuous exertion. *Journal of Sports Medicine, 26,* 306–319.

Brownell, K. D., & Rodin, J. (1992). Prevalence of eating disorders in athletes. In K. D. Brownell, J. Rodin, & J. H. Wilmore (Eds.), *Eating, body weight and performance in athletes. Disorders of modern society* (pp. 128–145). Philadelphia, PA: Lea & Febiger.

Brownell K. D., Steen S. N., & Wilmore J. H. (1987). Weight regulation practices in athletes: An analysis of metabolic and health effects. *Medicine and Science in Sports and Exercise, 19,* 546–556.

Bruch, H. (1978). *The golden cage.* Cambridge, MA: Harvard University Press.

Callen, K. E. (1983). Mental and emotional aspects of long distance running. *Psychosomatic Medicine, 24,* 133–152.

Campbell, J. (1985). Anorexia nervosa: Body dissatisfaction in a high risk population. *Canadian Association for Health, Physical Education and Recreation Journal, 52,* 36–41.

Cash, T. F., Winstrad, B. A., & Janda, I. M. (1986). The great American shape up. *Psychology Today, 20,* 30–34.

Cumming, D. C., & Wheeler, G. D. (1987). Opiates in exercise physiology. *Seminars in Reproductive Endocrinology, 5,* 171–179.

Davis, C. (1990). Body image and weight preoccupation: A comparison between exercising and non-exercising women. *Appetite, 15,* 13–21.

Davis, C., & Cowles, M. (1989). A comparison of weight and diet concerns and personality factors among female athletes and non-athletes. *Journal of Psychosomatic Research, 33*, 527–536.

Davis, C., Fox, J., Cowles, M., Hastings, P., & Schwass, K. (1990). The functional role of exercise in the development of weight and diet concerns in women. *Journal of Psychosomatic Research, 34*, 563–574.

DiNicola, V. F. (1990). Anorexia multiforms: Self-starvation in historical and cultural context: 2. Anorexia nervosa as a culture-reactive syndrome. *Transcultural Psychiatric Research Review, 27*, 245–286.

Drewnowski, A., & Yee, D. K. (1987). Men and body image: Are males satisfied with their body weight? *Psychosomatic Medicine, 49*, 626–634.

Drinkwater, B. L., Nilson, K., Chesnut, C. H., III, Bremner, W. J., Shainholtz, S., & Southworth, M. B. (1984). Bone mineral content of amenorrheic and eumenorrheic athletes. *New England Journal of Medicine, 311*, 277–281.

Dummer, G. M., Rosen, L. W., & Heusner, W. W. (1987). Pathogenic weight control behaviors of young competitive swimmers. *Physician and Sports Medicine, 15*, 75–85.

Edholm, O. G., Fletcher, J. G., Widdowson, E. M., & McCance, R. A. (1955). Energy expenditure and food intake of individual men. *British Journal of Nutrition, 9*, 286–300.

Edwards, H. T., Thorndike, A., & Dill, D. B. (1935). The energy requirement in strenuous muscle exercise. *New England Journal of Medicine, 33*, 532–536.

Elias, A. N., Iyer, K., Pandian, M. R., Weatherersbee, P., Stone, S., & Tobis, J. (1986). B-endorphin/B-Lipotropin release and gonadotropin secretion after acute exercise in normal males. *Journal of Applied Physiology Respiration and Environment, 61*, 2045–2049.

Enns, M. P, Drewnowski, A., & Grinker, J. A. (1987). Body composition, body size and attitudes towards eating in male college athletes. *Psychosomatic Medicine, 49*, 56–64.

Epling, W. F., & Pierce, W. D. (1984). Activity-based anorexia in rats as a function of opportunity to run on an activity wheel *Nutrition and Behavior, 2*, 37–49.

Epling, W. F., & Pierce, W. D. (1988). Activity-based anorexia: A biobehavioral perspective. *International Journal of Eating Disorders, 7*, 475–485.

Evers, C. L. (1987). Dietary intake and symptoms of anorexia nervosa in female university dancers. *Journal of the American Dietetic Association, 87*, 66–76.

Feldman, W., Hadgson, C., Corber, S., & Quinn, A. (1986). Health concerns and health-related behaviors of adolescents. *Canadian Medical Association Journal, 134*, 489–493.

Fishman, S. M., & Carr, D. B. (1983). Naloxone blocks exercise stimulated water intake in the rat. *Life Sciences, 32*, 2523–2527.

Friez, T. M., Olson, J. E., & Good, D. C. (1990). Perceived and actual discrimination in salaries of male and female managers. *Journal of Applied Social Psychology, 20*, 46–67

Gadpaille, W. J., Feicht-Sanborn, C., & Wagner, W. E. W. (1987). Athletic amenorrhea, major affective disorders and eating disorders. *American Journal of Psychiatry, 144*, 939–942.

Garner, D., & Garfinkel, P. (1980). Sociocultural factors in the development of anorexia nervosa. *Psychological Medicine, 10*, 646–656.

Garfinkel, P. E., Garner, D. M., & Olmstad, M. P. (1983). An overview of socio-cultural factors in the development of anorexia nervosa. In P. L. Darby, P. E. Garfinkel, D. M. Garner, & D. V. Coscina (Eds.), *Anorexia nervosa: Recend developments in research* (pp. 65–82). New York: Liss.

Grandison, L., & Guidotti, A. (1977). Stimulation of food intake by muscimol and beta-endorphin. *Neuropharmacology, 16*, 533–536.

Hamilton, L. H., Brooks-Gunn, J., & Warren, M. P. (1985). Sociocultural influences on eating disorders in professional female ballet dancers. *International Journal of Eating Disorders, 4*, 465–477.

Hamilton, L. H., Brooks-Gunn, J., & Warren, M. P. (1986). Nutritional intake of female dancers: A reflection of eating problems. *International Journal of Eating Disorders, 595*, 925–934.

Hamilton, L. H., Brooks-Gunn, J., Warren, M. P., & Hamilton., W. G. (1988). The role of selectivity in the pathogenesis of eating problems in ballet dancers. *Medicine and Science in Sports and Exercise, 20*, 560–565.

Hasan, M. K., & Tibbetts, R. W. (1977). Primary anorexia nervosa (weight phobia) in males. *Postgraduate Medical Journal, 53*, 146–151.

Henry, S. (1982, March). The price of perfection. *Runner*, 35–39.

Herman, C. D., & Polivy, J. (1985). Anxiety, restraint and eating behavior. *Journal of Abnormal Psychology, 84*, 666–672.

Hickson, J. F., Schrader, J., & Cunningham, L. (1986). Dietary intakes of female basketball and gymnastics athletes. *Journal of the American Dietetic Association, 86*, 251–253.

Hogan, W. M., Huerta, E., & Lucas, A. R. (1974). Diagnosing anorexia nervosa in males. *Psychosomatics, 15*, 122–126.

Holtzman, S. G. (1975). Effects of narcotic antagonists on fluid intake in the rat. *Life Sciences, 16*, 1465–1470.

Holtzman, S. G. (1979). Suppression of appetite behavior in the rat by naloxone: Lack of effect of prior morphine dependance. *Life Sciences, 24*, 219–226.

Jordan, H. A., Canavan, A. J., & Steer, R. A. (1986). Shifting gears: Self-reported attitudes and behaviors during times of weight loss, maintenance and gain. *Journal of Clinical Psychology, 42*, 77–81.

Kafman, M., & Sadeh, A. (1989). Anorexia nervosa in a kibbutz: Factors influencing the development of a monoideistic fixation. *International Journal of Eating Disorders, 8*, 33–53.

Katch, F. I., Michael, E. D., & Jones, E. M. (1969). Effect of physical training on the body composition and diet of females. *Research Quarterly, 40*, 99–103.

Katz, J. L. (1985). Some reflections on the nature of eating disorders: On the need for humility. *International Journal of Eating Disorders, 4*, 617–626.

Katz, J. L. (1986). Long distance running, anorexia nervosa and bulimia: A report of two cases. *Comprehensive Psychiatry, 27*, 74–78.

Kaye, W. H., Picker, D. M., Naber, D., & Ebert, M. H. (1982). Cerebrospinal fluid opioid activity in anorexia nervosa. *American Journal of Psychiatry, 139*, 643–645.

Keys, A., Brozek, J, Henschel, A., Mickelson, O., & Taylor, H. L. (1954). *The biology of human starvation*. Minneapolis: University of Minnesota Press.

Kidd, C. B., & Wood, J. F. (1966). Some observations on anorexia nervosa. *Postgraduate Medical Journal, 42*, 443–448.

King, A. (1963). Primary and secondary anorexia nervosa syndromes. *British Journal of Psychiatry, 109*, 470–479.

King, M. B., & Mezey, G. (1987). Eating behavior of male racing jockeys. *Psychological Medicine, 17*, 249–253.

Kirkham, T. C., & Blundell, J. E. (1984). Dual action of naloxone on feeding revealed by behavioral analysis: Separate effects on initiation and termination of eating. *Appetite, 5*, 47–54.

Kron, L., Katz, J. L., Gorzynski, G., & Weiner, H. (1978). Hyperactivity in anorexia nervosa: A fundamental clinical feature. *Comprehensive Psychiatry, 19*, 433–440.

Lammert, O., & Hansen, E. S. (1982). Effects of excessive caloric intake and caloric restriction on body weight and energy expenditure at rest and light exercise. *Acta Physiologica Scandinavica, 114*, 135–141.

Leibowitz, S. F., & Hor, L. (1982). Endorphinergic and alpha-adrenergic systems in the paraventricular nucleus: Effects on eating behavior. *Peptides, 3*, 421–428.

Leichner, P. (1986). Anorexia nervosa, bulimia and exercise. *Coaching Review*, 66–68.

Lindboe, C. F., & Slettebo, M. (1984). Are young female gymnasts malnourished? *European Journal of Applied Physiology, 52*, 457–462.

Little, J. C. (1969). The athlete's neurosis—A deprivation crisis. *Acta Physiologica Scandinavica, 101*, 187–197.

Little, J. C. (1981). Neurotic illness in fitness fanatics. *Psychological Abstracts, 66*, 49–56.

Maehlum, S., Grandmontagne, M., Newsholme, E. A , & Sejersted, O. M. (1986). Magnitude and duration of oxygen consumption in health young subjects. *Metabolism, 35*, 425–429.

Maikel, R. P., Brauch, M. C., & Zabik, J. E. (1977). The effects of various narcotic agonists and antagonists on deprivation induced fluid consumption. *Neuropharmacology, 16*, 863–866.

Manley, R. S. (1989, October). *What are anorexia nervosa and bulimia nervosa?* Symposium at Community Health Education Advisory Committee workshop, Vernon, BC.

Marcus, R., Cann, C., & Madvig, P. (1985). Menstrual function and bone mass in elite women distance runners. *Annals of Internal Medicine, 102*, 158–163.

Margules, D. L., Moisset, B., Lewis, M. J., Shibuya, H., & Pert, C. B. (1978). B-endorphin is associated with overeating in genetically obese mice (ob/ob) and rats (fa/fa). *Science, 202*, 988–991.

Marrazzi, M. A., & Luby, E. D. (1986). An auto-addiction opioid model of chronic anorexia nervosa. *International Journal of Eating Disorders, 5*, 191–208.

McKay, L. D., Kenney, N. J., Edens, N. K., Williams, R. H., & Woods, S. C. (1981). Intracerebroventricular beta-endorphin increases food intake in rats. *Life Sciences, 29*, 1429–1434.

Mellin, L. M., Sally, S., & Irwin, C. E. (1986, October). *Disordered eating characteristics in preadolescent girls.* Paper (abstract) presented at the meeting of the American Dietetic Association, Los Angeles, CA.

Moore, R., Mills, I. H., & Forster, A. (1981). Naloxone in the treatment of anorexia nervosa: Effect on weight gain and lipolysis. *Journal of the Royal Society of Medicine, 74,* 129–131.

Morgan, W. P. (1979). Negative addiction in runners. *Physician and Sports Medicine, 7,* 56–70.

Myerson, M., Gutin, B., Warren, M. P., May, M. T., Contento, I., Lee, M., Pi-Sunyer, F. X., Pierson, M. N., & Brooks-Gunn, J. (1991). Resting metabolic rate and energy balance in amenorrheic and eumenorrheic runners. *Medicine and Science in Sports and Exercise, 23,* 15–22.

Nasser, M. (1988). Culture and weight consciousness. *Journal of Psychosomatic Research, 32,* 573–577.

Nelson, M. E, Fisher, E. C., Catsos, P. D., Meridith, N., Turksoy, N., & Evans, W. J. (1986). Diet and bone status in amenorrheic runners. *American Journal of Clinical Nutrition, 43,* 910–916.

Nudelman, S., Rosen, J. C., & Leitenberg, H. (1988). Dissimilarities in eating attitudes, body image distortion, depression and self-esteem between high intensity male runners and women with anorexia nervosa. *International Journal of Eating Disorders, 7,* 625–634.

Nylander, I. (1971). The feeling of being fat and dieting in a school population. *Acta Sociomedica Scandinavica, 3,* 17–26.

Owens, R. G., & Slade, P. D. (1987). Running and anorexia nervosa: An empirical study. *International Journal of Eating Disorders, 6,* 771–775.

Phinney, S. D. (1985). The metabolic interaction between very low calorie diet and exercise. In G. L. Blackburn & G. A. Bray (Eds.), *Management of obesity by severe caloric restriction* (pp. 99–105). Littleton, MA: PSG.

Pierce, E. F., Daleng, M. L., & McGowan, R. W. (1993). Scores on exercise dependence among dancers. *Perceptual and Motor Skills, 176,* 531–535.

Pierce, W. D., & Epling, W. F. (1994). Activity anorexia: An interplay between basic and applied behavior analysis. *Behavior Analyst, 17,* 7–23.

Prince, R. (1985). Concept of culture-bound syndromes. *Social Science and Medicine, 21,* 197–203.

Richert, A. J., & Hummers, J. A. (1986). Patterns of physical activity in college students at possible risk for eating disorder. *International Journal of Eating Disorders, 5,* 757–763.

Rodin, J., & Larson, L. (1992). Social factors and the ideal body shape. In K. D. Brownell, J. Rodin, & J. H. Wilmore, (Eds.), *Eating, body weight and performance in athletes. Disorders of modern society* (pp. 146–158). Philadelphia, PA: Lea & Febiger.

Rodin, J., & Plante, T. (1989). The physiological effects of exercise. In R. S. Williams & A. G. Wallace (Eds.), *Biological effects of physical activity* (pp. 127–137). Champaign, IL: Human Kinetics.

Sanger, D. J., & McCarthy, P. S. (1980). Differential effect of morphine on food and water intake in food deprived and freely feeding rats. *Psychopharmacology, 72,* 103–106.

Selvini, P. (1965, April). *Interpretation of anorexia nervosa.* Paper presented at the Meyer and Feldman Symposium, Gottingen, Hanover, Germany.

Short, S. H., & Short, W. R. (1983). Four-year study of university athletes' dietary intake. *Journal of the American Dietetic Association, 82,* 632–645.

Smith, N. J. (1980). Excessive weight loss and food aversion simulating anorexia nervosa. *Pediatrics, 66,* 139–141.

Sours, J. A. (1980). *Starving to death in a sea of objects: The anorexia nervosa syndrome.* New York, London: Aronson.

Sours, J. A. (1981). Running, anorexia nervosa and perfection. In M. H. Sachs & M. L. Sachs (Eds.), *Psychology of running* (pp. 80–91). Champaign, IL: Human Kinetics.

Stainsby, M. (1995). Men falling prey to body image. *Edmonton Journal,* July 11.

Stevenson, T. T. (1990). Anorexia as a culture-bound syndrome. *Dissertation Abstracts International, 50*(8-A), 2553.

Sundgot-Borgen, J. (1994a). Eating disorders in female athletes. *Sports Medicine, 17,* 176–188.

Sundgot-Borgen, J. (1994b). Risk and trigger factors for the development of eating disorders in female elite athletes. *Medicine and Science in Sports and Exercise, 26,* 414–419.

Swann, I. (1977). Anorexia nervosa—A difficult diagnosis in boys. *Practitioner, 218,* 424–427.

Swartz, L. (1985). Anorexia nervosa as a culture-bound syndrome. *Social Science and Medicine, 20,* 725–730.

Thompson, R. A., & Sherman, R. T. (1993). *Helping athletes with eating disorders.* Leeds, UK: Human Kinetics.

Tokuyama, K., Saito, M., & Okuda, H. (1982). Effect of wheel running on food intake and weight gain of female rats. *Physiology and Behavior, 23,* 899–903.

Vitousek, K. B., & Hollon, S. D. (1990). The investigation of schematic content and processing in the eating disorders. *Cognitive Therapy and Research,* 191–214.

Warren, M. (1988, August). *Delayed menarche in athletes: The role of low energy intake and eating disorders and their relation to bone density.* Paper presented at the International Symposium on Hormones and Sport, Dubrovnik, Yugoslavia.

Warren, M. P., Stanton, A. L., & Blessing, D. L. (1990). Disordered eating patterns in competitive female athletes. *International Journal of Eating Disorders, 9,* 565–569.

Weight, L. M., & Noakes, T. D. (1987). Is running an analog of anorexia? A survey of the incidence of eating disorders in female distance runners. *Medicine and Science in Sports and Exercise, 19,* 213–217.

Welle, S. L., Amatruda, J. M., Forbes, G. B., & Lockwood, D. H. (1984). Resting metabolic rate of obese women after rapid weight loss. *Journal of Clinical Endocrinology and Metabolism, 59,* 41–44.

Wheeler, G. (1984). *Anorectic tendencies in high mileage runners.* Unpublished masters thesis, University of Alberta, Edmonton.

Wheeler, G. D., McFadyen, S. D., Symbaluk, D., Pierce, W. D., Epling, W. F., & Cumming, D. C. (1990). Effects of training on serum testosterone and cortisol levels in wrestlers. *Clinical Journal of Sports Medicine, 2,* 257–260.

Wheeler, G. D., Wall, S. R., Belcastro, A. N., & Cumming D. C. (1984). Reduced serum testosterone and prolactin levels in male distance runners. *Journal of the American Medical Association, 252,* 514–516.

Wheeler, G. D., Wall, S. R., Belcastro, A. N., Conger, P., & Cumming, D. C. (1986). Are anorexic tendencies prevalent in the habitual runner? *British Journal of Sport Medicine, 20,* 77–81.

Wheeler, G. D., Pierce, W. D., Epling, W. F., Singh, M., Smith, M., & Cumming D. C. (1989). *Dietary intake and hormonal levels in men and women in an endurance training program.* Unpublished doctoral dissertation, University of Alberta.

Wilson, G. T., & Eldredge, K. L. (1992). Pathology and development of eating disorders: Implications for athletes. In K. D. Brownell, J. Rodin, & J. H. Wilmore (Eds.), *Eating, body weight and performance in athletes. Disorders of modern society* (pp. 115–127). Philadelphia, PA: Lea & Febiger.

Yaeger, K. K., Agostini, R., Nattive, A., & Drinkwater, B. (1993). The female athlete triad: Disordered eating, amenorrhea, osteoporosis. *Medicine and Science in Sports and Exercise,* 775–777.

Yates, A. (1991). *Obligatory running and the eating disorders: Toward an integrated theory of activity.* New York: Brunner/Mazel.

Yates, A., Leehey, K., & Shisslak, C. M. (1983). Running—An analogue of anorexia? *New England Journal of Medicine, 308,* 251–255.

Yates, A., Shisslak, C., Allender, J., & Crago, M. (1992). Comparing obligatory and non-obligatory runners. *Psychosomatics, 33,* 180–189.

Yates, A., Shisslak, C., Crago, M., & Allender, J. (1994). Overcommitment to sports: Is there a relationship to eating disorders? *Clinical Journal of Sports Medicine, 4,* 39–46.

V

Clinical Observations
and Implications
of Activity Anorexia

14

Athletes, Eating Disorders, and the Overtraining Syndrome

Alayne Yates
University of Hawaii

Our work has focused on runners who became locked into their training regimen to the point where they lost control over the process (Yates, 1991, 1992; Yates, Leehey, & Shisslak, 1983; Yates, Shisslak, Allender, & Crago, 1992). These obligatory runners initiated an exercise or exercise-plus-diet program in the name of self-improvement. When they became locked in, they spent all of their free time running. Relationships suffered and divorce was not uncommon. Often dysphoric, the athletes felt controlled by the sport. Some had knowingly damaged the body by continuing to run on inflamed tendons or deteriorating cartilage. These athletes appeared rather strange, especially to older, nonathletic observers. But to many of their athletic age mates, they seemed like paradigms of virtue, role models for a healthy, productive life.

Because the association of compulsive athleticism with pathology remains tenuous, we preferred to define obligatory running operationally (Yates et al., 1992). We designated those runners who continued to run in spite of clear contraindications as *obligatory*. Twenty-seven of the 66 male and female runners in the study were obligatory by this definition. This was an unexpectedly high number. It may be that some of our runners were not truly obligatory. As 60% of runners experience musculoskeletal injuries (Paty, 1988), it may be that some of the obligatory runners ran only with less severe injuries but were able to stop running for more severe

ᵢer complications. Other studies suggest that about 10% of runners
ᵢtory or "addicted" category (Thaxton, 1982).

ᵎout, and sometimes met, runners who were more obligatory than
atory of our subjects. Again and again our subjects identified a few
ᵢnuᵢ.   ᵢ the community as "really hard core," or "far worse than I am."
Sometimes ᵤur subjects attempted to recruit these runners for the study. They
always refused. Participation in the study would take time away from their training.
Every available moment was already tagged and taken.

HIGH ACHIEVERS

Athletes exhibit personality traits of persistence, perfectionism, and high achievement (Gontang, Clitsome, & Kostrubala, 1977; Hauch & Blumenthal, 1992; Owens
& Slade, 1987; Puffer & McShane, 1992; Davis, Brewer & Ratusny, 1993). Our
subjects, obligatory and nonobligatory, certainly fit this description. Their average
educational attainment was better than 17 years, or first year in graduate school.
Even those who suffered from an emotional problem such as depression were
functioning extremely well in school or on the job. They strove for a personal best
in running just as they strove to make Dean's list or to become board certified in
another medical specialty. Running seemed to be part of a pattern of "workaholism."
Both the running and the workaholism were fueled by deep self-dissatisfaction and
the desire to improve. Some had begun to run at a time when they needed a challenge
(after graduation or when the children were all in school). Others began to run when
they were upset with their performance (failed marriage, low Graduate Record
Exam [GRE] scores).

There were clear differences between the obligatory and nonobligatory runners.
On semistructured interview, the obligatory runners appeared significantly more
concerned and rigid about weight control than did the nonobligatory athletes, $p >$
.004. Although they were already lean, they tended to follow a rigid, restrictive,
low fat, or fat-free "healthy" diet. For example, one athlete ate a piece of fruit and
rice cakes for breakfast, skipped lunch, and had pasta with tomato sauce and a salad
with low-calorie dressing for dinner. He consumed the same meals every day,
although the fruit could vary. He took minor liberties at Christmas parties and other
necessary celebrations. Another athlete ate only one meal a day, saying that he had
no time to waste on eating. Others followed "healthy" guidelines, but would binge
occasionally. Running helped them follow a diet: It stabilized their weight, and
when they ran they experienced less hunger. "Besides," said one athlete, "When I
run, I'm miles away from the refrigerator."

Nutritional history suggested that the calories the athletes consumed lagged far
behind the calories they were expending. They were all lean and a few appeared
emaciated, but in general their weight had not changed significantly in recent
months. This suggested that their bodies had become extremely efficient at utilizing
the nutrients available (Yates, 1992).

RELATIONSHIP TO THE EATING DISORDERS

Empirically, obligatory athletes fell into a bulimic or an anorectic exercise pattern. In the bulimic pattern, they ate more than they thought they should and then ran harder to get rid of the calories. In the anorectic pattern, they followed a stringent diet even though they were already very thin. They said they wanted to be "lean and mean," which meant reducing their percentage of body fat. When anorectic athletes increased their miles run, at the same time as they decreased fat (and total calories), they risked overtraining. The overtraining syndrome, or "staleness," is an exhausted state in which effort continues but performance diminishes. Because these runners often value performance above all else, the decline is a catastrophe. Not infrequently, they consider killing themselves.

At least one runner, Mary Wazeter, did make a serious suicide attempt. In her book *Dark Marathon* (Wazeter & Lewis, 1989), she described how she increased her effort and reduced her intake (through diet and purging) until her performance plummeted. In an attempt to recoup, she increased her training time, but her performance continued to deteriorate. Agitated and depressed, she threw herself from a bridge over the Susquehanna River onto the ice-covered water below. She did not die, but she did become a paraplegic and was permanently confined to a wheelchair.

Great athletes like Greg LeMond and Frank Shorter must conquer the body and control the need for food, rest, and care. They must concentrate single-mindedly on the goal and be acutely aware of minute changes in body function (body focus). They must be compulsive about training schedules and able to stay away from relationships that could interfere with training. Most athletes find some sort of balance, but under certain circumstances the need to control the body at all cost can place athletes at risk to develop an eating disorder.

Even though we had eliminated 11 subjects with current or past history of an eating disorder, 7 of our 66 subjects scored in the clinical range (> 30) on the Eating Attitudes Test (EAT). This finding is supported by many other studies that show an association between running and disturbed eating. As a group, athletes are more likely than nonathletes to fast, vomit, abuse diet medication, laxatives, and diuretics (DePalma et al., 1993; Davis, Brewer, & Ratusny, 1993). Fewer men than women are involved in these activities, but men are just as likely to have a distorted body image, to think of themselves as fat when they are not, and to feel out of control when they eat (Burckes-Miller & Black, 1988). Some of the men go on to develop an eating disorder (Katz, 1986). Of the athletes affected, most have eating-disordered symptoms rather than a full-fledged disorder (Pasman & Thompson, 1988; Wheeler, Wall, & Belcastro, 1986). Certain sports seem to foster problematic food behavior more than others: distance running, gymnastics, bodybuilding, wrestling, cycling, aerobics, dancing, figure skating, and diving. These tend to be individual sports that emphasize a personal best. In these activities, leanness is related to performance and the scantily clad body is often on display.

As noted, athletes are persistent and perfectionistic persons. They have also been described as somewhat rigid, strongly goal-oriented, and driven to excellence (Puffer & McShane, 1992). Women with eating disorders share these personality characteristics (Rothenberg, 1988; Silverstein, Perdue, Peterson, Vogel, & Fantini, 1986; Striegel-Moore, Silberstein, Grunberg, & Rodin, 1990; Vanderheyden, Fekken, & Boland, 1988), and perfectionism is an established risk factor for developing an eating disorder (Waller, Wood, Miller, & Slade, 1992). These traits foster overachievement in sport as well as in dieting. In our study we were unable to find eating-disordered women who ran who did not become obligatory. Even if they entered the sport just for fun, they soon became deadly serious about improving their performance. Most of the 38% to 75% of women with eating disorders who exercise must do so in an obligatory manner (Kron, Katz, Gorzynski, & Weiner, 1978).

Because of their personality characteristics, athletes and eating-disordered women have enormous concern about performance. They increase their effort when they think they have not improved enough or when faced with group urgency (as in aerobics), published standards of health or excellence, pressure from family or coach, or performance scores expressed in discrete units such as points, time, distance, and inches. The makers of Stairmaster, NordicTrack, and other exercise machines must be aware of this effect; they equip their units with readouts of calories burned, feet or floors climbed, and distance covered. These figures enhance the motivation of ordinary exercisers but can nudge obligatory athletes and eating disordered individuals over the line into senseless, driven activity.

When eating-disordered women embark on an exercise program such as running, the running "works" for them (Yates, Crago, Allender, & Shisslak, 1994). They like their bodies better after they begin to run. The body dissatisfaction that is the hallmark of the eating disorders diminishes or disappears entirely. They worry less about calories because the exercise allows them to eat whatever they want without gaining weight. However, they transfer their anxiety to performance, becoming as locked into personal best as they had been to weight loss. Body dissatisfaction becomes body preoccupation.

Obligatory runners were significantly more preoccupied with the body, $p > .00001$ than the nonobligatory runners. The preoccupation increased as they became locked into training. Preoccupation with the body displaced interest in family, social relationships, and personal pleasures. One of our subjects said: "My body *is* my life!" Where obligatory runners worry about how the body feels and functions, eating-disordered persons worry about how it looks and how much it weighs.

Obligatory runners were significantly more likely to run alone, $p > .01$ than were nonobligatory runners. The runners gave several reasons for this: No one else could run as long or as hard; they did not want to slow their pace; they preferred to revel in their own thoughts and fantasies; they wanted to maintain concentration or body focus. In other words, they wanted to maintain complete control, without interference or distraction. As they increased their training, they became more isolated, irritable, and compulsive. Anorectic women who starve themselves undergo a similar process as they withdraw from friends, prefer to eat alone, and spend every free moment focusing on the body. Davis (1990), and Davis, Fox, Cowles, Hastings, and Schwass (1990) described a similar process in women who engaged in a fitness program. These women developed an obsessive attitude toward weight control. As they became fit, they became more dissatisfied with the body, concerned with appearance, and they experienced a drop in emotional well-being. A comparable process was described in elite women runners (Gadpaille, Sanborn, & Wagner, 1987) and in women who diet (Drewnowski & Yee, 1989; Patton, 1992).

The preference of obligatory runners to run alone has led them to be rather pejoratively described as narcissistic. However, it was our impression that most had not been especially narcissistic before they became overcommitted to running and that the personality characteristics of aloofness, self-centeredness, and body preoccupation had intensified as they became obligatory.

HEALTH VERSUS PATHOLOGY

Even overcommitted or addicted athletes score in the healthy range on psychological tests. In, fact running addiction is associated with positive, rather than negative, psychological characteristics (Chapman & De Castro, 1990). This was so in our study also. With only a few exceptions, subjects scored in the healthy range on an extensive battery of psychological tests. In their view, running had helped them achieve positive changes in self-concept, $p > .002$ and a greater sense of control over their bodies and their lives, $p > .02$.

Even though the runners appeared psychologically healthy, they said and did things that seemed irrational. Why would psychologically healthy individuals knowingly cause permanent damage to joints, tendons, and marriages? How could healthy people say that if they could not run, they would commit suicide? Or that they would continue to run on crutches or in a cast? Were the tests in error, or did they not measure the "craziness" of the obligatory athlete?

We began to suspect that the runners were indeed healthy persons who were simply too well geared for success. Often reared by high-achieving parents, gifted in mind as well as body, blessed with the desire to do well (perfectionism) and the energy to continue in spite of setback (persistence), they had a burning need to achieve a personal best. As time progressed, some of them became locked in and unable to back off in spite of increasingly serious complications. There were factors in addition to personality traits that intensified the process. With this hypothesis, we began to look at how this might come to pass.

STRATEGIES AND THE RECIPROCAL
FEEDBACK LOOP

It is not easy to be a compulsive athlete, especially when running on injury. The no-pain-no-gain model is not for quitters. Without exception the obligatory runners in our study had developed complex cognitive strategies to keep themselves on track. They told themselves, "If I don't finish today, I'll give up and never run again;" "If I don't keep improving, I won't live to see 40;" "If I couldn't run, my life would be over;" "If I keep running, I'll never be depressed;" and, of course,

"Pain is the badge of the elite runner." They overvalued the sport, seeing it as the most gratifying aspect of life. They subscribed to superstitious beliefs: that increasing the total distance run would protect against aging or that running cleansed the soul and brought them closer to God. Some runners regularly devalued others who were overweight or out of shape. They viewed themselves as special—but only if they could keep on running.

Strategies are based on cognitive distortions, and the cognitive distortions are a major reason some athletes say and do irrational things. In reality they are struggling to maintain self-control in the face of pain and exhaustion. The strategies are a form of brainwashing designed to prevent any slacking in effort. These strategies are similar to those described in eating-disordered women (Garner, Rockert, Olmstead, Johnson, & Coscina, 1985) who are attempting a task at least as difficult as running a marathon: weight control in the face of readily available food and ravenous hunger.

Strategies contribute to the formation of a reciprocal feedback loop. The loop begins when an individual tries a sport and finds that he or she is good at it. This generates a sense of power and self-worth, providing the motivation to try even harder. The individual strives more, does better, and achieves an even greater sense of efficacy. Traits of perfectionism and persistence facilitate the process. The feedback loop serves as a powerful self-motivator and predictor of success (Bandura, 1986). Some individuals may become so caught up in the feedback loop that they are unable to get out. This places them at high risk for the overtraining syndrome, also called staleness.

OVERTRAINING SYNDROME

High achievers are known to be especially susceptible to the overtraining syndrome (Costill, 1986; O'Brien, 1988; Town, 1985) Overtraining occurs when there is too much exertion and not enough rest. The athlete tries harder but is able to do less. Fatigue, muscular soreness, stiffness, and loss of vigor follow. The athlete experiences irritability, depression, loss of muscle mass, and lack of desire for food. Concentration and memory are often affected (Fry, Morton, & Keast, 1991; Lehmann, Foster, & Keul, 1993; Puffer & McShane, 1992). The balance shifts from wanting to train (motivation) to having to train (compulsion). The clinical profile of overtrained endurance athletes is like that of persons with a reactive depression or chronic fatigue syndrome (Akiskal & McKinney, 1975; Wessely & Powell, 1990). Psychological factors contribute: unrealistic goals, demands of competition, fear of failure, and pressure from coach or family (Costill, 1986; Fry, Morton, & Keast, 1991).

Physiological changes associated with overtraining include reduced muscular strength and maximum oxygen uptake, reduced heart rate and lactic acid concentration after exertion, and immunosuppression with increased susceptibility to infection. There are profound changes in neurotransmitters and hormones. The heart becomes relatively unresponsive to catecholamine stimulation, and fewer catecholamines are secreted at night. The inhibitory neurotransmitters gamma-ami-nobutyric acid (GABA) and serotonin increase, accentuating the exhaustion the athlete experiences. A reduction in the anabolic hormone testosterone and an increase in the catabolic hormone cortisol foster a reduction in muscle mass. If the athlete continues to train in spite of exhaustion, the adrenals fail and cortisol drops (Costill, Flynn, & Kirwan, 1988; Fry et al., 1991; Lehmann, Foster, & Keul, 1993). Similar changes occur in starved anorectic patients (Yates, 1991).

For athletes the overtrained state is like hitting a wall. Trying harder does not work and the strategies are to no avail. The only cure is to rest from four to six weeks (Dishman, 1992; Fry et al., 1991). Rest is what compulsive athletes fear most. When they cannot run they experience severe anxiety and depression, confusion, psychic fragmentation, and feelings of bloatedness and body deteriora-tion (Chan & Grossman, 1988; Smith, Scott, O'Fallon, & Young, 1990). When told to rest they react in various ways. Some rest as long as necessary, realizing that there are no viable alternatives. Others rest for a week, start to train, and then rapidly deteriorate. Some refuse to rest and may consider suicide when their performance continues to deteriorate.

Two forms of overtraining syndrome are described in the literature: sympathetic and parasympathetic (Israel, 1976).The parasympathetic, or exhausted, form was just described. The sympathetic form is based on the same biophysiological changes, but is marked by restlessness and emotional instability. It used to be common but now is rare, perhaps because of the current emphasis on endurance sports. The paradoxical state of hyperactivity coupled with inanition is found in anorectic patients who are continuously active in spite of starvation.

ACTIVITY ANOREXIA

The overtraining syndrome is clearly related to activity anorexia, as described by Epling and Pierce (1988) and Pierce and Epling (1994). The semistarved rat, running itself to death on the activity wheel, appears somewhat like the overtrained athlete, close to collapse, who refuses to rest, and to the 72-pound anorectic who must work out for 45 minutes a day on the Stairmaster at maximum intensity. All three seem to be locked in by compulsion, controlled by the activity. When susceptible individuals combine dietary restriction with increased exercise, this generates biochemical and physiological changes that affect virtually every hor-mone and transmitter in the body, altering mood and cognition.

Changes in neuropeptides and neurotransmitters are likely to be involved in activity anorexia. For instance, exercise seems to induce an increase in hypotha-lamic norepinephrine secretion. Norepinephrine suppresses appetite and makes continued activity possible (Broocks, Liu, & Pirke, 1990). In activity anorexia there may be increases in vasopressin, a neurohypophyseal peptide hormone also known as antidiuretic hormone (ADH), to explain the increase in compulsivity. When vasopressin is administered to animals, it keeps them from unlearning behaviors they have previously learned (Van Ree, Hijman, Jolles, & DeWied, 1985). The animals continue to practice the behaviors even when there is no reason to do so. Vasopressin is elevated in obsessive compulsive disorder (OCD; Altemus et al., 1990), anorexia (Gold, Kaye, Robertson, & Ebert, 1983), and bulimia even after bulimics have abstained from purging for more than a month (Demitrack, Kalogeras, Altemus, Pigott, Listwak, & Gold, 1992). As vasopressin is sensitive to dehydration, one would expect there to be changes in vasopressin secondary to dehydration and rehydration in endurance sports such as running.

Many individuals could not develop activity anorexia if they tried. Some rats are not susceptible to activity anorexia either. Factors that protect against activity anorexia must be defined. Although animal research cannot tell us about changes in mood state or the development of cognitive distortions, it may be able to shed light on personality factors such as persistence and perfectionism. Animals that develop activity anorexia may be animals genetically loaded for compulsive traits. They would search longer and harder than other animals for grains of wheat hidden in the dirt or push the lever for food rewards longer, even when the food is gone.

CONCLUSION

Certain high-achieving individuals seem at risk for developing activity anorexia because of traits of persistence and perfectionism. They choose a diet or exercise program to enhance their self-worth in terms of current cultural values. They throw themselves into the activity just as they throw themselves into study or work. They are gratified by their excellent progress and inspired to try even harder. They become outstanding athletes and dieters, but if they combine these activities, they are at risk to develop activity anorexia. If activity anorexia develops, they experience a marked increase in driven, compulsive behavior. The activity regenerates itself and becomes resistant to change. As the process continues, they become more aloof, self-centered, depressed, and preoccupied with the body. If they persist, they may develop symptoms of the overtraining syndrome, marked by increased compulsion to train and a decline in performance. This places them at risk for severe depression and even suicide.

REFERENCES

Akiskal, H. S., & McKinney, W. T. (1975). Overview of recent research in depression: Integration of 10 conceptual models into a comprehensive clinical frame. *Archives of General Psychiatry, 32,* 285–305.

Altemus, M., Pigott, T. A., & Kalogeras, K. T., Demitrack, M. A., Oubbert, B., Murphy, D. L., & Gold, P. W. (1990). Elevations in arginine vasopressin and corticotropin-releasing hormone secretion in obsessive-compulsive disorder. *Archives of General Psychiatry, 49,* 9–20.

Bandura, A. (1986). *Social foundations of thought and action: A social cognitive theory.* Englewood Cliffs, NJ: Prentice-Hall.

Broocks, A., Liu, J., & Pirke, K. M. (1990). Semi-starvation induced hyperactivity compensates for decreased norepinephrine and dopamine turnover in the medio-basal hypothalamus of the rat. *Journal of Neurological Transmission, 79*, 113–124.

Burckes-Miller, M. E., & Black, D. R. (1988). Behaviors and attitudes associated with eating disorders: Perceptions of college athletes about food and weight. *Health Education Research, 3*, 203–208.

Chan, C. S., & Grossman, H. Y. (1988). Psychological effects of running loss on consistent runners. *Perceptual and Motor Skills, 66*, 875–883.

Chapman, C. L., & De Castro, J. M. (1990). Running addiction: Measurement and associated psychological characteristics. *Journal of Sports Medicine and Physical Fitness, 30*, 283–290.

Costill, D. L. (1986). *Inside running—Basics of sports physiology*. Indianapolis, IN: Benchmark Press.

Costill, D. L., Flynn, M. G., & Kirwan, J. P. (1988). Effects of repeated days of intensified training on muscle glycogen and swimming performance. *Medicine and Science in Sports and Exercise, 20*, 249–254.

Davis, C., Fox, J., Cowles, M., Hastings, P., & Schwass, K. (1990). The functional role of exercise in the development of weight and diet concerns in women. *Journal of Psychosomatic Research, 34*, 563–574.

Davis, C. (1990). Body image and weight preoccupation: A comparison between exercising and non-exercising women. *Appetite, 15*, 13–21.

Davis, C., Brewer, H. & Ratusny, D. (1993). Behavioral frequency and psychological commitment: Necessary concepts in the study of excessive exercising. *Journal of Behavioral Medicine, 16*, 611–628.

DePalma, M. T., Koszewski, W. M., Case, J. G., Barile, R. J., DePalma, B. F., & Oliaro, S. M. (1993). Weight control practices of lightweight football players. *Medicine and Science in Sports and Exercise, 25*, 694–701.

Demitrack, M. A., Kalogeras, K. T., & Altemus, M., Pigott, T. A., Listwak, S. T., & Gold, P. N. (1992). Plasma and cerebrospinal fluid measures of arginine vasopressin in patients with bulimia nervosa and in healthy subjects. *Journal of Clinical Endocrinology and Metabolism, 74*, 1277–1283.

Dishman, R. K. (1992). Physiological and psychological effects of overtraining. In K. D. Brownell, J. Rodin, & J. H. Wilmore (Eds.), *Eating, body weight, and performance in athletes* (pp. 248–272). Philadelphia, PA: Lea & Febiger.

Drewnowski, A., & Yee, D. K. (1987). Men and body image: Are males satisfied with their body weight? *Psychosomatic Medicine, 49*, 626–634.

Epling, W. F., & Pierce, W. D. (1988). Activity-based anorexia: A biobehavioral perspective. *International Journal of Eating Disorders, 7*, 475–485.

Fry, R. W., Morton, A. R., & Keast, D. (1991). Overtraining in athletes: An update. *Sports Medicine, 12*, 32–65.

Gadpaille, W. J., Sanborn, C. F., & Wagner, W. E. W. (1987). Athletic amenorrhea, major affective disorders, and eating disorders. *American Journal of Psychiatry, 144*, 939–942.

Garner, D. M., Rockert, W., Olmstead, M. P., Johnson, C., & Coscina, D. V. (1985). Psychoeducational principles in the treatment of bulimia and anorexia nervosa. In D. M. Garner & P. E. Garfinkel (Eds.), *Handbook of psychotherapy for anorexia nervosa and bulimia* (pp. 513–572). New York: Guilford.

Gold, P. W., Kaye, W., Robertson, G. L., & Ebert, M. (1983). Abnormalities in plasma and cerebrospinal fluid arginine vasopressin in patients with anorexia nervosa. *New England Journal of Medicine, 308*, 1117–1123.

Gontang, A., Clitsome, T., & Kostrubala, T. (1977). A psychological study of 50 sub-3-hour marathoners. *Annals of the New York Academy of Sciences, 30*, 1020–1028.

Hauch, E. R., & Blumenthal, J. A. (1992). Obsessive and compulsive traits in athletes. *Sports Medicine, 14*, 215–227.

Israel, S. (1976). Zur problematik des Ubertrainings aus internistischer und leistungsphysiolgisher sicht [The problem of overtraining from an internal medicine point of view and from a performance physiologic point of view]. *Medicine and Sport, 16*, 1–12.

Katz, J. L. (1986). Long distance running, anorexia nervosa, and bulimia: A report of two cases. *Comprehensive Psychiatry, 27*, 74–78.

Kron, L., Katz, J. L., Gorzynski, G., & Weiner, H. (1978); Hyperactivity in anorexia nervosa: A fundamental clinical feature. *Comprehensive Psychiatry, 19*, 433–440.

Lehmann, M., Foster, C., & Keul, J. (1993). Overtraining in endurance athletes: A brief review. *Medicine and Science in Sports and Exercise, 25*, 854–862.

O'Brien, A. (1988). Overtraining and sports psychology. In A. Dirix (Ed.), *The olympic book of sports medicine* (Vol. 1, pp. 635–645). Cambridge, MA: Blackwell Scientific Publications.

Owens, R. G., & Slade, P. D. (1987). Running and anorexia nervosa: An empirical study. *International Journal of Eating Disorders, 6*, 771–775.

Pasman, L., & Thompson, J. K. (1988). Body image and eating disturbance in obligatory runners, obligatory weightlifters, and sedentary individuals. *International Journal of Eating Disorders, 7*, 759–769.

Patton, G. C. (1992). Eating disorders: Antecedents, evolution, and course. *Annals of Medicine, 24*, 281–285.

Paty, J. G. (1988). Diagnosis and treatment of musculoskeletal injuries. *Seminars on Arthritis and Rheumatism, 18*, 48–60.

Pierce, W. D., & Epling, W. F. (1994). Activity anorexia: An interplay between basic and applied behavior analysis. *Behavior Analyst, 17*, 7–23.

Puffer, J. C., & McShane, J. M. (1992). Depression and chronic fatigue in athletes. *Clinics in Sports Medicine, 11*, 327–338.

Rothenberg, A. (1988). Differential diagnosis of anorexia nervosa and depressive illness: A review of 11 studies. *Comprehensive Psychiatry, 28*, 427–432.

Silverstein, B., Perdue, L., Peterson, B., Vogel, L., & Fantini, D. A. (1986). Possible causes of the thin standard of bodily attractiveness for women. *International Journal of Eating Disorders, 5*, 135–144.

Smith, A. M., Scott, S. G., O'Fallon, W. M., & Young, M. L. (1990). Emotional responses of athletes to injury. *Mayo Clinic Proceedings, 65*, 38–50.

Striegel-Moore, R. H., Silberstein, L. R., Grunberg, N. E., & Rodin, J. (1990). Competing on all fronts: Achievement orientation and disordered eating. *Sex Roles, 19*, 219–232.

Thaxton L. (1982). Physiological and psychological effects of short term exercise addiction on habitual runners. *Journal of Sports Psychology, 4*, 73–80.

Town, G. P. (1985). *Science of triathalon training and competition.* Champaign, IL: Human Kinetics Books.

Van Ree, J. M., Hijman, R., Jolles, J., & DeWied, D. (1985). Vasopressin and related peptides: Animal and human studies. *Neuro-psychopharmacology and Biological Psychiatry, 9*, 551–539.

Vanderheyden, D. A., Fekken, G. C., & Boland, F. J. (1988). Critical variables associated with binging and bulimia in a university population: A factor analytic study. *International Journal of Eating Disorders, 7*, 321–329.

Waller, G., Wood, A., Miller, G., & Slade, P. (1992). The development of neurotic perfectionism: A risk factor for unhealthy eating attitudes. *British Review of Bulimia and Anorexia Nervosa, 6*, 57–61.

Wazeter, M., & Lewis, G. (1989). *Dark marathon: The Mary Wazeter story.* Grand Rapids, MI: Zonderlean.

Wessely, S., & Powell, R. (1990) Fatigue syndromes: A comparison of chronic "post-viral" fatigue with neuromuscular and affective disorders. *Journal of Neurology, Neurosurgery and Psychiatry, 52*, 940–948.

Wheeler, G. D., Wall, S. R., & Belcastro, A. N. (Eds.). (1986). Are anorexic tendencies prevalent in the habitual runner? *British Journal of Sports Medicine, 20*, 77–81.

Yates A. (1991). *Obligatory running and the eating disorders: Toward an integrated theory of activity.* New York: Bruner/Mazel.

Yates, A. (1992). Biologic considerations in the etiology of the eating disorders. *Pediatric Annals, 21*, 739–745.

Yates, A., Crago, M., Allender, J., & Shisslak, C. (1994). Overcommittment to sport: Is there a relationship to the eating disorders? *Journal of Clinical and Sports Medicine, 4*, 39–46.

Yates, A., Leehey, K., & Shisslak, C. M. (1983). Running—An analogue of anorexia? *New England Journal of Medicine, 308*, 251–255.

Yates, A., Shisslak, C., Allender, J., & Crago, M. (1992). Comparing obligatory and nonobligatory runners. *Psychosomatics, 33*, 180–189.

15

The Problem of Excessive Physical Activity in Patients with Anorexia Nervosa

C. C. Beumont
P. J. V. Beumont
S. W. Touyz
University of Sydney

Excessive activity has long been recognized as a characteristic symptom of anorexia nervosa (AN), and seminal theorists such as Lasègue (1873/1964) and Gull (1964) referred to overactivity in their classic descriptions of the disorder. Janet (1929), in his distinction between hysterical and obsessional presentations of the illness, compared the use of exercise to lose weight in the obsessional form to exercise as a denial in the hysterical, whereas Bruch (1973) described obsessive hyperactivity as being one of the four cardinal features that characterize true AN. However, despite the longstanding recognition of the increased prevalence of hyperactivity in anorectic patients, many authors (Blinder, Freeman, & Stunkard 1970; Crisp 1965; Crisp, Hsu, Harding, & Hartshorn 1980; Halmi 1974; King 1963; Slade 1973; Thoma, 1967) appear to view the behavior as a secondary and seemingly unimportant feature of the illness, seeing excessive activity merely as one of a variety of behaviors used to bring about and maintain weight loss. Common explanations for its presence are that hyperactivity results from a conscious attempt by the patient to burn calories and speed up weight loss (Bruch, 1965) or that it acts as a "form of denial of the enervating effects of the excessive dieting" (Kron, Katz, Gorzynski, & Weiner, 1978, p. 433). In spite of this apparent lack of conviction that there may be a fundamental and reciprocal relationship between excessive exercise and AN, some researchers have investigated the matter further.

Stunkard (1960) demonstrated the use of pedometers as a valid measurement of excessive activity in man, and Blinder et al. (1970) attempted to quantify the extent of excessive activity in anorectic subjects using the same method. They demonstrated higher than average levels of activity in most of their anorectic patients.

Kron et al. (1978) surveyed medical charts of female patients hospitalized for treatment over a 10-year period and reported hyperactivity in 25 of 33 AN patients. Hyperactivity was judged to be present "when the patient clearly appeared to manifest a day-to-day level of physical activity that was far greater than most of her peers. This required . . . some form of strenuous daily exertion, e.g., jogging, swimming, tennis, biking" (p. 434). They stressed the apparent structure of the excessive exercise in the anorectic patients, explaining that although the patients' continual wandering around the hospital ward may appear to be aimless, this pacing of corridors is the main outlet for physical activity for hospitalized eating-disordered patients. Further, Kron et al. reported that excessive exercising was not merely a secondary symptom in hyperactive anorectic patients but rather that it usually preceded the onset of the illness, with 21 of the 25 patients identified described as being extremely active well before they had ever dieted or lost weight. Kron et al. managed to follow up 15 of the original 33 patients and reported that for 11 of these hyperactivity was still clearly present despite substantial weight recovery in 8. All the hyperactive patients contacted at follow-up described their current activity level as being goal-directed, organized, planned, tightly scheduled, and rigidly carried out. They concluded that hyperactivity is "an early and enduring clinical feature of AN and not merely secondary to either a conscious attempt to lose weight or weight loss per se" (p. 439).

Crisp et al. (1980) performed a similar retrospective analysis of the medical records of 102 anorectic patients and reported excessive activity in 38 cases, and King (1963) reported "intense athleticism" in up to 75% of AN sufferers.

Touyz, Beumont, and Hoek (1987) reviewed the clinical histories of 15 AN patients in whom overactivity had been noted as a cardinal feature. These patients were interviewed and compared with 17 anorectic patients in whom overactivity was not a predominant feature. They found that the initial motive for weight loss among the exercisers was a *pursuit of fitness* rather than a pursuit of thinness, and that 60% of the exercisers had started exercising excessively before engaging in dieting behaviors. Further, all but one of the exercisers were engaged in strenuous physical activity for more than two hours per day prior to their hospital admission, compared with none of the nonexercisers. Finally, they reported a clear relationship between caloric intake and physical activity, which they referred to as "debting," in all of the exercisers. (Debting involves an attempt to regulate energy input through eating against energy output through exercise so as always to remain in negative energy balance.) They commented further that all exercisers experienced marked withdrawal symptoms such as irritability, guilt, or anxiety when exercise was curtailed. A large number of the exercisers had sustained injuries as a result of their excessive activity, but continued to exercise regardless of pain. Many of the patients reported difficulty in controlling their activity when they returned home, and most were apparently unaware of the extent of their physical activity, tending to equate activity only with intense exercise. Touyz et al. concluded that for these exercising AN patients, overexercising was the major behavioral problem and suggested "some subjects with 'exercise addiction' eventually progress to frank AN while in other AN patients who start with abstinence behaviors, excessive exercising develops later as the major behavioral problem" (pp. 145-146).

Eisler and le Grange (1990) proposed four models to explain the link between excessive exercise and eating disorders. The first views excessive exercise and AN as distinct diagnostic groups and claims that although exercise may be a prominent feature of AN, it is principally a means of accelerating weight loss. According to this model, hospitalized anorectics using excessive activity as a means of facilitating weight loss will be more likely to complain about the increased food intake that hospitalization entails rather than the lack of physical activity. The second model proposes that AN and excessive exercise are overlapping groups and that excessive exercise can lead to the development of AN. This model proposes an additional causal link between excessive exercise and AN and is supported by the animal studies conducted by Routtenberg and Kuznesof (1967) and Epling, Pierce, and Stefan (1983). It has implications for prevention because it implies that people who exercise excessively are at risk of developing an eating disorder. The third model suggests that excessive exercise and AN are both related to some other underlying disorder, such as obsessive–compulsive disorder or affective disorder. There does not seem to be much evidence to support this hypothesis (Szmukler, 1987), and a more plausible suggestion is that another illness might be a predisposing factor for both eating disorders and excessive exercise.

The fourth model presented claims that excessive exercise is a variant of eating disorder, so that "the etiological factors (genetic, personality, familial, social) that might normally lead to the development of AN can lead in some cases to a disorder that is superficially different but is in effect the same disorder with different manifestations" (Eisler & le Grange, 1990, p. 380). This last model receives support from the argument put forward by Yates, Leehey, and Shisslak (1983) that the links between AN and excessive exercise can explain the observed female-to-male ratio observed in AN. According to the model, societal pressures are different for men and women, with women being praised for a slim, youthful appearance, whereas men are expected to display mastery and physical prowess. Thus the high value placed on thinness in women is analogous to the high emphasis on physical prowess in men, and vulnerable individuals respond to these pressures by either developing AN (in women) or excessive exercising (in males). Eisler and le Grange (1990) concede that the four models presented are not mutually exclusive and suggest that it is possible that the different models may apply to different individuals or different groups of people. They conclude their review by stating that more research is needed before the debate can be finalized.

OBLIGATORY EXERCISERS

A number of studies have been published dealing specifically with a subset of excessive exercisers referred to as obligatory runners, comparing these subjects with AN or bulimia nervosa (BN) patients (Blumenthal, O'Toole, & Chang, 1984;

Katz, 1986; Nudelman, Rosen, & Leitenberg 1988; Owens & Slade, 1987; Rippon, Nash, Myburgh, & Noakes, 1988; Yates et al., 1983). Yates et al. (1983) presented three (male) cases of obligatory runners (defined as people running over 80 km a week) and explored the similarities between them and anorectic women. They found marked similarities between the two groups in family background, socioeconomic class, and personality characteristics such as inhibition of anger, extraordinarily high self-expectations, high tolerance of physical discomfort, denial of potentially serious debility, and a tendency toward depression. It is quite common for anorectic women to demonstrate compulsive athleticism, and conversely "obligatory runners may demonstrate a bizarre preoccupation with food and an unusual emphasis on lean body mass" (p. 251). Both groups demonstrate an extreme degree of constriction, inflexibility, repetitive thoughts, adherence to rituals, and a need to control themselves and their environment, and in this way are able to be differentiated from those who diet or exercise for health purposes or to relieve anxiety.

Other studies have examined similarities and differences between eating-disordered patients and excessive exercisers (Blumenthal et al., 1984; Nudelman et al., 1988; Owens & Slade, 1987; Rippon et al., 1988). Owens and Slade (1987) administered the Setting Conditions for Anorexia Nervosa Scale (SCANS) questionnaire, a screening test used for identifying people at risk of developing an eating disorder, to 35 female marathon runners. They hypothesized that if excessive exercise was an analog of AN, then the SCANS scores of runners should resemble those of anorectic patients. Although seven of their sample obtained scores above the cutoff for the two scales in the questionnaire (Dissatisfaction and Perfectionism), the sample as a whole tended to obtain scores below the cutoff. Although many of the runners resembled anorectic patients on the Perfectionism scale of the questionnaire, their Dissatisfaction scores resembled those of normal people, suggesting that although superficial similarities may exist between obligatory runners and anorectic patients, "these do not reflect similarities at a more fundamental, causal level" (p. 771).

Blumenthal et al. (1984) compared female anorectics and male and female obligatory runners on the Minnesota Multiphasic Personality Inventory (MMPI). They defined obligatory runners as subjects who maintained a rigid schedule of intense exercise, resisted temptation to lapse into periods of no exercise, reported feelings of guilt when their exercise schedule was violated, compensated for periods of inactivity by increasing exercise, exercised even when tired or ill, were mentally preoccupied with exercising, and kept records of the amount and duration of exercise. Although the anorectics had significantly elevated scores on 8 of the 10 subscales of the MMPI, both male and female runners had normal profiles, suggesting that runners and women with AN are not similar in psychopathology.

Based on these findings reported by Blumenthal et al. (1984), Nudelman et al. (1988) administered the Eating Attitudes Test (EAT) and the Eating Disorders Inventory (EDI) to 20 high-intensity male runners, 20 sedentary-moderate exercising male controls, and 20 bulimic females in an attempt to establish whether runners shared any of the behavioral traits assumed to underlie eating disorders such as drive for thinness and negative body image. They reported that when compared with the female BN subjects on the two study tests, male runners did not display anxiety about eating, were not overly preoccupied with food, did not engage in binge eating and/or purging behavior, were not negatively preoccupied with their weight and intent on losing weight, did not score highly on the personality traits presumed to underlie eating disorders, did not display significant depression, and did not appear to have low self-esteem (as is often reported of eating-disordered patients). They concluded that high-intensity exercising in males is not analogous to either AN or BN, but did concede that a separate study would be required to demonstrate whether female runners resemble women with BN.

Rippon et al. (1988) surveyed female competitive runners and ballet dancers and compared them with professional female models using the EAT and EDI. All groups had elevated EAT and EDI scores; however, the presence of excessive exercise did not appear to be related to these scores, as half of the models in the study who did not use exercise as a means of maintaining their low body weight obtained scores that were not statistically different from those of either the competitive runners or the ballet dancers (both of which require subjects to engage in repetitive physical exercise).

Katz (1986) reported two cases of male excessive exercisers, both long-distance runners, in which extreme exercise precipitated AN. Both cases demonstrated a rapid increase in physical activity, followed by consistent weight loss and increased depression, and bingeing and vomiting when activity was restrained, leading Katz to conclude that extreme exercise can trigger and sustain an eating disorder. In an attempt to explain this phenomenon, Katz refers to a number of potential hypotheses including the animal studies described by Epling et al. (1983), increased narcissistic investment in the body, and elevated production of endorphins resulting in enhanced mood following exercise. This last hypothesis has received support from other studies in which increased production of endorphins is reported following exercise (Appenzeller 1981; Carr et al., 1981; Pangman & Baker, 1980). There has also been reference to the antidepressant and anxiety-reducing effects of regular exercise (Morgan, 1979; Ramsford, 1982).

ACTIVITY ANOREXIA
IN ANIMALS AND HUMANS

In 1983 Epling et al. introduced the term *activity anorexia* to describe the excessive exercising they believed was apparent in at least one third of cases of AN. Using animal models, they proposed a reciprocally interactive effect of activity and food ingestion to explain the phenomenon. They reviewed several studies such as that by Routtenberg and Kuznesof (1967), in which the opportunity to engage in physical activity interferes with eating, resulting in starvation and death of rats allowed free access to a running wheel while placed on a 60-minute per day food-deprivation cycle. Seventy-five percent of control animals that were not given access to the running wheel survived, leading the authors to conclude that activity is an essential component of the animal's self-starvation. Epling et al. (1983) replicated these findings with both mice and rats, further lending support to the hypothesis. A second experiment by the same researchers, investigating the interaction of food presentation and level of activity, indicated that restricting food supply while providing free access to an activity source significantly increased wheel running in rats and severely depressed their food intake, to the extent that the animals self-starved to 70% of their pre-experimental rate. These two experiments add further weight to the hypothesis presented by Routtenberg and Kuznesof, that animals placed on a restricted food schedule will dramatically reduce food consumption if given free access to engage in physical activity, thereby suggesting the possibility of an activity anorexia that exists across a number of different species.

Beumont (1984) reviewed the literature on animal models of AN. In respect to those models that involved hyperactivity, he noted that the key factor in both AN and the animals studied was that the increased activity occurs in a setting where food is restricted, and the expected compensation and adaptation to the situation cannot occur. Teleologically, there appears to be a potential benefit to the animal from the demonstrated increased activity resulting from restricted food. As food resources in the wild become scarce, the animal is prompted to become more active in order to search for food. Viewed in this way, the overactivity of AN patients, and the characteristically disturbed sleep pattern that is reversed on refeeding, may be seen as a direct effect of starvation. On the other hand, not all excess physical activity seen in anorectic patients can be attributed to this relationship. Excessive exercise is often the initial behavioral disturbance prompted by a desire to become fitter, rather than a secondary effect resulting from dietary restriction.

Epling et al. (1983) cited further examples where increased physical activity of animals reduces food intake. These studies can be linked to research conducted on human subjects, such as that of Edholm, Fletcher, Widdowson, and McCance (1955) in which male cadets were reported to consume less food on days of military training than on days of lower activity; that of Mayer, Roy, and Mitra (1956) who found that moderately active workers ate less than sedentary workers; and that of Epstein, Masek, and Marshall (1978) who reported that obese schoolchildren voluntarily reduced food intake after a prelunch exercise period. Finally, a number of human studies looking specifically at structured exercise programs (Holloszy, Skinner, Toro, & Cureton, 1964; Johnson, Mastropaolo, & Wharton, 1972; Katch, Michael, & Jones, 1969; Watt, Wiley, & Fletcher, 1976) indicated that, as demonstrated in animals, exercise reduces food intake in humans.

However, despite these findings, other animal studies have demonstrated that, given time, most subjects will adapt to increased activity levels when food intake is not restricted. According to Epling et al. (1983), this sort of adjustment would be expected to occur in most individuals who regularly engage in physically demanding exercise, such as long-distance runners or professional athletes.

Based on these studies, Epling et al. (1983) proposed that initially increased energy expenditure reduces food consumption, even under free food conditions. However, in activity anorexia, the strict dieting and restricted food schedule of the anorectic patient induce even greater levels of activity that in turn serve to further restrict intake and may well contribute to self-starvation. These variables are multiplicative rather than additive. They concluded their review by surmising that activity anorexia is a subset of the more general diagnostic category, AN, and that the pathology of activity anorexia is generated by the interaction between the effects of food deprivation on activity and also by the effects of activity on food consumption. Although not all people who simultaneously diet and increase their energy expenditure are susceptible to developing activity anorexia, a fast transition to an increased level of physical activity (e.g., sedentary to active sports participation) is likely to produce a vulnerability to this disorder.

IMPLICATIONS FOR TREATMENT

Most behavioral programs for AN severely restrict activity, but some authors have made use of activity in treatment. Blinder et al. (1970) suggested using access to physical activity as a reinforcer of weight gain. In a small series of 3 patients, they reported impressive weight gain with minimal confrontation when patients were permitted 6-hour periods of unrestricted activity outside the hospital on any day when the morning weight was at least half a pound above that of the previous day. A similar approach was discussed also by Liebman, Minuchin, and Baker (1974) and Garfinkel, Garner, and Moldofsky (1977).

Other authors have addressed the issue of specifically controlling exercise during the course of treatment. In an article that has been much quoted, Mavisskalian (1982) used a response prevention strategy in treating two anorexia patients in whom overexercising was a major problem. He included an hour of bed rest after meals to prevent the patients from attempting to "neutralize the obsessionally feared consequence of overweight." The staff supervisors reported that the patients experienced great discomfort in complying with the rest period. Mavisskalian stressed how difficult it was for them to overcome the compulsive overactivity: "It was only in the second part of hospitalization that continuous supervision during response prevention could be eased off . . . suggesting that the patients adapted to the condition only following a phenomenal number of sessions". Touyz and Beumont (1985) similarly included an hour of supervised bed rest after meals as part of a comprehensive treatment program so as to prevent compulsive overexercising as well as self-induced vomiting.

Pierce and Epling (1994) proposed a treatment program based specifically on their concept of activity anorexia. It consisted of three phases. In the first, treatment is directed at stopping excessive exercise and dieting by confinement to bed, forced or tube feeding, or drugs. Agents that block endogenous opiates such as naloxone are to be preferred, as they are thought to lower the motivation for physical activity and increase appetite. In phase 2, the theory of activity anorexia is explained to patients and their families as a part of a more general cognitive therapy approach. Specific attention is directed to the danger of combining stringent dieting with excessive exercise. Because findings from animal research show that the more frequent the meals the lower the tendency to exercise, patients are encouraged to eat frequently throughout the day.

Pierce and Epling (1994) endorsed the use of a conventional operant conditioning program, with negative reinforcement of weight loss by the loss of ward privileges. In addition, they advise training in "sensible and moderate exercise habits . . . [such as] allowing the anorectic to exercise for 20 minutes or less per day. If the patient exceeds 20 minutes, exercise is withheld on the following day. This is a fail-safe contingency, because the excessive exercise that generates activity anorexia is disrupted by the behavioral program." They do not support the use of exercise as a reinforcer for weight gain, claiming that the reinforcement effectiveness of exercise declines as the person gains weight (as they found in their work with laboratory rats). Further, they believe that physical activity at low body weight increases endogenous opiates that actually reduce appetite and further increase the drive to exercise, hence aggravating the anorectic illness.

In the third phase of treatment, patients are encouraged to maintain weight, eat appropriately, and exercise moderately. Family interactions are targeted to change those practices that encourage, albeit unwittingly, the recurrence of activity anorexia.

THE CLINICAL ASSESSMENT OF OVERACTIVITY IN AN PATIENTS

From the preceding review, it is clear that overactivity is an important and enduring feature in many anorectic patients, that there is some evidence of commonality of presentation between anorectic patients and obligatory runners, that interesting models have been proposed that link food restriction and increased activity in animals and humans, and that there has been a focus on anorectic patients' proclivity to overactivity in some treatment programs. But what are the clinical implications of overactivity in the assessment and management of anorexia patients? These issues were examined recently in a paper by Beumont, Arthur, Russell, and Touyz (1994) in the *International Journal of Eating Disorders*.

We argued in favor of a supervised program of exercise being included in the treatment of the anorectic patient. Although many programs totally prohibit exercise, we believe this to be both difficult to enforce and detrimental to recovery. Policing by staff adds further strain to the therapeutic relationship, creating a battle of wills that distracts both patients and staff from the major issue of therapy, which is to facilitate responsibility for self rather than increase feelings of helplessness, resentment, and dependence.

There is a basis of misinformation about the anorectic patient's behavior that is as true for beliefs concerning exercise as it is for the distorted views about food. These false beliefs should be challenged by providing accurate information on the type and level of activity necessary for optimal health, emphasizing the deleterious effects of excessive exercise in the presence of undernutrition.

The aim of therapy is to return the patient to a normal and healthy lifestyle. We believe that it is important to provide a model of healthy exercising that is not excessive while they are in hospital, which will serve as a basis for maintaining a reasonable and not excessive level of activity when they are discharged into the outside world, where high levels of exercise are portrayed as promoting health. On these grounds, we have designed a special program of supervised activity during inpatient treatment, which is is summarized in Beumont et al. (1994). Further details are available from the authors on request.

REFERENCES

Appenzeller, O. (1981). What makes us run? *New England Journal of Medicine, 305*, 578–580.
Beumont, P. J. V. (1984). A clinician looks at animal models of anorexia nervosa. In N. Bond (Ed.), *Animal Models of Psychopathology* (pp. 177–210). Sydney: Academic Press.

Beumont, P. J .V., Arthur, B., Russell, J. D., & Touyz, S. W. (1994). Excessive physical activity in dieting disorder patients: Proposals for a supervised exercise programme. *International Journal of Eating Disorders, 15*, 21–36.

Blinder, B. J., Freeman, D. M. A., & Stunkard, A. J. (1970). Behavior therapy of anorexia nervosa: Effectiveness of activity as a reinforcer of weight gain. *American Journal of Psychiatry, 126*, 1093–1098.

Blumenthal, J. A., O'Toole, L. C., & Chang, J. L. (1984). Is running an analog of anorexia nervosa? An empirical study of obligatory running and anorexia nervosa. *Journal of the American Medical Association, 252*, 520–523.

Bruch, H. (1965). Anorexia nervosa—Its differential diagnosis. *Journal of Mental and Nervous Disorders, 141*, 555–556.

Bruch, H. (1973). *Eating disorders: Obesity, anorexia nervosa, and the person within.* New York: Basic Books.

Carr, D. B., Bullen, B. A., Skrinar, G. S., Arnold, M. A., Rosenblatt, M., Beitins, I. Z., Martin, J. B., & McArthur, J. W. (1981). Physical conditioning facilitates the exercise-induced secretion of beta-endorphin and beta-lipotropin in women. *New England Journal of Medicine, 305*, 560–563.

Crisp, A. H. (1965). Clinical and therapeutic aspects of anorexia nervosa: A study of 30 cases. *Journal of Psychosomatic Research, 9*, 67–78.

Crisp, A. H., Hsu, L. K. G., Harding, B., & Hartshorn, J. (1980). Clinical features of anorexia nervosa: A study of a consecutive series of 102 female patients. *Journal of Psychosomatic Research, 24*, 179–191.

Edholm, O. G., Fletcher, J. G., Widdowson, E. M., & McCance, R. A. (1955). The energy expenditure and food intake of individual men. *British Journal of Nutrition, 9*, 286–300.

Eisler, I., & le Grange, D. (1990). Excessive exercise and anorexia nervosa. *International Journal of Eating Disorders, 9*, 377–386.

Epling, W. F., Pierce, W. D., & Stefan, L. (1983). A theory of activity-based anorexia. *International Journal of Eating Disorders, 3*, 27–46.

Epstein, L. H., Masek, B. J., & Marshall, W. R. A. (1978). A nutritionally based school program for control of eating in obese children. *Behavior Therapy, 9*, 766–778.

Garfinkel, P. E., Garner, D. M., & Moldofsky, H. (1977). The role of behavior modification in the treatment of anorexia nervosa. *Journal of Paediatric Psychology, 2*, 113–121.

Gull, W. W. (1964). Anorexia nervosa. In M. Kaufman & M. Heiman (Eds.), *Evolution of a psychosomatic concept: Anorexia nervosa* (pp. 132–140). New York: International Universities Press. (Original work published 1874)

Halmi, K. A. (1974). Anorexia nervosa: Demographic and clinical features in 94 cases. *Psychosomatic Medicine, 36*, 18–26.

Holloszy, J. O., Skinner, J. S., Toro, G., & Cureton, T. K. (1964). Effects of a six-month program of endurance exercise on the serum lipids of middle-aged men. *American Journal of Cardiology, 14*, 753–760.

Janet, P. (1929). *The major symptoms of hysteria* (2nd ed.). New York: Macmillan.

Johnson, R. E., Mastropaolo, J. A., & Wharton, M. A. (1972). Exercise, dietary intake, and body composition. *Journal of the American Dietetic Association, 61*, 399–403.

Katch, F. I., Michael, E. D., & Jones, E. M. (1969). Effects of physical training on the body composition and diet of females. *Research Quarterly, 40*, 99–104.

Katz, J. L. (1986). Long-distance running, anorexia nervosa, and bulimia: A report of two cases. *Comprehensive Psychiatry, 27*, 74–78.

King, A. (1963). Primary and secondary anorexia nervosa syndromes. *British Journal of Psychiatry, 109*, 470–479.

Kron, L., Katz, J. L., Gorzynski, G., & Weiner, H. (1978). Hyperactivity in anorexia nervosa: A fundamental clinical feature. *Comprehensive Psychiatry, 19*, 433–439.

Lasègue, C. H. (1964). De l'anorexie hysterique [On hysterical anorexia]. In M. Kaufman & M. Heiman (Eds.), *Evolution of a psychosomatic concept: Anorexia nervosa* (pp. 141–155). New York: International Universities Press. (Original work published 1873).

Liebman, R., Minuchin, S., & Baker, L. (1974). An integrated treatment program for anorexia nervosa. *American Journal of Psychiatry, 131*, 432–436,

Mavisskalian, M. (1982). Anorexia nervosa treated with response prevention and prolonged exposure. *Behavior Research and Therapy, 20*, 27–31.

Mayer, J., Roy, P., & Mitra, K. P. (1956). Relation between caloric intake, body weight, and physical work: Studies in an industrial male population in West Bengal. *American Journal of Clinical Nutrition, 4*, 169–175.

Morgan, W. P. (1979). Negative addiction in runners. *Physician Sportsmedicine, 7*, 57–70.

Nudelman, S., Rosen, J. C., & Leitenberg, H. (1988). Dissimilarities in eating attitudes, body image distortion, depression, and self-esteem between high-intensity male runners and women with bulimia nervosa. *International Journal of Eating Disorders, 7*, 625–634.

Owens, R. G., & Slade, P. D. (1987). Running and anorexia nervosa: An empirical study. *International Journal of Eating Disorders, 6*, 771–775.

Pangman, D., & Baker, M. C. (1980). Running high. *Journal of Drug Issues, 10*, 341–350.

Pierce, W. D., & Epling, W. F. (1994). Activity anorexia: An interplay between basic and applied behavior analysis. *Behavior Analyst, 17*, 7–23.

Ramsford, C. P. (1982). A role for amines in the antidepressant effect of exercise: A review. *Medicine, Science, Sports and Exercise, 14*, 1–10.

Rippon, C., Nash, J., Myburgh, K. H., & Noakes, T. D. (1988). Abnormal eating attitude test scores predict menstrual dysfunction in lean females. *International Journal of Eating Disorders, 7*, 617–624.

Routtenberg, A., & Kuznesof, A. W. (1967). "Self-starvation" of rats living in activity wheels on a restricted feeding schedule. *Journal of Comparative and Physiological Psychology, 64*, 414–421.

Slade, P. D. (1973). A short anorectic behavior scale. *British Journal of Psychiatry, 122*, 83–85.

Stunkard, A. J. (1960). A method of studying physical activity in man. *American Journal of Clinical Nutrition, 8*, 595–601.

Szmukler, G. I. (1987). Some comments on the link between anorexia nervosa and affective disorder. *International Journal of Eating Disorders, 6*, 181–189.

Thoma, H. (1967). *Anorexia nervosa*. New York: International Universities Press.

Touyz, S. W., & Beumont, P. J. V. (1985). A comprehensive multidisciplinary approach for the management of patients with eating disorders. In S. W. Touyz & P. J. V. Beumont (Eds.), *Eating Disorders: Prevalence and Treatment* (pp. 11–22). Sydney: Williams & Wilkins.

Touyz, S. W., Beumont, P. J. V., & Hoek, S. (1987). Exercise anorexia: A new dimension in anorexia nervosa? In P. J. V. Beumont, G. D. Burrows, & R. C. Casper (Eds.), *Handbook of Eating Disorders. Part 1: Anorexia and Bulimia Nervosa*. Amsterdam: Elsevier.

Watt, W. E., Wiley, J., & Fletcher, G. F. (1976). Effect of dietary control and exercise training on daily food intake and serum lipids in post-myocardial infarction patients. *American Journal of Clinical Nutrition, 29*, 900–904.

Yates, A., Leehey, K., & Shisslak, C. M. (1983). Running—An analogue of anorexia? *New England Journal of Medicine, 308*(5), 251–255.

16

Clinical Observations on the Physical Activity of Anorexia Nervosa

Jack L. Katz
*North Shore University Hospital
and Cornell University Medical College*

The traditional diagnostic wisdom regarding anorexia nervosa (AN) emphasizes that the conscious restriction of dietary intake and the consequent weight loss evolve out of a central fear of being unable to control one's eating and thus becoming (or remaining) overweight (Bruch, 1973; Crisp, 1983). Nevertheless, some clinical data suggest that another feature of AN is perhaps as fundamental to its pathogenesis as the dieting. Indeed, as long ago as 1970, Blinder, Freeman, and Stunkard (1970) demonstrated precisely how powerful exercise is in the mental economy of anorectic individuals. Employing access to exercise as a reinforcer for gaining weight in a small group of hospitalized anorectic women, they were able to achieve significant and rapid improvement in the weight of these patients. In a sense, the need to exercise overrode the need to restrict food intake.

The nature of the relationship between extensive exercise and AN remains controversial. Eisler and LeGrange (1990) proposed four explanatory models:

1. These are basically distinct phenomena, but have a seeming relationship because anorectic individuals use exercise to "work off" calories out of their fear of fatness, whereas athletes seek thin bodies out of their desire for optimal physical performance.
2. These are directly related phenomena in that one may be a risk or predisposing factor for developing the other.
3. These are indirectly related phenomena in that they are both related to some third variable (e.g., obsessive–compulsive tendencies, mood disorder, achievement striving, etc.) and thus will occur together with more than chance frequency.
4. These phenomena are essentially variants of each other, with developmental, gender, familial, and cultural factors accounting for why one or the other expression of the underlying proclivity (vulnerability?) occurs in a given person.

This chapter examines the reported nature of the activity seen in individuals during, before, and after the development of AN toward the goal of possibly narrowing the range of these conceivable explanations.

Because of the possibly more heterogeneous nature of bulimia nervosa (with some patients being underweight, others at normal weight, and still others overweight, and with many but not all having had a prior history of AN), this discussion is confined to the more classic and homogenous form of eating disorder, namely, AN. Anorexia nervosa itself, of course, can be complicated by the presence of bingeing and/or vomiting (American Psychiatric Association, 1994), but AN historically has had a clearer and better-documented relationship with activity than bulimia. The course of activity as AN evolves into bulimia nervosa (BN), however, is a matter worthy of further study.

Several clinical questions should be addressed in any attempt to understand activity in anorectic individuals:

1. What is the actual prevalence of elevated physical activity during the active illness?
2. What is the nature of this excessive physical activity?
3. Does excessive physical activity precede, begin with, or follow the onset of the anorectic dieting (i.e., is it antecedent, concomitant, or consequence)?
4. What is the long-term course of the physical activity in relation to the long-term course of the other important clinical features of the disorder?

PREVALENCE OF THE ELEVATED PHYSICAL ACTIVITY

Although it is commonly stated that elevated physical activity is a frequent characteristic of active-phase AN, there is not an abundance of studies that specifically quantify this frequency. Indeed, much of the data in this regard come from earlier reports when the various clinical features of the syndrome were still being delineated. Reported frequencies of excessive exercise in anorectic patients have ranged from 33% (Halmi, 1974), to 38% (Crisp, Hsu, Harding, & Hartshorn, 1980), to 67% (Litt & Glader, 1986), to 75% (King, 1963; Kron, Katz, Gorzynski, & Weiner, 1978), to 100% (Beumont, Booth, Abraham, Griffiths, & Turner, 1983). Interestingly, a recent study by Sharp, Clark, Dunan, Blackwood, and Shapiro (1994), which compared clinical features in matched groups of 14 male and 25 female anorectic patients, found excessive exercise present in 67% of the males and 44% of the females.

It should be noted that these studies generally examined rates in hospitalized anorectic patients. One could argue that this introduces the biases of severity and confinement, but the presence of these variables may mean that the true prevalence of excessive exercise among all anorectics is actually even higher, as those not ill enough to be in a hospital might logically be expected to be able to exercise even more readily. Indeed, Falk, Halmi, and Tryon (1985), who found an increase in physical activity level in anorectic patients in conjunction with weight gain during the first two weeks of hospitalization, concede that severity and weakness at admission may have produced this seemingly paradoxical finding. In any event, the available data clearly document a substantial prevalence of excessive exercise among acutely anorectic subjects, probably between 65% and 75%.

There are, however, two noteworthy problems with the prevalence figures reported in anorexia nervosa. Although the previously cited percentages (33%–100%) would seem striking, all the studies fail to provide control data. Thus we do not know what percentage of normal female adolescents can be categorized as extreme exercisers. It is, however, common clinical experience on inpatient services that house anorectic patients with either other psychiatric or other medical patients that the anorectic subjects are readily identifiable as being "different," not simply because of their emaciated appearances, but because their relentless robust walking or calisthenic activity dramatically exceeds that of their peers.

The second issue, one that Kron et al. (1978) and Leon (1984) noted, is even thornier, namely, how does one define "elevated" or "excessive" physical activity? Is it activity that is qualitatively unusually strenuous, such as intense running, swimming, or calisthenics? Is it activity that quantitatively exceeds that commonly performed by adolescents, such as running, swimming, or calisthenics that simply occur for more hours of the day or more days of the week than the same activity engaged in by normal peers? Or does it entail some combination of both qualitative and quantitative elements? Unfortunately, although there may be descriptions of frenetic exercising in case reports, this issue is rarely considered, much less addressed, in reports of exercise prevalence in anorectic cohorts (although Blinder et al., 1970 did use pedometers to measure miles walked per day during the acute phase). Of course, many experienced clinicians might well argue that when it comes to assessing the presence of excessively elevated physical activity, "You know when you see it." The nature of the physical activity described in the literature on AN is further examined later.

Finally, one other issue merits comment. Given that probably 50% of eating disorderred patients manifest diagnosable concomitant major depression (Strober & Katz, 1988), and that elevated psychomotor activity can occur as part of a depressive disorder, can it be assumed that on an inpatient service where one cannot, for example, swim or play tennis that the pacing or calisthenics in which the anorectic patient engages is not the equivalent of depressive agitation? Indeed, one might even ponder whether depressive agitation might be related to the depressed person's typically diminished food intake. These questions are raised to alert the reader that there remain aspects of the activity question in AN that frequently have not been addressed, much less clarified.

THE NATURE OF THE ELEVATED PHYSICAL ACTIVITY

Several books now describe in rich detail factual or fictionalized accounts of the adolescent's descent into AN (Bruch, 1973; Huebner, 1993; Levenkron, 1978; Sours, 1980). All these accounts are consistent not only in noting the presence of excessive exercise, but in their general description of the nature of the exercise. The systematic, albeit retrospective, examination of exercise in the report by Kron et al. (1978) offers a similar picture, one that characterized virtually all the excessively active 25 patients in their total group of 33 anorectic young women. Finally, the recent review by Beumont, Arthur, Russell, and Touyz (1994) provided further verification of this picture, which is now summarized.

During the prodromal phase, prior exercise routines become intensified. Running, swimming, gymnastics, tennis, and so forth become more rigidly scheduled, more prolonged, and more meticulously carried out. But they are orderly and would not be viewed by a spectator as odd or unusual in form or nature.

As Beumont et al. (1994) observed, the exercise increasingly becomes titrated against caloric intake. More exercise permits more food to be eaten, but when more food is eaten, this demands further increase in exercise. In effect, the patient constantly strives to be in caloric debt, and failure to maintain a debt raises the anxiety level in the evolving anorectic adolescent. But this underlying dynamic becomes progressively less conscious and more automatically and compulsively expressed as the process accelerates.

As the dieting and weight loss progress, the exercise becomes more driven, more intense, more frenetic. Moreover, it becomes less goal-directed; it is aimed not so much at achieving a specific end—for example, better tennis serve, better swimming lap time—but at extending the duration of the exercise as a goal in itself. The individual begins to experience a diffuse restlessness, which is almost invariably associated with progressive insomnia; she is virtually unable to sit still and cannot read or watch television for more than several minutes. The casual observer would now be able to discern the agitated, disorganized, bizarre, and excessive nature of the exercise.

There is one other characteristic of the exercise pattern in AN that I have observed (as have others, undoubtedly) but that has received little note in the literature, although Beumont et al. (1994) did passingly allude to it. This is the schizoid nature of the exercise, whether premorbidly, prodromally, or during the acute, fulminating phase. The exercise is characteristically confined to such individual activities as running, gymnastics, calisthenics, swimming, or dance. Even when anorectic individuals are involved in so-called team sports, these are really sports in which the team is composed of individual performers, for example, track, swimming, wrestling (in cases of males), or tennis (singles). It is strikingly rare to find an anorectic patient who elevates his or her level of participation in, for example, softball, basketball, or volleyball. Whether this reflects the utility of individual sports for controlling and increasing one's exercise level, particularly the level of aerobic activity, or whether the loneness of the individual sports presents a ready defense against the social interactions required in genuine team sports, or both, is a matter that remains open to conjecture.

THE PRESENCE OF ELEVATED PHYSICAL ACTIVITY PREMORBIDLY

In the report of Kron et al. (1978), 21 of 33 anorectic subjects reported being extremely active physically well before their dieting and weight loss. Of course, these were subjective, retrospective self-descriptions, and their reliability might be questioned. But, based on detailed exercise histories that I routinely take, it would seem likely that well over half of all anorectic patients are serious exercisers (or athletes) premorbidly. Of course, two important questions remain unanswered: What percentage of female adolescents in the general population are significant exercisers, and what percentage of those who are and those who are not go on to develop an eating disorder?

That elevated physical activity can evolve into classical anorexia nervosa has been documented. Katz (1986) described in detail two male long-distance runners whose entry into running clearly preceded the onset of their eating disorder, which first appeared when they began to expand their weekly mileage. Interestingly, when in both instances physical injuries consequent to their excessive running forced curtailment of their training, both men became depressed and bulimic for the first time. This sequence was also described by Sundgot-Borgen (1994) in a study of risk factors and triggers for eating disorders in 603 elite female athletes in Norway.

On the other hand, that food restriction may be the trigger that elicits increased physical activity is suggested by the report of Beumont et al. (1983). Based on meticulous interviewing of 25 anorectic patients (both inpatients and outpatients), these researchers found six symptoms present in 90% to 100% of their patients as AN unfolded: increased sports activity (100%), adoption of recognized diet plan (96%), strict adherence to diet (96%), preoccupation with weight (96%), and obsessive dieting (92%). The general sequence was dieting and food restriction occurring at the outset, followed relatively early by increased sports activity, followed by more irregular eating, followed by exercising alone and obsessively. This report thus strongly hints at the intimate relationship between food restriction and elevated exercise level. It is not simply that exercise and dieting coexisted in this group, but that a reduction in food intake was followed by an increase in physical activity, and then the increase in physical activity was followed by a further reduction in food intake.

THE COURSE OF ELEVATED PHYSICAL ACTIVITY IN RELATION TO THE COURSE OF AN

Clearly any attempt to understand the relationship between AN and physical activity requires knowledge about the course of both over time. The study of Kron et al. (1978), which obtained follow up data on 15 women who were 15 to 120 months posthospital treatment for AN, is helpful in this regard. In each of these 15 subjects, elevated exercise level had been present at the time of hospital admission. At follow up, 2 of the women had died (one of an overdose, the other of complications of malnutrition); 10 of the remaining 13 women still displayed elevated physical activity at the time of follow up, despite substantial weight recovery in 8 of these women, including full clinical recovery in 3.

Among the 3 who were not exercising excessively, 2 were doing poorly and attributed the reduction in exercise to "exhaustion." Only the remaining patient saw the reduction in activity level as part of a significant global improvement in her condition. Among the still-exercising but weight-improved 8 patients, their activity had returned to its preanorexia nature: tightly scheduled and rigidly carried out, but goal-directed, organized, and planned. Thus the frenetic, diffuse, almost chaotic quality of the exercising during the acute period had gradually dissipated as nutrition and weight progressively improved.

It might also be noted that Halmi (1974), in her study of 94 cases of AN, found hyperactivity to be equally prevalent in good- and poor-outcome cases, suggesting that it was a core feature of the syndrome and without special prognostic significance. Kaye, Gwirstman, George, Ebert, and Petersen (1986) found that a return to normal activity took at least 6 months in the group of weight-recovered anorectic patients they studied, again suggesting that weight restoration alone does not quickly normalize activity level.

Patients typically explain their elevated physical activity as reflecting the conscious desire to "work off calories" and thus lose weight. Again, however, the study of Kron et al. (1978), which found 21 of 33 anorectic women to be hyperactive before the manifest onset of AN and 8 of 9 to be so after weight restoration (to at least 90% of ideal body weight), suggests a more complex underlying relationship between exercise and dieting in individuals vulnerable to AN.

However, we must also note that weight restoration per se is not identical with nutritional restoration. It is well known, for instance, that normal-weight bulimic individuals can still be biologically starving (Pirke, Pahl, & Schweiger, 1985). Clearly one must search for the correlation between exercise and both full psychological and full biological recovery, not merely restoration of a "normal" weight (which may actually be significantly less than the patient's premorbid weight).

DISCUSSION

The studies and observations reviewed here suggest that the following descriptions of elevated physical activity in relation to AN are reasonably reliable.

1. Exercise plays an important role in the physical and mental lives of the majority of anorectic individuals prior to the onset of the manifest eating disorder.

2. The prominence and importance of exercise increase even further concomitant with the onset of the significant nutritional restriction that characterizes AN, and previous nonexercisers may now also begin to exercise rigorously; furthermore, there may often be an upsurge of physical activity as an acute antecedent of the dieting and then again as an early consequence of it.

3. The nature of the exercise prior to dietary restriction tends to be organized and tightly scheduled, and typically involves individual effort, even when part of a team, rather than participation in a teamwork sport (e.g., running or swimming vs. baseball or lacrosse).

4. With the progression of dietary restraint and weight loss, the activity becomes not only extraordinarily increased in quantity but qualitatively frenetic, disorganized, chaotic, almost beyond the individual's control; calisthenics and running, perhaps because of their ready availability and aerobic nature, are particularly common.

5. The exercise can continue well into the emaciated phase, often defying the logic of what an emaciated person is presumed capable of enduring.

6. The importance of exercise for the anorectic person during the acute phase can rival that of the food restriction itself.

7. Weight restoration can be followed by a gradual reduction in the random, chaotic nature of the exercising, but it does not necessarily translate into a full subsidence of signifcant exercising.

This scenario, classic in its consistency and frequency in individuals who develop AN, suggests a complex interplay among behavioral, psychological, and biological variables with regard to the relationship between exercise and dietary restriction. The high frequency of reported premorbid exercising suggests that this may well be a predisposing factor for developing AN. However, considering the increasingly high prevalence of athletic participation by young women in today's world and that the lifetime incidence of AN among females is about 1% (Lucas, Beard, O'Fallon, & Kurland, 1991), we must assume either that exercise as a risk factor must occur in conjunction with other risk factors (e.g., premorbid personal or family weight concerns, conflicts or doubts about sense of self, family enmeshment, extreme achievement orientation, etc.) or that the exercise must also further and significantly accelerate to be a relatively singular risk factor. The work of Pierce and Epling (1994) on activity anorexia clearly provides a pathophysiologic basis for such a phenomenon (see also chapter 3, this volume).

The transformation of controlled, organized, regimented physical activity into more frenetic, chaotic, and extreme exercising, as the dieting of AN becomes more extreme, suggests that the reduced nutritional intake can in turn feed back upon and further intensify the drive to activity. Again, the model proposed by Pierce and Epling (1994) would be consistent with this clinical observation.

If extreme exercise or extreme dieting can each serve as an inducing factor for the other, we are still confronted with the extraordinary fashion in which both of these ordinarily uncomfortable activities are perpetuated. As noted earlier, clinical experience indicates that the exercising, like the dieting, can continue unabated for many months, virtually to the point of physical collapse (as it can in animals). What initially appeared to be a conscious, quasi-understandable decision becomes an irrational, out-of-control behavior. Perhaps the most inviting hypothesis to account for this perpetuation is that offered by Huebner (1993). He proposes that a rise in endorphins, elicited by both starvation and exercise, fuels an autoaddiction, that is; it creates a drive to recapture the initial high by progressively intensifying both the dieting and the exercising. The evidence for this is indirect and inferential, but the clinical picture is clearly compatible with the hypothesis.

Finally, there remains the questions of whether similar predisposing traits or conflicts can lead to either compulsive exercising or compulsive dieting (the choice depending on other variables), and whether such exercising and dieting are essentially variants of each other. Yates (1991) has discussed these possibilities in elegant detail (see also chapter 14, this volume), but here, too, the clinical data are helpful. The fact that most of Kron et al.'s (1978) anorectic subjects continued to be highly active even after clinical recovery, and that Katz's (1986) two anorectic subjects became depressed and bulimic after physical injury forced curtailment of their long-distance running, suggests that the relationship between AN and exercise is not merely coincidental or mechanical. In some fashion, both activities appear to develop in response to certain common premorbid psychological, body image, sociocultural, familial, and biological needs. But as they also can precipitate, intensify, and perpetuate each other, they should be regarded as phenomena having more than merely a common lineage; exercise and anorexia nervosa are indeed intimately connected, perhaps more like spouses than siblings.

REFERENCES

American Psychiatric Association. (1994). *Diagnostic and statistical manual of mental disorders* (4th ed.). Washington, DC: Author.

Beumont, P. J. V., Arthur, B., Russell, J. D., & Touyz, S. W. (1994). Excessive physical activity in dieting disorder patients: Proposals for a supervised exercise program. *International Journal of Eating Disorders, 15*, 21–36.

Beumont, P. J. V, Booth, A. L., Abraham, S. F., Griffiths, D. A., & Turner, T. R. (1983). Temporal sequence of symptoms in patients with anorexia nervosa: A preliminary report. In P. L. Darby, P. E. Garfinkel, D. M. Garner, & D. V. Coscina (Eds.), *Anorexia nervosa: Recent developments in research* (pp. 129–136). New York: Liss.

Blinder, B. J., Freeman, D. M. A., & Stunkard, A. J. (1970). Behavior therapy of anorexia nervosa: Effectiveness of activity as a reinforcer of weight gain. *American Journal of Psychiatry, 126*, 1093–1098.

Bruch, H. (1973). *Eating disorders: Obesity, anorexia nervosa, and the person within.* New York: Basic Books.

Crisp, A. H. (1983). Some aspects of the psychopathology of anorexia nervosa. In P. L. Darby, P. E. Garfinkel, D. M. Gardner, & D. V. Coscina (Eds.), *Anorexia nervosa: Recent developments in research* (pp. 15–28). New York: Liss.

Crisp, A. H., Hsu, L. K. G., Harding, B., & Hartshorn, J. (1980). Clinical features of anorexia nervosa: A study of a consecutive series of 102 female patients. *Journal of Psychosomatic Research, 24*, 179–191.

Eisler, I., & LeGrange, D. (1990). Excessive exercise and anorexia nervosa. *International Journal of Eating Disorders, 9*, 377–386.

Falk, J. R., Halmi, K. A., & Tryon, W. W. (1985). Activity measures in anorexia nervosa. *Archives of General Psychiatry, 42*, 811–814.

Halmi, K. A. (1974). Anorexia nervosa: Demographic and clinical features in 94 cases. *Psychosomatic Medicine, 36*, 18–26.

Huebner, H. F. (1993). *Endorphins, eating disorders and other addictive behaviors.* New York: Norton.

Katz, J. L. (1986). Long-distance running, anorexia nervosa, and bulimia: A report of two cases. *Comprehensive Psychiatry, 27*, 74–78.

Kaye, W. H., Gwirstman, H., George, T., Ebert, M. H., & Petersen, R. (1986). Caloric consumption and activity levels after weight recovery in anorexia nervosa: A prolonged delay in normalization. *International Journal of Eating Disorders, 5*, 489–502.

King, A. (1963). Primary and secondary anorexia nervosa syndromes. *British Journal of Psychiatry, 109*, 470–479.

Kron, L., Katz, J. L., Gorzynski, G., & Weiner, H. (1978). Hyperactivity in anorexia nervosa: A fundamental clinical feature. *Comprehensive Psychiatry, 19*, 433–440.

Leon, G. R. (1984). Anorexia and sports activity. *Behavior Analyst, 7*, 9–10.

Levenkron, S. (1978). *The best little girl in the world.* Chicago, IL: Contemporary Books.

Litt, I. F., & Glader, L. (1986): Anorexia nervosa, athletics, and amenorrhea. *Journal of Pediatrics, 109*, 150–153.

Lucas, A. R., Beard C. M., O'Fallon, W. M., & Kurland, L. I. (1991). 50 year trends in the incidence of anorexia nervosa in Rochester, Minn: A population-based study. *American Journal of Psychiatry, 148*, 917–922.

Pierce, W. D., & Epling, W. F. (1994). Activity anorexia: An interplay between basic and applied behavior analysis. *Behavior Analyst, 17*, 7–23.

Pirke, K. M., Pahl, J., & Schweiger, U. (1985). Metabolic and endocrine indices of starvation in bulimia: A comparison with anorexia nervosa. *Psychiatry Research, 14*, 33–39.

Sharp, C. W., Clark, S. A., Dunan, J. R., Blackwood, D. H., & Shapiro, C. M. (1994). Clinical presentation of anorexia nervosa in males: 24 new cases. *International Journal of Eating Disorders, 15*, 125–134.

Sours, J. A. (1980). *Starving to death in a sea of objects.* New York: Jason Aronson.

Strober, M., & Katz, J. L. (1988). Depression in the eating disorders: A review and analysis of descriptive, family, and biological findings. In P. E. Garfinkel & D. M. Garner (Eds.), *Diagnostic issues in anorexia nervosa and bulimia nervosa* (pp. 80–111). New York: Bruner/Mazel.

Sundgot-Borgen, J. (1994). Risk and trigger factors for the development of eating disorders in female elite athletes. *Medicine and Science in Sports and Exercise, 26*, 414–419.

Yates, A. (1991). *Compulsive exercise and the eating disorders.* New York: Bruner/Mazel.

17

The Interdependence of Obsessive–Compulsiveness, Physical Activity, and Starvation: A Model for Anorexia Nervosa

Caroline Davis
York University

COMMONALITIES BETWEEN OBSESSIVE–COMPULSIVE DISORDER AND THE EATING DISORDERS

Although the clinical similarities between obsessive–compulsive disorder (OCD) and the eating disorders were first reported over 50 years ago (Palmer & Jones, 1939), and a smattering of later studies has also identified an association (Crisp, 1967; Rothenberg, 1986; Solyom, Thomas, Freeman, & Miles, 1983), research linking these syndromes has burgeoned considerably in the past five years or so (Bulik, Beidel, Duchmann, Weltzin, & Kaye, 1992; Fahy, Osacar, & Marks, 1993; Holden, 1990; Hsu, Kaye, Weltzin, 1993; Kaye, Weltzin, Hsu, 1993; Rastam, Gillberg, & Gillberg, 1995; Rubenstein, Altemus, Pigott, Hess & Murphy, 1995;

Thiel, Broocks, Ohlmeier, Jacoby, & Schussler, 1995). Based largely on the similarity of symptom profiles, there is now general agreement of a substantial comorbidity between the two. Nevertheless, studies that have specifically examined prevalence rates are far from consistent. For example, some report that the occurrence of OCD in anorexia nervosa (AN) and bulimia nervosa (BN) is 10% or less (Schwalberg, Barlow, Alger, & Howard, 1992; Halmi et al., 1991). On the other hand, more recent studies have found that at least a third of eating-disordered patients meet diagnostic criteria for OCD (Rastam et al., 1995; Thiel et al., 1995). Furthermore, although some studies claim that OCD prevalence is higher among AN than BN patients (Hudson, Pope, Jonas, & Yurgelun-Todd, 1983; Laessle, Wittchen, Fichter, & Pirke, 1989), others have found no significant differences among the various subgroups (Thiel et al., 1995).

Not only are there psychopathological parallels between the eating disorders and OCD, there also appears to be a marked neurochemical correspondence. In particular, a number of studies provide evidence of altered serotonergic (5-HT) function in OCD patients, although the specific mechanisms of dysfunction are still not entirely clear (Barr, Goodman, Price, McDougle, & Charney, 1992; Bastani, Nash, & Meltzer, 1990; Kaye, Weltzin, Hsu, & Bulik, 1991; Marazziti, Hollander, Lensi, Ravagli, & Cassano, 1992). It should be noted, however, that much of this evidence is indirect and has been inferred, in large part, from drug-response data. For example, chemical agents such as fluoxetine, fluvoxamine, and sertraline, that elevate intrasynaptic 5-HT or directly activate 5-HT receptors, have shown impressive efficacy in the treatment of OCD (Apter et al., 1994; Jenike, Buttolph, Baer, Ricciardi, & Holland, 1989).

In addition, the critical importance of 5-HT in appetite control is now well established (see Curzon, 1992 for a review). Specifically, interventions that increase 5-HT activation have consistently been shown to diminish hunger and reduce food intake in laboratory animals (Leibowitz, 1990). Although clinical studies of 5-HT status in eating-disordered patients are not plentiful, the research that does exist also suggests functional alterations in cases of AN and BN (Kaye et al., 1993; Hsu et al., 1993). However, both increased and decreased activity in this system has been reported, a fact that renders much of the data confusing. There is, for example, evidence of hyperactivity in weight-restored anorectics, and hypoactivity in BN patients (see Jarry & Vaccarino, in press, for a review).

Jarry and Vaccarino (in press) present an interesting model of OCD and the eating disorders that integrate these apparently contradictory findings. They propose that both OCD and the eating disorders occur along a continuum. At one end, both syndromes are characterized by high behavioral and cognitive inhibition, such as the prolonged starvation and generalized control seen in AN patients of the restricting type, and in those OCD patients with classical symptoms such as checking and washing; this is matched by elevated 5-HT functioning in both disorders. At the other end of the continuum, both are characterized by insufficient inhibition, as seen in the impulsive behavior of bulimics and in those OCD patients who manifest violent or socially inappropriate thoughts, here matched by lowered 5-HT activity.

HYPERACTIVITY, OBSESSIONALITY, AND THE EATING DISORDERS

Generalized hyperactivity and/or excessive exercising are common features of AN and of particular relevance in its link with OCD. Since the earliest reports of the disorder, clinicians have recognized the relentless physical activity that is characteristic of many eating-disordered patients, even in the face of severe emaciation (Bruch, 1965; Gull's study, as cited in Warah, 1993; Yates, 1991). In fact, it has been reported that hyperactivity is one of the first symptoms to appear after the occurrence of substantial weight loss (Kron, Katz, Gorzynski, & Weiner, 1978). For the most part this behavior has been viewed as a *consequence* of an extreme desire for thinness, in other words, simply as a means of expending unwanted calories. More recently, however, some have speculated that physical activity may have a causal significance in the pathogenesis of the disorder (Kron et al., 1978; Katz, 1986).

Central to this position is the biobehavioral, activity-induced model of AN proposed by Epling and Pierce (1988; 1992). They claim that for many anorectics the disorder is not a *nervosa*, but a physiologically mediated phenomenon. They propose that strict calorie restriction and strenuous exercise are mutually reinforcing behaviors that eventually become self-perpetuating and resistant to change. This theory was formulated on the basis of a body of well-controlled animal research conducted since the mid-1960s. Using a standard experimental paradigm, it has been reliably demonstrated that food-restricted experimental rats with free access to a running wheel will reduce their food intake and their body weight in almost direct proportion to an increase in physical activity (Epling & Pierce, 1984; Routtenberg & Kuznesof, 1967; Russell, Epling, Pierce, Amy, & Boer, 1987). In fact, in the original experiments—and over a relatively short period of time—the animals literally ran themselves to death!

In this context, it is important to consider the relatively high prevalence of eating pathologies that have been reported among female athletes, particularly those involved in high-level competition (Brownell, Rodin, & Wilmore, 1992). For example, one study found that 15% of the female athletes tested, compared with 4% of a control group, had scores on the Drive-for-Thinness subscale of the Eating Disorder Inventory in excess of the mean score reported for anorectic patients (Davis, 1992). There is also evidence indicating that a high percentage of female athletes report using potentially harmful weight-loss techniques, despite the fact that a large proportion of them are, by objective standards, of normal weight or even underweight (Dummer, Rosen, Heusner, Roberts, & Counsilman, 1987). Almost by definition, competitive athletes in any sport are heavily invested in a high-intensity, physically taxing training regimen. In addition, however, many female athletes are chronically subjected to strong pressures to maintain a low level of body fat. Not only does this confer a performance advantage—up to a point—but it helps achieve the ultraslender body shape that has become the ideal in many sports such as gymnastics, figure skating, and dance.

Except for a number of case reports—and a certain amount of anecdote—little in the way of systematic research has assessed the validity and occurrence of the activity-induced model of AN in the human condition (Epling & Pierce, 1992; Yates, 1991). Recently we initiated an in-depth study of hospitalized eating-disordered patients in order to investigate these issues, namely, whether participation in physical activity is a significant factor in the etiology of eating disorders (Davis, Kennedy, Ralevski, & Dionne, 1994). In this endeavor, it was our intention to obtain a lifetime sport and exercise profile of patients, to compare the premorbid and morbid levels of physical activity between these patients and a group of age- and sex-matched peers, to establish the relative frequency with which exercising predated dieting and weight loss among these patients, and in particular, to test the specific hypothesis of Epling and Pierce (1988, 1992) that in many cases weight loss and exercise become mutually reinforcing behaviors that are inversely related with respect to intensity and degree.

Qualitative methods (based on patient interviews) and quantitative data were used in the analyses. The combined results of this study strongly supported the hypothesis that participation in sport and exercise can play a central, even a causal, role in the development and maintenance of eating disorders. For example, we found (a) that on average patients were more physically active than control subjects from early adolescence onward, and prior to the onset of the primary diagnostic symptoms or characteristics of AN; (b) that 60% of patients had been competitive athletes or in dance before the onset of their disorder; (c) that more than half the patients were involved in regular sport or exercise participation before they ever began to diet; (d) that 78% described their physical activity, during the acute phase of their disorder as "excessive;" (e) that 93% of the patients described their exercise behavior as "out of control" and "compulsive;" and importantly, (f) that 75% reported that during the period of maximum weight loss, their level of physical activity was steadily increasing as their weight and food intake decreased in the same manner.

Taken together, these factors militate against the assertion that the hyperactivity observed among eating-disordered women is merely a benign form of purgation initiated in response to a pathological drive for thinness and fear of weight gain. Furthermore, the finding that a large number of women with AN reported an inverse relationship between physical activity and food intake maps closely onto the behavior observed in experimental animals. At this point, it is fair to conclude that we now have compelling evidence, both from animal experimentation and from clinical data, that indicates that strenuous exercise and severe calorie restriction in combination act synergistically and potentiate one another.

Several neurochemical mechanisms have been proposed to explain this exercise-induced weight-loss syndrome. It has been noted that the behavioral response to starvation, in the form of heightened locomotion and arousal, is identical to that produced by amphetamine (AMPH, Mills, 1985). Phenylethylamine (PEA) is a trace amine in the brain that is structurally similar to AMPH, and both produce hyperactivity and anorexia in laboratory rats. There is evidence to suggest that PEA is an endogenous AMPH, the hyperactive effects of which are produced primarily by enhancing the dopamine system in the central nervous system, and the anorectic effects of which are mediated via enhanced central 5-HT activity (Popplewell, Coffey, Montgomery, & Burton, 1986). More recent research also suggests that

5-HT dysfunction occurs in the exercise-induced weight-loss syndrome as it does in AN, and that these changes are specific to the syndrome and not a general consequence either of weight loss or of exercise on its own (Aravich, Rieg, Ahmed, & Lauterio, 1993). Other research has indicated that this syndrome is also associated with specific ß-endorphin abnormalities, and that this is consistent with the possibility that a ß-endorphin autoaddiction occurs during the development of this syndrome that serves to maintain the maladaptive behaviors of overactivity and self-starvation (Aravich, Rieg, Lauterio, & Doerries, 1993).

Recently, Altemus, Glowa, and Murphy (1993) have argued that the food-restriction-induced hyperactivity observed in experimental animals may also be a valid animal model for OCD, as well as for AN. Experimentally, they found that, compared with saline- or imipramine-treated rats, those pretreated with fluoxetine showed a significant attenuation of hyperactivity and weight loss when subjected to the food-restriction procedures described previously. They point out that in many ways the increasing, almost perpetual, running observed in this syndrome resembles the compulsive and maladaptive behaviors seen in people with OCD. For example, the behavior is clearly repetitive and purposeful, and obviously excessive. On balance, the animal research just reviewed suggests, albeit indirectly, that strenuous exercise in combination with substantial calorie restriction increases obsessionality by means of altered 5-HT functioning and ß-endorphin abnormalities.

AN INTERACTIVE MODEL
OF EATING DISORDERS

Yates (1991) made a strong case, based on considerable case-report data and psychological assessments, that excessive exercising and the eating disorders are sister activities that share, among other characteristics, a strong relationship to obsessionality. She found that excessive exercisers typically display a compulsive behavior pattern, and that they are characterized by an obsessional and rigid personality profile. Others also found that heightened trait obsessionality was not changed in a group of anorectic individuals after weight restoration, even though there was a diminution in obsessive–compulsive symptomatology (Sohlberg & Strober, 1994).

In support of this viewpoint, a small body of nonclinical research has demonstrated an association between obsessive–compulsive personality style and various aspects of exercising (Davis, Brewer, & Ratusny, 1993; Goldfarb & Plante, 1984; Kagan, 1987). In addition, an obligatory commitment to exercise was positively related to weight preoccupation in both men and women (Davis et al., 1993). In another study we also found a positive relationship between obsessive–compulsive symptomatology and exercise frequency in a group of high-level exercising women, as well as among females diagnosed with AN (Davis, Kennedy, et al., 1995). Furthermore, in the patient group, weight preoccupation was positively associated with the frequency of exercising, with obligatory attitudes to exercise (e.g., feelings of guilt associated with missed exercise sessions), and with pathological attitudes to exercise (e.g., exercising when sick or injured). In the high-level exercising group, weight preoccupation was only associated with obligatory attitudes.

Prompted by the results of the present study, and by the various studies linking OCD and AN, my colleagues and I have recently proposed a nonrecursive, interactive model that integrates, in a dynamic sense, obsessive–compulsiveness, physical activity, and starvation in the pathogenesis of some eating disorders (Davis, Kennedy, et al., 1995). Figure 17.1 presents a graphical representation of these associations. Although this model shares similarities with that proposed earlier by Epling and Pierce (1988, 1992), we have extended the scope of their model by taking account of influential psychological factors. We have suggested that in the context of a sport or fitness environment, the combination of excessive weight preoccupation and obsessive–compulsive tendencies are likely to increase the frequency and duration of one's physical activity and to exacerbate the obligatory nature of a commitment to this behavior. In turn, increased physical activity itself may foster greater food restriction by virtue of its appetite-suppressing effects (Rivest & Richard, 1990) and by encouraging a narcissistic focus on appearance, weight, and performance (Davis, 1992; Katz, 1986). Furthermore, as we have seen, strenuous physical activity and food restriction in concert have been shown to alter 5-HT functioning (Altemus et al., 1993; Aravich, Rieg, Ahmed, & Lauterio, 1993), and to increase obsessionality (Davis et al., 1994; Kaye et al., 1991), a factor that then contributes to even greater increases in physical activity and more rigorous starvation. As a consequence, one's commitment to exercise may become more pathological as obsessionality increases.

In proposing this dynamic process as a model of AN, it is important to be mindful that the etiology of eating disorders is highly complex and indeed variable across cases. For these reasons it is acknowledged that the model may explain only one aspect of the pathogenesis of AN, and then only for some individuals. Clearly this model says little about the motivations that initially trigger exaggerated weight and

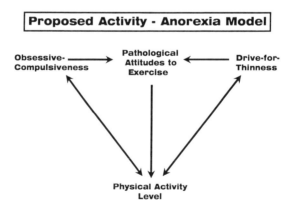

FIG. 17.1.   A proposed interactive model of AN based on interrelationships among starvation, physical activity, and obsessive–compulsiveness.

diet concerns, nor does it address the complexity of factors that predispose certain individuals, and not others, to invest heavily in athletics and exercise.

We are all too familiar with the numerous pressures on women to try to achieve an unrealistically thin body shape. These are especially pervasive in media-dominated societies such as those in most Western cultures. However, excessive body image concerns do not occur simply because of externally imposed standards. Certain personality vulnerabilities amplify some individuals' responses to these factors. Body disparagement and disordered eating behaviors have been associated, in particular, with low self-esteem, high anxiety, and a perfectionistic personal style (see Davis, in press, for a review).

The relationship between exercise and dieting has also been the subject of an increasing body of research over the past decade, an interest sparked, no doubt, by the popularity of the fitness movement and the increasing prevalence of eating pathologies among women. Considerable research has demonstrated that weight control is one of the principal reasons reported for exercising, especially among young women (Davis, Fox, et al., 1995; Markland & Hardy, 1993; McDonald & Thompson, 1992). This may reflect, in part, the increasing promotion by the media of exercise as a weight-loss method. Since the mid-1980s, for example, the number of articles in popular women's magazines that recommend exercise for slimming has surpassed those recommending traditional calorie-reduced dieting (Wiseman, Gray, Mosimann, & Ahrens, 1992).

In summary, and in conclusion, it is proposed that the relationships among physical activity, self-starvation, and obsessive–compulsiveness tend to be reciprocal and dynamic. In other words, in combination they tend to potentiate one another in a destructive feedback–feedforward loop that can become self-perpetuating and operational beyond the level of wilful cognitive control. There is now good reason to believe that this process is a significant influence in the development and maintenance of eating disorders for some women.

REFERENCES

Altemus, M., Glowa, J. R., & Murphy, D. L. (1993). Attenuation of food-restriction-induced running by chronic fluoxetine treatment. *Psychopharmacology Bulletin, 29*, 397–400.

Apter, A., Ratzoni, G., King, R. A., Weizman, A., Iancu, I., Binder, M., & Riddle, M. A. (1994). Fluoxamine open-label treatment of adolescent inpatients with obsessive-compulsive disorder or depression. *Journal of the American Academy of Child and Adolescent Psychiatry, 33*, 342–348.

Aravich, P. F., Rieg, T. S., Ahmed, I., & Lauterio, T. J. (1993). Fluoxetine induces vasopressin and oxytocin abnormalities in food-restricted rats given voluntary exercise: Relationship to anorexia nervosa. *Brain Research, 612*, 180–189.

Aravich, P. F., Rieg, T. S., Lauterio, T. J., & Doerries, L. E. (1993). Beta-endorphin and dynorphin abnormalities in rats subjected to exercise and restricted feeding: Relationship to anorexia nervosa. *Brain Research, 622*, 1–8.

Barr, L. C., Goodman, W. K., Price, L. H., McDougle, C. J., & Charney, D. S. (1992). The serotonin hypothesis of obsessive compulsive disorder: Implications of pharmacologic challenge studies. *Journal of Clinical Psychiatry, 53*, 17–28.

Bastani, B., Nash, F., & Meltzer, H. Y. (1990). Prolactin and cortisol responses to MK-212, a serotonin agonist, in obsessive-compulsive disorder. *Archives of General Psychiatry, 47*, 833–839.

Brownell, K. D., Rodin, J., & Wilmore, J. H. (Eds.). (1992). *Eating, body weight, and performance.* Philadelphia, PA: Lea & Febiger.

Bruch, H. (1965). Anorexia nervosa—Its differential diagnosis. *Journal of Mental and Nervous Disorders, 141,* 555–566.

Bulik, C. M., Beidel, D. C., Duchmann, E., Weltzin, T. E., & Kaye, W. H. (1992) Comparative psychopathology of women with bulimia nervosa and obsessive-compulsive disorder. *Comprehensive Psychiatry, 33,* 262–268.

Crisp, A. H. (1967). The possible significance of some behavioral correlates of weight and carbohydrate intake. *Journal of Psychosomatic Research, 11,* 117–131.

Curzon, G. (1992). Serotonin and eating disorders: Pharmacological relationships. *International Academy of Biomedical Drug Research, 1,* 112–128.

Davis, C. (1992). Body image, dieting behaviors, and personality factors: A study of high-performance female athletes. *International Journal of Sport Psychology, 23,* 179–192.

Davis, C. (in press). Body image, exercise, and eating behaviors. In K. R. Fox (Ed.), *The physical self: From motivation to well-being.* Champaign, IL: Human Kinetics.

Davis, C., Brewer, H., & Ratusny, D. (1993). Behavioral frequency and psychological commitment: Necessary concepts in the study of excessive exercising. *Journal of Behavioral Medicine, 16,* 611–628.

Davis, C., Fox, J., Brewer, H., & Ratusny, D. (1995). Motivations to exercise as a function of personality characteristics, age, and gender. *Personality and Individual Differences, 19,* 165–174.

Davis, C., Kennedy, S. H., Ralevski, E., & Dionne, M. (1994). The role of physical activity in the development and maintenance of eating disorders. *Psychological Medicine, 24,* 957–967.

Davis, C., Kennedy, S. H., Ralevski, E., Dionne, M., Brewer, H., Neitzert, C., & Ratusny, D. (1995). Obsessive-compulsiveness in anorexia nervosa and high-level exercising. *Journal of Psychosomatic Research, 39,* 967–976.

Dummer, G. M., Rosen, L. W., Heusner, W. W., Roberts, P. J., & Counsilman, J. E. (1987). Pathogenic weight-control behaviors of young competitive swimmers. *Physician and Sportsmedicine, 15,* 75–84.

Epling, W. F., & Pierce, W. D. (1984). Activity-based anorexia in rats as a function of opportunity to run on an activity wheel. *Nutrition and Behavior, 2,* 37–49.

Epling, W. F., & Pierce, W. D. (1988). Activity-based anorexia: A biobehavioral perspective. *International Journal of Eating Disorders, 7,* 475–485.

Epling, W. F., & Pierce, W. D. (1992). *Solving the anorexia puzzle.* Toronto, ON: Hogrefe & Huber.

Fahy, T. A., Osacar, A., & Marks, I. (1993). History of eating disorders in female patients with obsessive-compulsive disorder. *International Journal of Eating Disorders, 14,* 439–443.

Goldfarb, L. A., & Plante, T. G. (1984). Fear of fat in runners: An examination of the connection between anorexia nervosa and distance running. *Psychological Reports, 55,* 296.

Gull, W. W. (1874). Anorexia nervosa. *Transactions of the Clinical Society of London, 7,* 22–28.

Halmi, K. A., Eckert, E., Marchi, P., Sampugnaro, V., Apple, R., & Cohen, J. (1991). Comorbidity of psychiatric diagnoses in anorexia nervosa. *Archives of General Psychiatry, 48,* 712–718.

Holden, N. L. (1990). Is anorexia nervosa an obsessive-compulsive disorder? *British Journal of Psychiatry, 157,* 1–5.

Hsu, L. K. G., Kaye, W., & Weltzin, T. (1993). Are the eating disorders related to obsessive compulsive disorder? *International Journal of Eating Disorders, 14,* 305–318.

Hudson, J. I., Pope, H. G., Jonas, J. M., & Yurgelun-Todd, D. (1983). Phenomenologic relationship of eating disorders to major affective disorder. *Psychiatric Research, 9,* 345–354.

Jarry, J. L., & Vaccarino, F. J. (in press). Eating disorder and obsessive-compulsive disorder: Neurochemical and phenomenological commonalities. *Journal of Psychiatry and Neuroscience.*

Jenike, M. A., Buttolph, L., Baer, L., Ricciardi, J., & Holland, A. (1989). Open trial of fluoxetine in obsessive-compulsive disorder. *American Journal of Psychiatry, 146,* 909–911.

Kagan, D. (1987). Addictive personality factors. *Journal of Psychology, 121,* 533–538.

Katz, J. L. (1986). Long-distance running, anorexia nervosa, and bulimia: A report of two cases. *Comprehensive Psychiatry, 27,* 74–78.

Kaye, W. H., Weltzin, T., & Hsu, L. K. G. (1993). Relationship between anorexia nervosa and obsessive and compulsive behaviors. *Psychiatric Annals, 23,* 365–373.

Kaye, W. H., Weltzin, T., Hsu, L. K. G., & Bulik, C. (1991). An open trial of fluoxetine in patients with anorexia nervosa. *Journal of Clinical Psychiatry, 52,* 464–471.

Kron, L., Katz, J. L., Gorzynski, G., & Weiner, W. (1978). Hyperactivity in anorexia nervosa: A fundamental clinical feature. *Comprehensive Psychiatry, 19,* 433–439.

Laessle, R. G., Wittchen, H. U., Fichter, M. M., & Pirke, K. M. (1989). The significance of subgroups of bulimia and anorexia nervosa: Lifetime frequency of psychiatric disorders. *International Journal of Eating Disorders, 8*, 569–574.

Leibowitz, S.F. (1990). The role of serotonin in eating disorders. *Drugs, 39*(Suppl. 3), 33–48.

Marazziti, D., Hollander, E., Lensi, P., Ravagli, S., & Cassano, G.B. (1992). Peripheral markers of serotonin and dopamine function in obsessive-compulsive disorder. *Psychiatry Research, 42*, 41–51.

Markland, D., & Hardy, L. (1993). The exercise motivations inventory: Preliminary development and validity of a measure of individuals' reasons for participation in regular physical exercise. *Personality and Individual Differences, 15*, 289–296.

McDonald, K., & Thompson, J. K. (1992). Eating disturbance, body image dissatisfaction, and reasons for exercising: Gender differences and correlational findings. *International Journal of Eating Disorders, 11*, 289–292.

Mills, I. H. (1985). The neuronal basis of compulsive behavior in anorexia nervosa. *Journal of Psychiatric Research, 19*, 231–235.

Palmer, H. D., & Jones, M. S. (1939). Anorexia nervosa as a manifestation of compulsive neurosis. *Archives of Neurological Psychiatry, 41*, 856–860.

Popplewell, D. A., Coffey, P. J., Montgomery, A. M. J., & Burton, M. J. (1986). A behavioral and pharmacological examination of phenylethylamine-induced anorexia and hyperactivity—Comparisons with amphetamine. *Pharmacology Biochemistry and Behavior, 25*, 711–716.

Rastam, M., Gillberg, I. C., & Gillberg, C. (1995). Anorexia nervosa 6 years after onset: Part II. Comorbid psychiatric problems. *Comprehensive Psychiatry, 36*, 70–76.

Rivest, S., & Richard D. (1990). Involvement of corticotropin-releasing factor in the anorexia induced by exercise. *Brain Research Bulletin, 25*, 169–172.

Rothenberg, A. (1986). Eating disorder as a modern obsessive-compulsive syndrome. *Psychiatry, 49*, 45–53.

Routtenberg, A., & Kuznesof, A. W. (1967). Self-starvation of rats living in activity wheels on a restricted feeding schedule. *Journal of Comparative and Physiological Psychology, 64*, 414–421.

Rubenstein, C. S., Altemus, M., Pigott, T. A., Hess, A., & Murphy, D. L. (1995). Symptom overlap between OCD and bulimia nervosa. *Journal of Anxiety Disorders, 9*, 1–9.

Russell, J. C., Epling, W. F., Pierce, W. D., Amy, R. M., & Boer, D. P. (1987). Induction of voluntary prolonged running in rats. *Journal of Applied Physiology, 63*, 2549–2553.

Schwalberg, M. D., Barlow, D. H., Alger, S. A., & Howard, L. J. (1992). Comparison of bulimics, obese binge eaters, social phobics and individuals with panic disorder on comorbidity across DSM-III-R anxiety disorders. *Journal of Abnormal Psychology, 10*, 675–681.

Sohlberg, S., & Strober, M. (1994) Personality in anorexia nervosa: An update and a theoretical integration. *Acta Psychiatrica Scandinavica, 89*, 1–15.

Solyom, L., Thomas, C. D., Freeman, R. J., & Miles, J. E. (1983). Anorexia nervosa: Obsessive-compulsive disorder or phobia? A comparative study. In P. L. Darby, P. E. Garfinkel, D. M. Garner, & D. V. Coscina. (Eds.), *Anorexia nervosa: Recent developments in research* (pp. 137–147). New York: Liss.

Thiel, A., Broocks, A., Ohlmeier, M., Jacoby, G. E., & Schussler, G. (1995). Obsessive-compulsive disorder among patients with anorexia nervosa and bulimia nervosa. *American Journal of Psychiatry, 152*, 72–75.

Warah, A. (1993). Overactivity and boundary setting in anorexia nervosa: An existential perspective. *Journal of Adolescence, 16*, 93–100.

Wiseman, C. V., Gray, J. J., Mosimann, J. E., & Ahrens, A. H. (1992). Cultural expectations of thinness in women: An update. *International Journal of Eating Disorders, 11*, 85–89.

Yates, A. (1991). *Compulsive exercise and the eating disorders.* New York: Bruner/Mazel.

Author Index

219

Subject Index